BEYOND THE
HORIZON

BEYOND THE HORIZON

EXTREME ADVENTURES
AT THE EDGE OF THE WORLD

RICHARD PARKS

with Michael Aylwin

SPHERE

First published in Great Britain in 2014 by Sphere

Copyright © 2014 by Richard Parks

A CIP catalogue record for this book
is available from the British Library.

HB ISBN 978-0-7515-5539-4
C format ISBN 978-0-7515-5606-3

Typeset in Sabon by M Rules
Printed and bound in Great Britain by
Clays Ltd, St Ives plc

Papers used by Sphere are from well-managed forests
and other responsible sources.

MIX
Paper from
responsible sources
FSC® C104740

Sphere
An imprint of
Little, Brown Book Group
100 Victoria Embankment
London EC4Y 0DY

An Hachette UK Company
www.hachette.co.uk

www.littlebrown.co.uk

In memory of my nana and uncle

Gwendoline Celeste Webb 1928–2007
Terry Albert Parks 1938–1985

North Pole

Denali

Double Brutal

Jungle Ultra

Aconcagua

Project X

Mount Vinson

South Pole

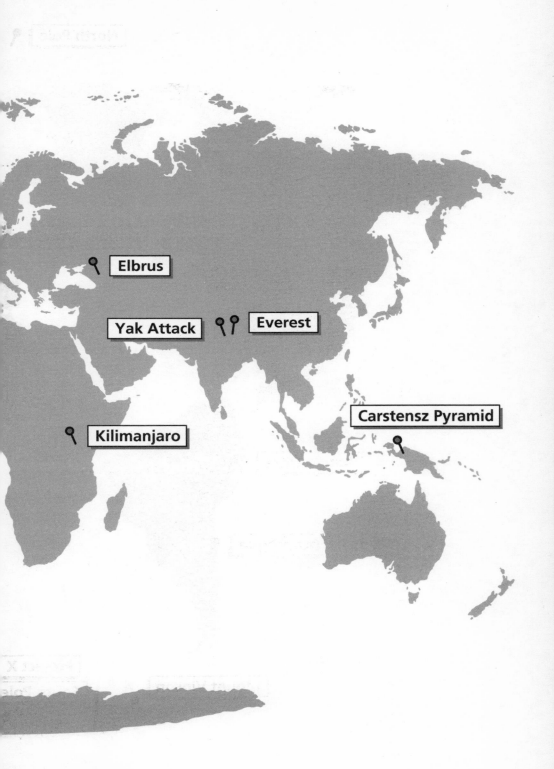

1

The top of a mountain is no place for an agoraphobic. Nor is the top, or bottom, of the world. The horizon stretches further from these places than anywhere else. To stand at them is to take in as much of the Earth as it is possible to see without leaving its surface. For that reason, I find that it moves you closer to the planet and, somehow, to whatever else there might be that is bigger than us. It takes an effort of the will to embrace all that, maybe even as much as it does to reach these places in a physical sense. Well, almost.

Strange, then, to be able to say that my journey began with me curled up in a small room suffering from agoraphobia. I see that room now as a tunnel that led from my previous existence as a professional rugby player to the brilliant whiteness of mountains, wildernesses and the unknown. It was terrible in that room, wrestling with the fact that my rugby

1

career was over, trying to control the fears that had always been in attendance but now rose up and threatened to drag me down.

Fear had informed every move of my playing career. When I started out, winning was the most important thing, and the accompanying fear of losing, but as I matured (in other words, lost a few times) it became the fear of making mistakes, being dropped and, worst of all, letting down my team-mates. What a terrible waste of energy, I realised in that room, now that it was all over. How restricting, to let your horizons close in like that. What's the point of being scared of something that you're not going to do because you're scared of doing it? Be scared by all means, but only of the challenges you have resolved to take on.

No sportsman knows how he will handle the end of his playing days. Not many will even think about it. I had entertained the idea from time to time, but never for long. It was too terrifying. Besides, in a contact sport like rugby, if you think too much about that sort of thing you lay yourself open to doubt and vulnerability, and that can bring about the end in itself. I found it better not to think. Everything is laid on for you: an elite environment, a vigorous routine to live your life by, a direction and a purpose. All you have to do is to focus on the next session and the next game.

If only it could last for ever. Sometimes it feels as if it will. But the end must arrive some time – and it could be the next session, it could be the next game.

Sure enough, my time came suddenly and without argument. I was left with no choice. And, as it turned out, I handled it very badly, shutting myself away in that room for

2

twenty-one days. The only time I went outside was for an operation on my ruined shoulder.

It was a cold and unfamiliar room in the small two-bedroom house my parents were renting in Newport while they were renovating their new home. When I'd moved out of my previous house a few weeks earlier, I had taken it, the room at the back. Little did I know it would become purgatory to me, a kind of halfway house between the life I had led and the one I was about to lead.

I remember the room well. Its bare walls were smooth and white. The bed on which I lay was white. The fitted wardrobe at the foot of it was white. The only window looked out on to the side of the steep hill on which the house was built. When I ventured to look out, the houses on the next street up seemed to gather round and peer down at me, so I tended to keep the curtains drawn. On the floor, my bags overflowed with kit, the trappings of the only life I'd known, all of it now so suddenly redundant.

What did I do in there for so long? Nothing. At least, nothing constructive. There was a lot of fear and self-loathing. Towards the end, I started reading a book. I also had a laptop with a painfully slow internet connection. And there was, and still is, a tattoo on the inside of my left arm. Together, those items would haul me out of the state of agoraphobia and depression I'd fallen into. Until they did, though, I passed the time enduring the emotions and thoughts that visited me, scanning the perfect walls for a crack to slip into, or just a blemish to identify with.

My shoulder was painful and incapacitated, so that it woke me every time I rolled on to it. A few days after my operation, it was time to take off the sling and begin the rehabilitation exercises they had issued me with, but I couldn't bring myself to do them. What was the point? My career was over.

My parents would check on me every now and then. I knew they were deeply worried, but they didn't pander to me or try to force me into anything. They let me be. Just knowing they were there on the other side of that white door was the only comfort I held on to throughout the twenty-one days, even if I wasn't able to let them in emotionally. You could say that, despite my thirty-one years, there was precious little difference between me then and the teenager who won't come out of his room. My predicament might have been more serious, the emotions more intense and the thoughts darker and scarier, but on a superficial level the reaction was indistinguishable.

I couldn't have seen that, though. When I feel vulnerable I do tend to withdraw. Things were bad, so I retreated into the proverbial cave. And I didn't want, or couldn't have, anyone in there. Mum and Dad knew that.

What I can see now, although I didn't grasp it at the time, was that I had subconsciously associated the end of my rugby career with the end of everything. That was why I had never dared confront the idea. It was like a dark shadow lurking in the back of my mind. Just ignore it. Next session, next game. You're indestructible, remember.

When I returned to Wales for the start of the new season in 2007, I was more focused than I had ever been. Maybe too focused. Maybe even desperate. I had lost a sense of perspective. It felt as if my whole career as a rugby player, which means my whole life as an adult, was converging on this two-year contract I'd been offered by the Dragons, the Welsh region centred on Newport, my home town.

I was desperate – yes, that is the right word – to play for Wales again. I'd won the last of my four caps in 2003 and since then I'd played elsewhere, first at my beloved Leeds, then for one difficult year at Perpignan in France. Now I was returning. I'd turned thirty a couple of weeks before the season started. Age has never concerned me, but maybe that milestone heightened the sense that this was it, my last chance.

To begin with, I played the best rugby of my life. My coach, Paul Turner, told me the Wales coaches were talking to him about me. There were no autumn internationals that year, because of the World Cup, but it seemed I was back in the thinking of the people who mattered. I almost forgot about the shadow in my head.

Then, a knee injury on Boxing Day put me out for a few months, and so began the downward spiral that would lead to the room in my parents' house a year and a half later. I'm no stranger to injury, and each time I've come back stronger, but this one felt different. Deep down, I knew my body and my mind were not right. I've always been a terrible invalid, but now I seemed to be panicking, too. As I strove to regain fitness, it was as if I were gasping for air whenever I thought about the precious days and weeks ticking by. This hadn't been the plan; this was not why I'd come back.

That injury was just a precursor, though. In the second match of the following season, a home game against the Llanelli Scarlets, I was crouching over a tackled player trying to win the ball when I was cleared out from the side by one of the opposition. I felt a searing pain in my shoulder. I would later find out that I had suffered what's known as a subluxation, a partial dislocation, and in this case the head of my humerus had knocked a chunk of cartilage away from the socket.

The idea of injury striking me down again was unthinkable. No way. I hadn't yet won that fifth Wales cap, and this was now year two of my campaign to earn it.

I played on for the rest of the game and the rest of the month and the month after that. I've never minded pain. Truth be told, I've been known to thrive on it. I'm not a masochist, but I like to feel I'm pushing myself, and sometimes that means it hurts. Besides, if you play professional rugby, pain is something you get used to.

But, if the pain was just about bearable, my range of movement was deteriorating steadily, so that by the end of October I couldn't lift my arm above shoulder height. That was more of a problem, as was living with the unhealthy dosage of painkillers. I had a scan, which revealed the extent of the problem. The piece of cartilage that had been knocked off had been floating in the socket and, because I'd played on, it had chipped away at other areas. So by now I had quite a few bits of cartilage floating round and an area of the shoulder joint where it was bone on bone – hence the restricted movement.

My panic had been growing again as the mobility of my shoulder worsened. Now I was back where I had been the year before with my knee. This time I needed an operation. Geoff Graham is one of the leading shoulder specialists in the country, and we soon got to know each other very well. He scheduled a procedure called microfracture, whereby they drill into the bone, which stimulates the growth of fibrous cartilage.

Fibrocartilage is never as strong as hyaline cartilage, which is what joints are made out of, but this has become a popular procedure among sportsmen. It was tried and tested on knees but less so on shoulders. If I wanted to play on, however, it was my only option.

When I came round, Geoff told me the operation had gone well. But he also had to tell me that the situation was more serious than he'd thought. I was feeling groggy because of the anaesthetic, but I doubt I would have taken in what he was saying, whatever my clarity of consciousness. I honestly can't tell you what the cause for concern was because I just didn't want to know. I listened to everything he said and accepted it on an intellectual level – then I must have locked it away in a cellar of my mind.

What drives you in a sport like rugby isn't intellect. I have been known to overthink things, but I am a man driven by the heart. If you lived your life by intellect alone you wouldn't play rugby at all. You wouldn't smash each other up on a Saturday afternoon. Or, if you did, you would surely have some serious issues!

For all the analysis and preparation, it pays not to think too much in a sporting context – and especially when you daren't confront the thought in question. I had no time for concerns about my condition. I'd always been indestructible. I would be fine.

I played again towards the end of February, and it was OK. By this stage of the season, with the Six Nations under way and then the knock-out phases of Europe and the cup, games are irregularly dotted throughout the calendar. I played in our one game in March and then again in the next at the start of

April. Something was not right, but I couldn't put my finger on it. Those occupational pains were there. Nothing new about that, but maybe there was something qualitatively different about them now. Maybe Geoff's words were festering in that cellar of my mind. Or maybe I was just haunted by a premonition of the end.

On 26 April 2009, a Sunday, I played in our home game against Connacht. I can't actually remember how it happened. I just remember the crack, the crunch and the grind. I could hear it as well as feel it. And I knew. It had gone again. With five minutes to go before the end of the match, I walked off a rugby field for what would prove to be the last time.

I organised an appointment with Geoff as soon as I could, which ended up being the following Wednesday. Dan Martin, the physio at the Dragons, accompanied me. I remember odd little details, like noticing as we walked in that Geoff drove a Subaru Impreza, which seemed a bit 'boy racer' for a leading orthopaedic surgeon. If only I could remember as clearly the details of what he said to me in his clinic, after I told him what had happened and shown him how immobile my shoulder had become again, but I think it went something like this:

'I feared this would happen. Your shoulder is irreversibly damaged and will only get worse. It's going to impact upon the way you live your life. My advice to you as a medical professional and as a friend is that you should stop playing.'

He said it as if he were speaking to a ten-year-old. We knew each other pretty well by now, and he wanted to make sure that I heard this and heard it properly.

I had nothing to say. I'd gone. I'd been lifted out of myself, and I was somewhere else. It's grief. I've lost family and friends, and receiving this news was the same feeling. I didn't argue, I had no questions, because it was what I knew. I'd feared this moment for so long. That dark shadow in my head came out to claim its dues. Well, it's got me now, was all I could think.

In order to have any kind of quality of life in the future, I would need another operation. Once outside, I agitated with Dan over how quickly I could have it. For a moment, I instinctively believed that the operation might save my career. In the car park, we discussed it. I would have to wait until the off-season for the Dragons to be able to process it, so Dan suggested I did it on my own medical insurance, if I had any. I did, I remembered. I had a policy from a previous club. Right, let's get this sorted straightaway. Find the policy number. Make arrangements.

I bounded to my car, but this burst of decisiveness was short-lived. I pulled out of Geoff's clinic in Cardiff. Almost immediately, I knew I shouldn't be driving. When you're in shock you go into a kind of trance. You stare at something and yet stare through it; your focus is out. I turned on to a side road and tried to compose myself. What the fuck is going on, I said to myself. This was not the plan. This was *not* the plan.

I rang Dee Clark, the Dragons' team doctor, who was so much more than that to many of us. She recognised the fragility behind all that machismo in a testosterone-rich environment and understood the importance of pastoral care. I told her everything. As ever, she was perfectly level-headed and explained that I needed to get my policy number off Bupa. That was something to focus on, so I rang them.

I'm not sure I'd ever used the policy before, and I'd moved so many times since it had been opened I didn't know what address it would be registered under. The conversation took a surreal turn as I sat in my car and recited the addresses of all the places I'd ever lived, a kind of whistle-stop tour of my now-former career, with the Bupa guy sitting in judgement.

'41 Madrid House?' I said.

'No.'

'How about 23 North Lane?'

'No.'

When we'd finally found the right policy, I rang Geoff's secretary, Helen, to give her the number. Then, when I'd composed myself, which was probably about half an hour later, but seemed like days, I drove home and told Mum and Dad.

My parents were as shocked as I was by the news. They knew I'd been hurt, but it was not exactly for the first time. Mum and Dad had lived every twist and turn of my career as if they'd been playing, too, so it was the end of a significant period of their lives as well. They remained strong and, most importantly, there for me. I don't know if I would have made it through the weeks that followed without them. Not that I let them in or allowed them to help, but they were physically there, and the constancy they provided and represented was the one thing I clung to as everything else fell away.

I must also have told my mates Kev Morgan and Sonny Parker because I do remember the following Friday night. Kev suggested we go out for a couple of beers in Cardiff. We went for a pizza and ended up in a nightclub. I completely wrote myself off and behaved in a way that embarrasses me even to think about, let alone write down. I hope I'm not a dick when I'm drunk – I'm pretty sure I'm not – but I was that night. In the club, I fell into an argument with a group and threw a drink over a girl. When the bouncers came to throw me out I tried to fight them, as if they were the cruel world itself. And I did it all one-handed.

As well-known rugby players from the area, the three of us knew the manager, and he knew us. Kev told him my news and he took me into his office. And there, in the manager's office in a nightclub in Cardiff, I gave in to my emotions for the first time. Among the boxes and crates, I broke down and wept.

He let me return to the bar, where I sat on a stool for a while, not wanting to go home. I was a thirty-one-year-old living in a spare room at his parents' house. I would soon have no income, and I no longer had the ability to practise my only trade. The illusion of security that comes from being an elite performer had just been put out as if by a switch. I didn't know where to go.

So I went round to my ex-girlfriend's house. I hadn't seen her for weeks, but I'm sure this did not make me the first drunk on hard times to do something silly. After sleeping in my own vomit on her bathroom floor, though, it was clear that our relationship was now every bit as finished as my rugby career.

My reclusiveness began then. The embarrassment of that night out was the superficial trigger, and it was very real, but in came many other emotions, so strong and well-formed that they must have been building all the while.

I was angry, so angry. Fuck Geoff. What does he know? When have I ever listened to a consultant anyway? I've gone against the advice of all of them. Why shouldn't I again?

Because, in my heart, I knew he was right, which led to the frustration. I wasn't ready to retire. I had so much more to give, so much more I wanted to achieve.

Which led to the embarrassment. I hadn't accomplished what I'd set out to do. I hadn't played for Wales again. Everyone at the club knew that that was the goal I'd set myself, so how could I ever show my face there again, now that I had officially failed? My body had proven too weak, and now I had failed them as well, my comrades-in-arms.

Which led to the sadness, the crushing melancholy, at the realisation I would never again know the inside of a changing room. The energy, anticipation and nerves on the eve of combat, and then the aftermath – you've emptied yourself, you're hurting, cut and broken, hopefully you've won, and your eyes meet those of a team-mate. That's all. That's all it needs to be. The feeling that you're part of something bigger. The team, the club, the town, the country. To be cut loose from that …

I withdrew into the room. My operation was scheduled for 8 May, and I sat tight waiting for it. I couldn't bring myself to go down to the club. I didn't want to see any of them. There was no mechanism at the Dragons – or, I believe, in rugby generally – to provide the kind of support, emotional, educational or otherwise, that a player in my situation needed, even if he'd been open to seeking it. But I will be for ever grateful to the Dragons for what they could and did do for me. Just the paperwork, for example, was enough to bewilder me. I couldn't motivate myself to get out of bed, so why would I fill out a form? The Dragons did all of that for me. They drew up a statement to announce my retirement, and let me edit it and add to it, to thank all the people I wanted to over the course of my career. Then, when it was ready, they asked me when I wanted the statement put out. Do it now, I said of a document that felt like a kind of contract with the end. Just get it out there.

The operation was the same procedure as the previous one, a microfracture, but this time there was a larger area of cartilage that had been broken off the bone. I went back to the room to recuperate and was lying in bed, feeling woozy and in pain, when the phone calls started to come in. Friends, newspapers, magazines. The press release had gone out, and now the end of my career was public knowledge. That was when it became real. Any subconscious hope I may have been harbouring that it had all been a joke, or that they would open me up and find they had made a mistake, or that it would just get better, vanished at that point. That day, all those emotions I'd been wrestling with since the diagnosis were replaced by one, which was uncomplicated and devastating. All those emotions were replaced by fear.

I had become institutionalised, which is the way it is with any performer in an elite team environment. Rugby had controlled every decision of my adult life. I had sacrificed so much – happily and gratefully, I must make clear – to be the best that I could be. I'd chosen to drop out of a dental degree so I could focus on professional rugby. My sister's wedding had clashed with my first cap for Wales, which came in South Africa. Rugby had determined when I ate and slept. Ninety per cent of my social life was in rugby. And now it was gone, with no chance of coming back. I was petrified. What do I do? Where do I go? Who am I?

And so began the spiral into depression. The embarrassment caused by the failings of my body and, as I saw it, my career, compounded by the way I'd behaved that Friday night, crystallised into extreme self-loathing and the exhausting lethargy that accompanied it. I just didn't want to do anything, which made me hate me all the more. Hadn't I always been a man of action, if nothing else?

I went to some really dark places. I contemplated the very worst. And my self-hatred went to another level again for doing so. I feel guilty now about even considering it. I do believe that life and everything in it is a gift. That I thought about throwing it away troubles me still.

Mum and Dad were my fixed points. They were clearly worried about me, but they let me be there, in my cave, trusting that I'd find a way out. They were the one constant I had left. They're the only thing in my life that's ever been constant. No matter how crazy the world becomes, there has always been one rock: home. It's not a place, either, it's an emotion. All the things parents do for you …

I'm lucky to have a wonderful relationship with them. We argue, but we are friends more than anything. My dad, Derek, is Welsh, and my mum, Lee, is Jamaican. I am the only child they had together, although I have two brothers and two sisters, one sister through Mum, the others through Dad. They'd been together for a while before I was born. I guess I was an accident, but I've always quite liked the idea of being a love child!

Much of my youth was spent living in a tent out of the back of our car. From Friday to Sunday, they would take me to motocross races all over the country. Dad bought me a 50cc bike when I was six, and we never looked back. Every weekend, I would race at the South Wales Schoolboy Scramblers Club. Dad would help mark the course and act as my mechanic; Mum would write the report for the local paper and make bacon sarnies for everyone in the vicinity of our car/tent. As I improved and attracted some sponsorship, it became a van/tent. If I raced well, we would stop off at a Little Chef on the way home, and Mum and Dad would let me have a cherry pancake. We'd be back home in time for *Catchphrase*. What awesome times! I would go back there in a heartbeat if I could.

Growing up, I never idolised the usual stars, but I always admired Mum and Dad. They were my heroes. They couldn't really have been more different from each other. Mum is passionate and emotional. She's the engine of the house, always on the go. Dad is calm and relaxed with an adventurous spirit. Both were strict but understanding. They make a great team, and from them I learned the values of kindness, a work ethic and doing a job properly. They instilled those values by being rock-solid, without ever being pushy. Even when I was confronted with that crunch decision, which any professional sportsman will face at some point, whether to turn away from a 'normal' life and pursue sport for a living, they left me to decide. In 2000, three years into a five-year dentistry degree at Cardiff University, Pontypridd offered me a contract. I took a two-year sabbatical from the course (which I never returned to!) and signed the contract. Despite the sacrifices my parents had made to provide me with the kind of opportunities they had never had in life, there was nothing but support from them – and the belief that I could make it.

I was privately educated, to some people's surprise, considering my accent, tattoos and colour, but I would describe myself as coming from a working-middle-class background. Dad is an engineer and is still working, well into his seventies. Mum has usually worked with Dad, running the books, even driving the lorries when required. Now she is a magistrate. They have pretty much always been self-employed. They worked so hard they were able to send me to Monmouth School as a day boy. When I played junior rugby at Pontypool, I was seen as the public-school boy, and the fact that I went to public school I felt worked against me when I played for Wales Schools, far more so than the colour of my skin. It helped to foster the impression I had of myself as an outsider.

I would not describe myself as a rebel, but I have always felt a bit different, as if I didn't fit in anywhere. That is not a sob story – on the contrary, I have loved walking my own path. Although its repercussions were crushing during those dark days at the end of my rugby career, it has been the making of me. I learned to be independent and to think for myself from a young age. I was proudly Welsh yet of mixed race, an only child yet with four half-siblings, always around people yet never quite one of them.

That impression continued throughout my adolescence as a schoolboy and rugby player, further heightened by the fact that I was always the youngest of my peers, having been born in August. Just after I'd turned eighteen, I spent a year in South Africa on a sporting scholarship to Michaelhouse School in Durban. It was their centenary year and barely a year after the end of apartheid. I imagine – although I don't know this – that I was offered it because of my rugby and my colour. It was one of the best years of my life. For the first time I was striding out somewhere completely different and on my own. I grew up six years in one. That was where I embraced the idea of 'professionalism' in my approach to sport, the first time I'd applied to sport the lessons my parents had taught me. Schoolboy rugby was massive out there, akin to college football in the States. We played one game in front of 14,000 people. I was the only black pupil in the Michaelhouse first XV and, I'm proud to say, the first ever to receive the school colours.

If I'd always felt a misfit I was by now conditioned by rugby to feel happy as part of a collective and to feel inspired by it. Some of the greatest times of my life followed. I returned to play for Newport and represented Wales at sevens. A broken back put me out for a season, but after a year playing for Cardiff Meds at university I joined the rugby club at Pontypridd, the town of my birth. Here I fell in with a crop of talented youngsters. Some of my fondest rugby memories are of that club. We quickly became one of the best teams in the country. In 2002, we won the Principality Cup and reached the final of the European Challenge Cup. And that year five of us won our first caps. Mine came in Bloemfontein on 8 June when I became the 1001st Wales international on the summer tour to South Africa. If only it hadn't clashed with my sister Debbie's wedding – but rugby had long since been dictating the terms of my life by that point.

I won three more caps in the year or so following the first, but I missed out on selection for the World Cup in 2003. That same year, Pontypridd merged with Bridgend, during the restructuring of Welsh professional rugby, to form the ill-fated Celtic Warriors. Despite a really promising first season on the field, the powers that be closed us down after just a year. I could write a book about that turbulent period alone. We were broken up and auctioned off, I felt like we were cattle. Phil Davies rescued me with a contract at Leeds, and so began another happy spell, which included Leeds' first piece of major silverware in the shape of the Powergen Cup in 2005. Then, after the pain of relegation a year later, I joined Perpignan on my biggest contract yet, but I wasn't myself. I remember turning up more anxious to make friends than to play hard. Perhaps, deep down, I thought I'd made it.

I hadn't. I didn't play well in my first couple of games, by which time they make their mind up about you over there. I was injured in my third game and then became a fixture on the bench. I fell out with the president and watched a year of my life pass by. When Paul Turner offered me the chance to return to Wales with the Dragons I took it with more gratitude than he'll ever know.

Regrets over my time at Perpignan recurred throughout the agonising in that room. What a golden opportunity. Why hadn't I been myself down there? No matter how much I tried I couldn't stop myself going over moment after moment of my elapsed career, and not just the big decisions but little choices or mistakes I'd made in games I thought I'd forgotten about a long time ago. I sometimes have trouble remembering what happened yesterday, but vivid recollections of incidents from years back started appearing in my head. Why did I force that pass, why drop that ball? The ghosts of matches past reared up and crowded in on me. Had I been the best I could be?

It pained me so much to go over it again and again in my mind. But it wasn't just the missed opportunities, however large or small, that made the room so hellish. The regret itself tore me up. I hated myself for the inertia of it, the introspection. I was unmanned.

The turning point came while I was lying in bed, staring at the ceiling. I couldn't tell you what prompted it, or what I was thinking about when it happened. I just remember the moment.

My nana had died about two years earlier. I was very close to her. We all were. She used to live with my parents and was like a second mother to me. She was Mum's mother and her best friend. Mum struggles with her loss to this day.

Her funeral passed in the blink of an eye. I negotiated it on auto-pilot, not even particularly emotional on the day. I didn't take in much during the service. It was if the whole thing were playing with the volume turned down. But, for one line, someone turned it up.

'The horizon is only the limit of our sight.'

It was the vicar who said it. I don't know what he'd been saying before it, I don't know what he went on to say after, but it was a line that leaped out at me from the white noise of the funeral. Since then I've come to believe, from the bottom of my heart, that somehow, if people can do that, my nan was speaking to me through those words. I believe she could see through me, to my fears, and beyond, to what was waiting down the road.

I didn't know what the line meant; I just knew it was important, so important. And within two weeks I'd had it tattooed on my arm. I just had to have it somehow, to keep it on me at all times, never to forget it. Why I needed to, at that point, I had no idea.

So, for the following two years, every time I looked at the inside of my left forearm, there it was, this strange, enigmatic sentence. And now, lying in bed, with my other arm immobile, some process in my head, chemical or electrical, emotional or spiritual, completed itself, and I suddenly understood it. The horizon is only the limit of our sight. There's much more beyond that we can't see, but not being able to see it doesn't mean it's not there. I wanted to live freely. No more fear. I'd spent my life being scared of what I couldn't see, of the future and of dark shadows in my head. I was sick of it. For once I was going to stand up and embrace them.

I have since had months and months in a tent to think this all through, and I have come to the realisation that rugby had been all I'd ever seen, particularly in those furiously focused, desperate last couple of years. I'd regarded the return to Wales with the Dragons as my one last chance. It was all or nothing. I couldn't conceive of a life beyond rugby, nor did I dare to try. I was holding on to everything I knew so tightly, desperate not to lose any of it. As my body, rugby career and relationship began to shut down, my horizons closed in. Now, for the first time, I could see that there might be more.

That was the point I picked myself up. Next, I picked up Sir Ranulph Fiennes's book *Mad, Bad and Dangerous to Know*. About a year earlier, someone had given it to me, and now I started reading.

I was captivated by his stories, the hardship and perseverance, the environment he performed in. It stirred something in me.

I never actually finished it, though. The first third was all I needed, it was so powerful. I really should read the whole thing one day, what with the way it changed my life. People have approached me to compare notes on a book that has clearly inspired so many others. 'I love the bit when ...' they say, and I laugh along nervously, too ashamed to admit that I haven't actually made it so far as to read that episode.

I used to feel embarrassed about that; now I don't mind so much. I read the first third of the book, and I was inspired. It gave me a taste, but I didn't want to read on and see someone else climb the mountain. I wanted to get out and climb it for myself.

2

First things first, though. No one launches off in a new direction anywhere these days without first consulting the internet.

I reached over for my laptop, ready for my next brush with death by progress bar. Time slowed to a crawl in that white room, and the same went for the internet connection. But I had the first inklings of a purpose now. I'd made out a peephole to my future. I reached over for that laptop feeling, at last, something other than emptiness and pain. And soon (well, as soon as the bitrate would allow) I had come across a site dedicated to the Seven Summits – the highest mountain on each of the seven continents.

That very instant I learned of them I knew I was going to climb them. In fact, I was so sure it was as if, in a strange way, I had already done it. Another piece of me loosened; another packet of hope unfolded.

It was then that I went downstairs and made myself a coffee.

There was no plan, of course, no thought of timeframes or records at this stage. All that mattered was that it was a new way of life and that it wasn't rugby. My vision did not involve a career path or a way of financing it, but that was fine. This was nothing more or less than the way out of that room. And I wanted to throw myself into it.

Already I was in thrall to the mountains. They are so much more than big lumps of rock. Their mystique is powerful, even in a small white room with a slow internet connection and a life of no direction. Particularly then. I knew little about mountains, but I felt the fear of them as much as anyone. My rugby career had been haunted by fear of failure. I had come to that realisation in this very room, but it was too late to do anything about that now. The fear of mountains, though – that could be embraced. I was angry with my body and I wanted to push it again. The idea of striving for something in an atmosphere with 20 per cent of the oxygen we breathe down here was just the kind of challenge I wanted. I needed to know that my body was not the failure, the broken wreck that had ended my rugby career. The path out of that room was now clear to me, and it led up mountains.

I can't say I was consciously aware of any of this reasoning, but I was driven all of a sudden. That same day, I looked into the kinds of organisations that could teach me the relevant skills. Which was another important point. I had to do this properly. I had no interest in being hauled up a mountain by a commercial enterprise, who would charge me a fortune for the privilege and leave me at the end of it barely changed from the man at the start. More than anything else, I wanted to learn a new skill. I fired off emails to a handful of companies, explaining my background, what I wanted to do, which was to climb the Seven Summits, and why I wanted to do it.

And the next day I pulled on a pair of shoes and left the house.

When you're in a fragile state of mind like I was, little things become so important. All I'd done was send some emails, but at the time it felt as if I'd, well, climbed Everest. I felt so much better. It was the first time since the injury that I'd helped myself, the first positive step I'd taken, having contemplated the worst. You can look back over a time like that, which obviously I have, and ask yourself why you didn't just pull yourself together sooner, send those emails on day one in the room, rather than on day twenty-one. I don't know. Maybe you just have to go through it all. But I'd been through it, and now I wanted to help myself.

Sure enough, when you resolve to help yourself, your positivity quickly attracts others to your side. I don't remember how or why my wanderings had brought me there, but I was standing outside the Welsh Shop in Cardiff, across the road from the castle, when my phone rang. A voice on the other end introduced himself as Tom Briggs of Jagged Globe, one of the companies I had emailed only the day before. He invited me up to Sheffield, where they are based, to meet Simon Lowe, the managing director.

'Simon's away next week,' he said, 'so how about in two weeks' time?'

'How about tomorrow?' I replied.

I didn't want to wait two weeks. There was a fresh momentum I could feel behind me at this point, which had been so lacking, and I had to ride it now. The next day, just two days out of the white room, I was driving up to Sheffield.

Mountaineers, I have since learned, come in all shapes and sizes – there's no stereotype. And you would not look at Simon Lowe and think, 'Ah, here's a conqueror of mountains, if ever I saw one'. The man I met in Sheffield that day was in his late forties, I would say, grey-haired and bespectacled. I warmed to him immediately. One of the reasons mountaineers need not conform physically is that so much of the strength required of them is mental. It was obvious that Simon was passionate about his trade – honest and direct.

The latter qualities I particularly valued. Simon receives hundreds of enquiries from people who want to climb mountains. Once he's talked them through what is involved, he won't hear from many of them again. I drove up to see him in Sheffield, and he spent most of our first meeting trying to talk me out of it. He spent most of our second meeting doing much the same thing. I appreciated it, and I think he appreciated my response to it. He has a military background, and his eye for detail, which is meticulous, was never better demonstrated as he laid out the dangers to be faced, the techniques to be mastered and, not least, the finances to be mustered. His integrity was obvious. He would not take any shortcuts. I knew quickly that this was the company I wanted to learn with, then to work with. And I would not be cowed by his efforts to test my resolve.

It was then that I set to work on my shoulder exercises.

Within a week of my first meeting with Simon, I had another call from Tom (who *is* the sort of big, broad fellow you might imagine astride a mountain top). They'd had a cancellation. Would I be interested in taking their Alpine introduction course in two weeks' time? It would involve ten days in the Alps, learning basic mountaineering techniques – crampons, rope work, glacier travel, and so on. Then if I wanted to, I could stay on for another four or five days and attempt Mont Blanc. Knowing Simon as I do now, I wouldn't be surprised if he threw it at me as a first test. The normal programme they suggest to bring somebody of my mountaineering experience at the time, which is to say none, to a stage where they might attempt Everest is three years. I had made it clear I wanted to devote myself to any such journey and to complete the Seven Summits, including Everest, in less time than that. Well, now, with this invitation, they would see just how serious I was about it. I'm sure they expected me to decline on the grounds of late notice, but I said yes without a thought.

It was my next step away from the room. I was living in the moment, without consideration for the long term, but I was living. There was cash in the bank. An insurance pay-out for my career-ending injury made up the bulk of it, but I also had some savings from my rugby days. Not a huge amount, but enough to let me take a leap like this. And, anyway, what else did I have to do?

It was an awesome two weeks in the Alps. I loved it. Just being outside was such a blessing. The Alps is a powerful place to be regardless of what you're doing, the opposite of being in that little room for so long. But to be there learning a new skill, at however rudimentary a level, and channelling my energies into something positive, while meeting new and interesting people, did wonders to move me on.

At the end of it, four of us stayed to climb Mont Blanc, and I was the least experienced by far. Our guide was a Matterhorn specialist, which means he likes to climb fast, the safest way to attempt the Matterhorn. We reached the Tête Rousse Hut (at 3167m altitude), which is the launch point for the summit of Mont Blanc. The weather had closed in, and we settled for the night. Normally, you attempt Mont Blanc (4807m) from the Tête Rousse Hut and return to the Goûter Hut (3835m), or set off from the Goûter and return to the Tête Rousse. But we set off from the Tête Rousse and returned there too, all in the same day. The conditions were good, and we were quick. We summited in six hours, which was the fastest ascent by a Jagged Globe team that year. But it was tough, my first experience of pushing so hard for so long and at that altitude. I might have been a professional sportsman, but in rugby you perform for eighty minutes. Here, we were on it for ten or eleven hours. It was exhausting, physically and mentally, but I felt confident throughout. When I returned to the UK, I rang Simon to tell him I was still in the game. Indeed, I was clearer than ever that this was what I wanted to do. I had passed my first test. Simon could move me into the category marked 'Not a joker'.

At this point, my plan was to climb two of the Seven Summits a year for the next three years. Before I went any further down that path, though, it was important that I got back into shape. I worked with my mate Kevin Morgan, who was now conditioning coach at Neath Rugby Club, on a basic endurance programme to help me transition from the power athlete I had once been.

My physical condition was one thing. Financially, I had even more work to do. The Welsh rugby community is strong and reaches into many walks of life. I had hoped that I might be able to source some sponsorship from within that network. I spoke to a few companies about funding. They all listened respectfully, but you can tell when people's eyes are glazing over. Nobody came in with anything concrete. It quickly became clear that my plan was too difficult to market. Three years was far too long to take over a challenge whose successful completion was becoming increasingly commonplace. I had been introduced to a company called Limegreentangerine, a design agency in Cardiff whose owners, Andy and Bev Rees, have become good friends of mine. They were the first of many who would come on board and give their time so enthusiastically and to such great effect. It was in our first brainstorming session (all four hours of it!) that we struck upon the notion of climbing the Seven Summits in seven months. It wasn't a world first – a handful of others had achieved it at that point – but it was a more credible project, and 'Challenge 77' was a snappy name for my life's new direction, at least. I was just so grateful to have that life back, and my confidence. The next chapter of it was starting to take shape. I had something to work towards, in the boardroom and out on the trails.

I can't remember what Simon's reaction was to this latest development. Drama is not his style, so it would have been measured. Either way, he didn't laugh in my face, which he would have had every right to. In his calm, meticulous way, he advised me that the next test would be to climb more technically, beyond 5000m. He suggested the volcanoes in Ecuador, where there are a few such peaks to be scaled. This opportunity would arise in a trip over Christmas and New Year.

Until then, I hit the trails with the best training partner a man could have – Ben, my beloved dog. We ran and we ran through – and up and down – the Welsh countryside. The gym was off limits. I was sick of it and I didn't want to be reminded of the rugby career I'd been forced to abandon. At this point, the energy driving me in this enterprise was anti-rugby, anti-rugby.

I have always been a dedicated trainer, but now it was becoming a form of therapy for me. I was pushing myself hard. Kev organised for me to undergo VO_2 max testing at the University of South Wales with Professor Bruce Davies. The VO_2 max test measures the maximum rate at which your body takes up oxygen during intense exercise, in other words how fit you are. On this occasion, mine involved pounding on a treadmill at an ever-increasing speed and incline, breathing through a sealed tube, until I could go on no more. We didn't learn a huge amount from the test that we didn't know already, but it was a useful and enlightening experience to force my body to the point of collapse. What we did learn, though, is that I have an irregular heartbeat. This is quite common, apparently, for elite sportsmen. When the resting heart rate falls below sixty-five beats per minute, residue can collect in the bottom of the ventricle, which is thrown up with each beat. My resting heart rate is fifty-two. It is also common for sportsmen to have an enlarged ventricle. Less common, though, is what it turns out I have, which is two enlarged ventricles. Bruce was quite concerned about the irregular heartbeat and put me through further tests, but his finding was that my heart is strong. Indeed, as soon as the heartbeat increases, it becomes regular. My heart is actually happier, it seems, when I'm exercising.

Another thing I learned in the Alps, and then in Ecuador, is that I seem to acclimatise to altitude well. Whether or not this is linked to Bruce's findings is unknown. Science has not yet unravelled the mysteries of altitude acclimatisation, which, besides, are vicious and unpredictable. I have since got to know one of Britain's best mountaineers, a tiny but super-strong woman called Adele Pennington. She is the first British woman to have climbed Everest twice and is on her way to becoming the first to summit all fourteen of the world's 8000m mountains. She is a phenomenon. Then, suddenly in 2010, near the summit of Makalu in the Himalaya, she suffered a pulmonary oedema, fluid within the lung. She had to be flown off the mountain for life-saving surgery. (Incredibly, she returned to Makalu the following year and summited.) You can acclimatise at a certain altitude as many times as you like, but there is no guarantee for the next time. So many factors play a part. Experience counts a great deal on a psychological level, but, physiologically, the body has no memory when it comes to altitude acclimatisation.

By now, Simon was beginning to believe in me. Not that he ever said it, but he started to discuss the kinds of skills I would need if I hoped to achieve what I wanted to in the timeframe we had chosen. I had to be self-sufficient, regardless of whether or not I planned to climb with others. I had to acquire a 'toolbox' of skills, some of which might not in theory be required. Although they may be the highest, the Seven

Summits are not technically the hardest mountains on their respective continents, but I would be pushing so hard to climb them all within seven months that I had to train as if they were. Before we set off for Ecuador, I signed up for some ice-climbing in Italy almost as soon as we got back, and then further training expeditions in the Alps and in the Scottish Highlands.

But the final endorsement, the moment I knew Simon had seen something in me, came after we returned from Ecuador in January. Simon and I had shared a tent, so we got to know each other a lot better. I learned from him, and he was able to see how I conducted myself – that I was neither gung-ho nor wanting to cut corners. I was the only one of Jagged Globe's clients on that trip, among whom were some experienced mountaineers, to summit all of the 5000m peaks we tackled. I felt strong on all of them.

So, when we returned to the UK, Simon suggested one further tweak to my project. How about we throw in the two poles? If I climbed the Seven Summits and skied the last degree to the North and South Poles all in seven months, that would be a world first. Indeed, no one had stood at all nine places in the same calendar year, let alone in seven months. Seven Summits, three poles (Everest is known as the third pole), seven months – the 737 Challenge was born.

I was like a bottle of pop, I was so excited. It immediately felt right. This was a genuine world first. What a privilege to be able to attempt it! And this, six months after I'd retired from a life as a rugby player who had never climbed a mountain.

We escalated my training programme. In January I learned

to ice-climb in Cogne, Italy; in February I returned to the Alps; in March I went to Scotland to develop my climbing skills; and in April I joined an expedition on the sea ice in Greenland.

There were a lot of moving parts in this project, a challenge of logistics, as well as the obvious others. We drew up a running order of peaks and poles for the Challenge. It was complicated, and I ceded control of it to Simon. Each location has a season, outside which it is impossible to attempt an assault, and of course each has a specific geographical position on the globe. Taking all of it into account, we came up with the following itinerary: the South Pole (geographic), Vinson (4897m, Antarctica), Aconcagua (6959m, South America), Kilimanjaro (5895m, Africa), Carstensz Pyramid (4884m, Australasia), the North Pole (geographic), Everest (8848m, Asia), Denali (6194m, North America) and Elbrus (5642m, Europe). The Challenge would officially begin on New Year's Day 2011 on the South Pole. All being well, I would complete it sometime in July at the top of Elbrus.

Margins were tight throughout, as you would expect of something no one had ever tried before, but one section of the Challenge stood out as particularly precarious, not to mention brutal. The North Pole, Everest and Denali legs were the most difficult legs individually, and they all fell within the same weather window. I would have to complete them between 1 April, when the North Pole season opens, and July, when Denali's closes. This would leave very little margin for error, injury, illness or weather delays. Considering most people take months to recover from an expedition up Everest, the Denali leg looked especially tough, as the one that followed. At that

32

stage Simon was hoping to accompany me, but it was not inconceivable that I would have to climb it alone. It was therefore essential that I had gained experience of this treacherous mountain beforehand. To that end, Simon organised for me to join Jagged Globe's expedition in May.

I remember Tom briefing me about the mountain before I left, over a coffee at Jagged Globe's offices, and I was amped with nerves and adrenaline. Denali, in its own right, is a serious proposition to a climber, every bit as serious as Everest, if not more so. It doesn't have Everest's altitude, but at 6194m, the third highest mountain of the Seven Summits, it's enough to be getting on with. Besides, in terms of atmosphere and thus acclimatisation, it equates to a height closer to 7000m, relative to the Himalaya, because of the lower barometric pressure towards the poles. Which is another distinguishing feature – its proximity to the Arctic Circle. Denali is the most northerly mountain of the Seven Summits. Of all the things it is famous for, perhaps its weather is the most dangerous. Not only does the mountain skirt the Arctic Circle, but it sits just to the north-east of the Aleutian Islands, home of the Aleutian Low, a semi-permanent area of low pressure and one of a handful of places around the world where weather systems are formed. That means storms can whip up without notice. In the Alps and the Himalaya, weather comes across from the Atlantic, so you have longer to gather forecasts, but on Denali you can go from one extreme to the other in days. It is the coldest of the world's major mountains, with temperatures dropping to −40°C routinely and winds sometimes exceeding 100mph.

It is also known as Mount McKinley, but the native name, Denali, has become the more widely used. It means 'Great One' in the Koyukon Athabaskan language. Indeed, from base to tip, it is the world's highest mountain on dry land. The vertical gain of 4000m from base camp to peak is greater than that on Everest. Not only that, but, because of its remoteness, you have to carry everything with you and you carry it yourself. The limit per person is 125lb (9st) across a rucksack and sled (or pulk, as we call them, the Norwegian word for sled). In other words, you're dragging a decently sized teenager with you.

That expedition was the making of me. It was at that point that people who know about mountains began to think: he might just do this. I had spent the past few months building up my toolbox of skills, learning as much as I could from as many different experts, but there's no substitute for experiencing the real thing. Denali has a reputation for her weather, and she lived up to it. We were hit with the worst of that season. The first storm struck just under Motorcycle Hill. Then we had to sit out another, higher up, for seven days. On one of the first days, I made the mistake of leaving the zip open on the vestibule of my tent – not much, only an inch. As we hunkered down that night, the vestibule quietly filled with snow. My boots and rucksack were covered. That was the kind of mistake that could cost me on the Challenge without the luxury of extra days to dry things out. Always do your zips up.

I also experienced for the first time the chilling proximity of a fellow climber's death. A French guy in a group ahead of us had taken his pulk up to Windy Corner at 13,000ft (everything's in feet on Denali – that's about 4000m). Absolutely shattered, he sat down on it to take a breather, lost his footing and rode it off the side of the mountain. It's the end of days when you do that. No way you can stop. Horrific.

Our leader on that trip was a guy called Rob Durnell, or Durny, a super-experienced leader on Denali and one of the best big-mountain skiers in the world. He taught me so much. It is such a privilege to be on mountains with these people. I try to make the most of every moment with them.

Summit day for us was tough – and at more than eighteen hours another new experience for a sportsman from the eighty-minute school of exertion. We had left High Camp (5200m) and negotiated most of the final push to the summit, up the Autobahn, through Denali Pass, past Archdeacon's Tower and across the Football Field. The names on Denali are colourful, if nothing else. There, at the foot of Pig Hill, the last steep climb to the summit ridge, the weather closed in. By now our group had dwindled from twelve to four. The wind chill was close to −40°C and visibility was poor. Conditions were marginal, but Durny decided we could push on to the summit.

It was on the way back down that things started to go wrong. We'd negotiated the summit ridge in really difficult conditions. Visibility was down to 20m or so. But, when you're edging along a ridge with the best part of a kilometre drop down one side and half a kilometre down the other, not being able to see very far has its advantages. Still, a narrow ridge at 6000m in freezing cloud is an environment fraught with danger. People fall from that ridge quite regularly.

We were in two rope teams. The one I was in was leading on the way back from the summit. We thought the other team were right behind us, but when we got down to the top of Pig Hill and waited there was no sign.

You fear the worst in those situations. We climbed back up the summit ridge. Thankfully, the other team were alive and

well, but one of the guys wore prescription goggles. These consist of two pairs of lenses, hermetically sealed. They are supposed to be anti-fog, but it was so cold that the lenses had frozen over not only on the inside and out, where they could be scraped, but between the lenses, where they could not. So he'd had to take them off, which meant he could barely see. The others were having to guide him off the ridge as if he were blind.

So we reorganised our rope teams, this time with Durny and our other guide, Caitlin – a very pretty Alaskan, hard as nails – helping this guy off the ridge. Durny asked me to lead the other team down. I was amped. Bricking it, but amped. And super-proud. For him to put that level of trust in me. It was only for about half an hour, but it was the biggest step in my evolution so far.

When we reached the top of Pig Hill again, we regathered and composed ourselves. If the conditions in which we summited had been difficult, they were now deteriorating even further. You could see no further than 10 to 15m. We were in rope teams of three, and I could make out only the silhouette of the next guy, as the rope disappeared into the white. Things were so bad that other professional guides had waited with their groups at the top of Pig Hill for Durny to break the trail back to High Camp. Only someone with intimate knowledge of the mountain could navigate in these conditions, and Durny was that man. He was like the Pied Piper, with around twenty people following him now.

It was a painful descent; they often are. You've been climbing for hours. Eighty per cent of accidents happen on the way down. One of our team was really struggling with the altitude and fatigue. He had quite a few falls. Twice Durny and I had to effect an ice-axe arrest to save all three of us.

It was epic. And I loved it. The deprivation. I think everyone has a masochistic streak in them, but I would say mine is particularly pronounced. And to be around professional mountaineers who were finding it tough came as a massive boost to my confidence. Because I felt all right. Clearly, it was about as far removed from a walk in the park as you could imagine, but I was coping. More than that, I felt I was thriving.

I came off Denali like a man restored. Physically I was shattered, but life felt good again. I had a purpose, and the belief that I would fulfil it was now hardening into confidence. Still, there was plenty more to endure before I could even think about setting off. In June, Simon arranged for me to undergo cold-water-immersion testing at the University of Portsmouth. It was a three-day study on different types of survival blanket. I was to be the test dummy.

Simon had organised it through a few contacts of his. They were interested in their blankets; Simon and I were interested in preparing me for the possibility of a fall into the icy waters of the Arctic Ocean on the North Pole leg. It was genuinely horrible. As a rugby player, I was used to ice baths, but this was a new level of pain. I was supposed to be immersed for an hour, or until clinical hypothermia set in, whichever came first. My body fat is pretty low, so it was hypothermia for me.

Three days running.

With a thermometer up my arse.

I don't know which was worse. We laughed about it on day one, as they presented me with this thermometer the length of a drinking straw, a tub of Vaseline and a room where I could be on my own. By day three, the laughing had stopped. But it's by far the best way to measure your core temperature, and I appreciated the importance of ensuring an accurate reading.

The first thing that happens when you are lowered into the pool is that your survival instincts kick in. The body goes into shock. The blood vessels constrict, placing the heart under pressure. The most common cause of cold-water deaths is heart attack. Next, your mind says, stop, get me out of here. The challenge – and the reason I was doing it – is to manage the panic and control the mind. It is a neat analogy for so much of what an endurance athlete does. You are engaged in a non-stop dialogue with your body, constantly overriding its defence mechanisms to drive yourself on. Because after the head has bleated about its discomfort you enter the stage where, physiologically, your whole body is starting to protest. In other words, it's really hurting. Again, the answer is an exercise in suppression and exertion of will. I just don't give myself the option. For all the conversations you can have with yourself about coping strategies, escape plans, worst-case scenarios, when it is all stripped away the final question, the raw, naked crux of the matter, is that you do it or you don't. With a test like that, I go into lockdown. I'm in here. I'm in here until they pull me out. And that's it.

Obviously, it's one thing to think like that when surrounded by scientists with a thermometer up your bottom and another on your own in one of the world's frozen wildernesses, but the experience gained from the former is invaluable, as is the knowledge of what can be endured. I now know what it feels like to be hypothermic – and, just as importantly, what it feels like when you're not yet.

I ended up lasting around about fifty minutes in the tank each time, before my body's temperature dropped below 35°C – hypothermia. This is when the test begins for the scientists. They pull you out, wrap you in a shiny survival blanket and lie you on a piece of foam in a cold room for an hour. That part was even worse, because you become colder before you become warmer. You are shivering uncontrollably, unable to speak or even react, and they leave you on your back for an hour. There's no threshold to be activated this time, no point at which you can be hauled out. You just have to endure. It's a long hour. On the third day they adjusted the oxygen levels in the chamber, so we did it all at the equivalent of 3000m in altitude.

At the end of the hour you feel cold but more comfortable (the survival blankets work!), whereupon the process of rewarming begins. They place you in a bath at a very specific temperature – pretty cold by normal standards, but on the return from hypothermia it feels nice and warm. Then, over the course of another hour or so, they gradually warm it up.

All in all, it's the best part of three hours. The process didn't change me physiologically, but it transformed me mentally. Resilience is a trainable skill, like any other. So much of what we do physically is driven by our mental fitness. Here was further evidence that these extreme environments could be endured.

It was now June. I was due to leave for the South Pole in December, six months away. The 737 Challenge was in the public domain, but I still had no funding in place. My positivity was all very well, but without the more prosaic support structures of sponsorship and publicity I was as unfit to take this thing on as I had been a year earlier, when I'd never climbed a mountain in my life.

I've already introduced some of the key members of the team that I had put together so far – Simon; Bev and Andy at Limegreentangerine; my parents, whose role was to become so important – but not yet Tracy Pinder, my PR manager and rock of support. She and I had met earlier in the year, when a mutual friend had asked her to produce a promotional video for the Challenge. We got on like a house on fire and after she'd organised for me and a few of the boys to go to the Moto GP in Catalonia – and get on the grid – that was it. She was never going to get rid of Parksy!

When I'd left for Denali in May, I had a very crude plan in place. But while I'd been away, Tracy had discovered the extent of the Challenge's commercial shortcomings.

We arranged to meet for a picnic in the New Forest, straight after my last dose of hypothermia. It was a sweltering day, something my poor body did not appreciate after what it had just been through. But we sat down and talked it all through. I drew a diagram of my ideal team, some of which was already in place, and Tracy, or Pinders, as I sometimes call her, pressed home the need to get things moving.

I had already decided by then that I wanted to raise funds in aid of Marie Curie Cancer Care and was working with Karen Jones, the fundraising manager of Penarth Hospice. It was important to me that the Challenge left a positive legacy. As for many, cancer has loomed large in my family. My dad has survived it, as have my sister and brother-in-law. I lost my Uncle Terry to it when I was young. While I was preparing for the Challenge, my cousin, Joy, was losing her battle in the

Marie Curie hospice in Penarth. It was there that I met Karen, and she and I hit it off from the start.

It just so happened that Sir Ranulph Fiennes was supporting Marie Curie, too. Karen was able to introduce me to him, when she frogmarched me to the front of a queue of people waiting to speak to him after a talk he'd been giving at a Marie Curie event in London. I was amazed by how interested he seemed in the Challenge, taking a moment out of his book-signing session to talk to me about it. I had with me that precious copy of his book, which had played such a part in helping me out of the white room. He signed it, and underneath wrote his email address. Don't hesitate, he said. It was insane. Later, I went to his home to interview him for a promotional video for the Challenge. He had considered climbing Vinson with me, but it never happened. Regardless, I was so grateful for his support and his words of wisdom on the video.

'You must remember,' he said, 'the part that luck plays in everything we do.'

So true. As I have learned for myself since, and continue to learn.

But you also need to make your own luck. When it came to the funding of the Challenge, I had not been doing that until Tracy helped focus my efforts over the picnic in the forest. It was no use having everything in my head; I needed to delegate, something that I have never found easy. And so came together the best team a person could wish for, a team of people who pulled together on nothing more tangible than belief. They gave their time and energy for free, and in some cases, even more than that: they risked their own capital. Tracy was to manage my PR; Simon oversaw the logistics and acted as technical consultant;

Andy and Bev designed my website and branding; Gemma Hutton of Gusto Events became events manager and all-round bottle of pop; Lindsey Bridgeman and Carwyn Williams worked on fundraising and sponsorship; Emma Assender looked after admin and schools; Rob James was commercial director; Gareth Thomas managed the books, along with Mum; and Mum and Dad oversaw the whole thing. We held meetings at the Cameo Club, where a room with sandwiches was provided by the owner, Huw Davies, an old friend of mine. We were a happy little team, greater than the sum of our parts, and I am genuinely as proud of what we achieved as I am of anything else that followed. All the money I had at that point – from my insurance pay-out and my savings – had gone into my training, so we had to build a brand and a website without any backing, and then try to win sponsorship. A person with any kind of pedigree in this field would do it the other way round – put together a game plan and secure sponsorship before they go public – but I had no pedigree, as evidenced by the fact I had gone public a while ago. I pulled together my team and then set them what might have been considered an unreasonable task.

What a lot I was asking, and how they responded with a passion and belief that humbles me to think about still! Two years later, we won a prestigious fundraising award for our efforts. Limegreentangerine would also win a design award for their work on the 737 Challenge website.

With people like this in my corner, I knew I had every chance.

I had two more mountains to climb before I left. One of them was 8201m high; the other, well, it was a mere 886m, but I climbed it seven times.

At the end of July, as part of my deprivation training I'd set myself the task of a twenty-four-hour climb in the Brecon Beacons. I chose Pen y Fan, and the plan was simple: start at 3 p.m., walk to the top, then back down, then back up, and so on, and keep doing it until 3 p.m. the next day. It was a simple test of mental resilience. There was no science to it. In the end, I managed seven legs. I was accompanied for some of them. Tracy and Kev did one each, but during the night I had to make do with sheep for company. I had grown used to the sight of their eyes glowing in the beam from my head torch. At 4 a.m., though, I thought I must be hallucinating when I saw a couple of eyes start dancing and jiggling about. It turned out to be the head torches of Ollie and Rob from Boulders, an indoor climbing centre in Cardiff. They'd brought golf clubs, so we ended up firing a few balls off the top of Pen y Fan as the sun came up.

But the first ascent was special because I was accompanied by Captain Anthony Harris, who had lost a leg in Helmand province. He was in so much pain on the way up. He'd only just learned to walk again, and his prosthesis was rubbing the stump of his leg raw. But he made it. There are so many amazing people out there, each with their own mountain to climb. Whenever I struggled for the rest of that twenty-four-hour climb, I thought of Anthony. Then, when I finished, I headed into Cardiff for Kev's engagement party and fell asleep talking to my old Ponty team-mate Ceri Sweeney. But he's used to that!

My final test before the Challenge would take me to new heights. At 8201m, Cho Oyu, in the Himalaya, is the sixth highest mountain in the world. Simon considered it important

43

that I experience the kind of altitude I would have to operate in on Everest. And, more than that, I had to if I wanted to climb Everest with Jagged Globe. One of their conditions for it was that climbers have experience of an 8000m expedition.

Cho Oyu did become an important mountain for me, although not necessarily for that reason. It provided another demonstration of the power of luck.

I left for the Himalaya in September with Matt Parkes from Jagged Globe and Steve Williams, the Olympic oarsman. Steve would be joining me on the North Pole and Everest legs. We had already trained together on the sea ice of Greenland, and now we were taking our 8000m test.

Our leader was Rob Anderson, an American climber who is the only man to have climbed the Seven Summits solo, making it to the top of Everest at the ninth attempt, fourteen years after he'd started his mission. As such, he was the perfect man to accompany us on this expedition. Because this was a new and powerful lesson. This was my first experience of not making it to the summit.

The reality is that you don't always, as Rob knew well. You have to manage that disappointment, which is unlike pro sport, where everything is so clear-cut – you win or you lose. In mountaineering, the tapestry is richer.

The problem was a rare shift in the prevailing wind, and more specifically the threat of avalanche. Usually, Cho Oyu is about as accessible as an 8000m mountain gets, which is not very, obviously, but it is unheard of for nobody to have summited by late September, as was the case here. There had been huge blizzards. The snow sat bloated and threatening on the higher slopes. It was beautiful to behold, even if the air was thick with tension. We made it up to Camp 3, which is at 7300m, but the snow was knee-deep, and I could see the concern in the eyes of Rob and Matt. A team just behind us had been caught in an avalanche, and another big one struck a couple of days later above Camp 3. Remarkably, a team of Sherpas fixing ropes at 8000m survived that one. They were swept 400m down the slope and would have fallen to their deaths had the rope linking them not looped over a protruding rock, to leave them dangling either side of it.

It was clear that the mountain was unstable. The dynamics of an avalanche have been well studied, but, even for the most experienced and well-informed, trying to second-guess them is a form of Russian roulette. The Tibetans decided to close the mountain, which is extremely rare on Cho Oyu.

So they decided to hold a party. Management of the mountain is shared out among the major commercial teams, whose Sherpas come together to fix the ropes. Because none had been fixed that season above Camp 3, there was a surplus in the rope budget, which the Tibetan authorities decided to spend on beer! They sent it up the mountain on a yak train. It was the most bizarre party I have ever been to. At 5700m, Cho Oyu's is the most elevated base camp in the world, so this had to be the highest party ever held – music, beer and Sherpa dancing.

We all left the mountain the next day, bar three climbers. Two of them became the only people to summit Cho Oyu that year. The third was killed in the attempt by an avalanche.

I came away with mixed feelings – heavy with disappointment that we hadn't made the summit but so grateful to be safe and alive. I had learned a valuable lesson here, at an early stage in my development, which wouldn't have happened had the summit attempt been successful. It's not about conquering mountains; it's about working with them. Sometimes the mountain says no. Always the mountain is boss.

Still, I'd climbed beyond 7000m now without any trouble (or supplementary oxygen). This was an important threshold to cross.

The 737 Challenge was on. I was to leave in two months' time.

3

Of all the places the 737 Challenge would take me – and they include some of the most legendary on Earth – it was the first that made the deepest impression.

Antarctica.

It seems ridiculous to describe Antarctica as a 'place'. It's a continent. A vast tract of land, twice the size of Australia, splayed out across the bottom of the globe. It's a wilderness, the coldest, driest and windiest continent on Earth. On average, it is the highest above sea level, as well. And, of course, it is by far the least populated. For that reason, I feel happy calling it a special 'place'. Vast it may be, but very few people have been there. And no one can call it home.

Over the preceding eighteen months of preparation, friends had given me books about the heroic age of the early twentieth century, when the ice of Antarctica was first breached by the human race. As with Sir Ranulph Fiennes's book, I was captivated by the stories of incredible men. I spent hours poring over the maps in these books of a stretch of land that is overlooked in more ways than one by the rest of the world and yet represents one of our planet's seven continents – the fifth largest, as it happens, bigger than Europe or Australasia. On your average globe it's almost impossible to study it properly, because that's where they attach the globe to its axis. Many of them don't even bother to show it at all.

I consider that a shocking lack of respect for a continent that is no less remarkable for the fact that nothing can live there. Indeed, its beauty, hostility and inaccessibility inclines me to consider it the most remarkable of our seven continents, or at least the one to respect above all others. Before I left on the Challenge, it blew my mind to think that I was heading to a place that barely a hundred years ago no one had ever been to before.

It was poignant to me, then, that by sheer coincidence I set off on my adventure from Cardiff Bay exactly a hundred years after Scott's ill-fated *Terra Nova* expedition embarked for the South Pole from the same place. I was touched, too, by the part Wales had played in Scott's endeavours. Not only had they set sail from Cardiff Bay, but Taff Evans, a sailor from Swansea, became one of Scott's most valued team members for his physical strength and manual expertise. He was one of the final team of four Scott took with him to the South Pole. None of them returned. The figurehead of the *Terra Nova* has ended up in the National Museum in Cardiff and the binnacle in the Pierhead Building. And it was from the Pierhead Building, after a reception at the Senedd, home of the Welsh Assembly, that I set off on my quest on 12 December 2010.

Of course, the similarities between me and these heroic pioneers ended there. Where they left to negotiate a treacherous, six-month journey via New Zealand just to reach Antarctica, I got to sit back on a plane. It is only in the last few years that a challenge such as mine has become even remotely feasible – and the passenger jet is as crucial a tool as any. But I wouldn't want to disparage my journey to Antarctica too much. Anyone with an ounce of adventure in their spirit would have been stirred by my five-day journey to the ice. Cardiff, Heathrow, Madrid, Santiago and finally to pretty much the last outpost of civilisation on the South American continent, Punta Arenas. There is life beyond Punta, but not much. It is the last city you reach as you travel south through Chile and much bigger than the two settlements across the border in Argentina that vie for the title of the world's most southerly city. Again, a look on the map is instructive – right at the end of that narrow tip at the bottom of the Americas. And you really do feel as if you're out on a limb when you arrive there, genuinely at the bottom of the world. I love it. It's barren, it's cold and it's windy – a sort of geographical and cultural airlock between the 'real' world and the one I was heading to.

I spent a few days there, my excitement building in the debrief meetings, bag-weighing sessions and breakfasts that helped to pass the time. My OCD tendencies are well known to those who spend any time with me, and they really come into their own in the build-up to an expedition. I must have hundreds of photos on my computer of hotel beds around the world hidden beneath an array of clothing, food and equipment, neatly laid out in the correct order for packing. Unless, of course, I decide that it's not in the correct order, in which case I will rearrange. Then photograph again. People laugh at it, myself included, but I was learning by now that this kind of attention to detail is something for which you are hugely grateful deep into an expedition when it's blowing a gale in the wilderness and you know precisely where that life-saving square of flapjack is. And sometimes, when the straits are dire enough, a sure grasp of where something is really can prove life-saving.

It's a waiting game at Punta. You are on standby indefinitely, hoping for a weather window to open the way to Antarctica, expected to mobilise at half an hour's notice. Antarctic Logistics and Expeditions (ALE) are the company to go to for all things operational in Antarctica. I've never known an organisation like them. They are a British/Australian concern based in America, who work with anyone who needs logistical support out there, from governments at the Antarctic Treaty level all the way down to tourists who want to see the penguins. A dedicated subsidiary company called Adventure Network International (ANI) deal with the non-government operations, and they are the ones who round you up as soon as that weather window appears. You dash off to the local airport in a shuttle bus and pile into the belly of an Ilyushin II-76, a Russian freight plane. They are vast, heavy air tankers, deafeningly noisy and incredibly exciting. Like something out of a war movie. And there you sit, among the crates, machinery and nervous faces, for four and a half hours, until they let you out into the coldest, most desolate wilderness on Earth.

They drop you at ALE's logistical base, a semi-permanent

village on Union Glacier, nestled among the southern stretch of the Ellsworth Mountains, 600 miles 'west' of the South Pole. (Notions of east and west are difficult to get your head round in Antarctica, where technically everything is north of the South Pole, but Union Glacier sits just off the 82nd meridian west, on the underside of the globe's western hemisphere. In other words, on a map of Antarctica, with the Greenwich Meridian taken as twelve o'clock, it is off to the left of the Pole.)

I had joined one of ALE's commercial groups. There were four of us, including the expedition leader, Chris Nance, each with his own reason for wanting to ski the last degree to the South Pole. We pitched our tents among the much larger ones that ALE set up each 'summer' and waited for the next weather window, so that we could be flown to the last degree of latitude, from where we would ski to the Pole. The prognosis was not good for the next few days, but unexpectedly, after two days of tweaking gear and systems, a window appeared. We leaped aboard a Twin Otter and flew off to the 89th degree. A Twin Otter is a much smaller aircraft – and it has windows you can look out of.

Which is exactly what you do. The flight lasted three hours. Three hours of gazing at nothingness. Not a single living thing and barely a feature, bar the odd outcrop of rock. The heart races when the sheer scale of it is laid out before you like that; the imagination runs wild with childish wonder.

Then suddenly and for no obvious reason the plane landed on the whiteness, and the pilot told us that this was our stop. The 89th degree. We climbed out of the plane, which was when it hit me. The blinding white that stretches in all directions; the thin air that is cold, so cold. The South Pole sits on

51

a plateau roughly 3000m above sea level, the elevation of a higher-than-average Alp. Where we were dropped is pretty much at the start of it. The wind whips across the wasteland from the Pole, then begins to pick up serious speed as it tumbles down towards the coast. The temperature with wind chill was close to −30°C when we climbed out of that plane. When your body generates warmth it burns oxygen, which at that altitude is already in short supply. In fact, the air feels rarer than it would at 3000m anywhere else, because the atmosphere is thinner towards the Earth's poles. And you've just arrived straight from sea level. The net effect is that you slow down a little, both in body and mind. Before you know it, you are gathering yourself and your gear, and the plane is taking off, to leave you more isolated than you have ever been before. It is a culture shock. We pulled up our hoods and our face masks, strapped on our skis, harnessed up our 50kg pulks and headed off into the headwind, on a bearing to the South Pole.

Even now I buzz just thinking about it. The adventure of a lifetime was under way, the culmination of a year and a half of planning and preparation, countless man hours and many thousands of pounds. The way out of that white room and the despair within it had led me here – to more whiteness certainly but to a horizon that had never seemed wider and, for now, a perfect sky. Before I'd even taken a step I knew that this was more than the exorcism of my demons. This was where I was supposed to be.

Over the course of the next six days that we spent skiing to the South Pole, I vowed in my diary that I would return to Antarctica. The last degree is sixty nautical miles, a nautical mile being ⅟₆₀th of a degree of latitude, which is roughly sixty-nine statute miles, or 111km. I was aware that this journey across the last degree of latitude is the minimum requirement, really, for anyone who wants to claim to have skied to the South Pole, but I had to complete the Challenge in seven months, which would make a full coast-to-pole expedition for the North and South Poles impossible. We were just scratching the surface of this great continent. I knew I would have to return.

Still, those six days we spent pulling our pulks across the wilderness were as brutal as anything I had tried till then. Quite apart from the fact that I was getting through the calorific equivalent of a marathon a day, it is the constant mental challenge that is so exhausting. The weather we had that year was as good as it gets – and at times breathtakingly beautiful – but that just means the wind was brisk, rather than ferocious. Antarctica is a desert, so it rarely snows, particularly on the plateau, which sees less annual precipitation than the Sahara. But any snow that does fall never melts. It just sits there and becomes 'dry' and powdery, like sand, and the wind scours it into ridges and troughs called sastrugi. All of which makes pulling your pulk much harder than it should be.

It may not snow much, but poor visibility is commonplace – from flat light, when you lose all contrast and shadows, to a whiteout, when the cloud gathers round and you cannot see a thing, not even the ground beneath your skis. It is alarming how a lack of visual stimuli can bend the mind. All you can do is march on by your compass (or the back of the person in front of you) into the whiteness. And on and on and on, for hours on end.

Under those circumstances, you look forward to pitching

your tent at the end of each day. At that time of year, the sun never sets, so the idea of the end of a day is arbitrary, but of course you must observe one. You quickly lose any sense of time, particularly when all the world's time zones have converged to make any differences between them meaningless.

Which means it's easy to forget that it's Christmas. One of our team, Ralf, was German, so he wanted to celebrate Christmas Eve and did so by producing a flask of sixteen-year-old single-malt whisky. Weight is crucial on these trips. Everything you take you have to carry, and it is not long before you feel every last gram. But it is customary (at least, it is for me) to allow yourself one luxury. We were all grateful for Ralf's. A flask of whisky might well have been my choice, too. Often it's Jelly Bellies. Or an iPod. But this time my mum insisted that I take a Christmas card as my one luxury item. This was the second Christmas in a row I was spending away from home, so I relented. After the emotional scenes leaving Mum and Dad at Heathrow, I was looking forward to opening the card on Christmas Day, imagining there to be an inspiring message inside. Maybe even a £20 note. But no. 'To Richard,' it read, 'Happy Christmas. Love, Mum and Dad.' And that was it! I'd denied myself something edible or audible for that! I've never let anyone else choose my luxury item since.

But we were close to the South Pole now, only 22km away. And on Boxing Day, after five days of hauling through the relentless emptiness, feeling as if we were going nowhere, we caught our first glimpse of the Amundsen–Scott Station. It was an incredible feeling. Ralf spotted it first, a tiny speck in the distance, about 17km away. He was suffering from frostbite of the nose by now and was absolutely shattered. For a commercial team, we had been pulling really hard. Kilometre-wise, we made it into the late teens most days, and some of the guys were struggling now. With our goal in sight, I was keen to push on, but we pitched camp for a couple of hours at the end of Boxing Day, 9km from the Pole. By the time we'd covered those last kilometres, we'd been on the march for more than seventeen hours, including our tent break.

There are so many regulations governing the South Pole and surrounding area, with sectors all over the place – the Clean Air Sector, the Quiet Sector, the Dark Sector, and so on. Travellers can only approach the Pole down a specific corridor, about a kilometre long. The 'tourist' camp is at the mouth of it. The other two in our group were so exhausted they decided to pitch their tent and collapse into it. Chris stayed with them, but I didn't want to wait. My emotions welling, I trudged on along the corridor towards the Pole. A hundred years ago, no one had been here. People have given their lives to pave the way.

After a week in the wilderness, the assault of colours was overwhelming. Huge NASA-like buildings rear up on pillars above the ice. The flags of the Treaty nations flutter in a semi-circle around the ceremonial marker, a kind of podium that supports a waist-high silver sphere. In retrospect, I was glad to have this moment to myself. At 3.10 a.m., Chilean time, on 27 December, with the sun overhead and lumps of ice in my beard, I reached the South Pole and the first destination of my 737 Challenge.

Except that I was not alone. There was a film crew there waiting for the outcome of a race between two teams of celebrities, one German, one Austrian, who had set out on a 400-mile race to the Pole from somewhere out on the plateau. And so would begin an extraordinary few days.

The film crew were able to take footage of me arriving (again) at the South Pole for the documentary of the Challenge that BBC Wales had commissioned. I was staying at the Pole until New Year's Day, when the Challenge would officially begin, but the rest of my team left on the 28th. And on the 29th the team of celebrity Austrians, who included the legendary skier Hermann Maier, arrived to win the race.

By now I was keeping company with another of ALE's guides, a wild American called Scott Woolums. Didn't own a car. Did own a plane. In the middle of nowhere we may have been, but things were never boring with Scott around, which made him fairly typical of the sort of person you tend to meet in Antarctica. There are not many of them, but by definition no one is dull.

That includes the scientists. They allow 'tourists' into the Amundsen–Scott Station only at their discretion. Every year they hold a competition among the crew in the station to design the sculpture that sits on top of the marker of the actual geographical pole, which lies about 50m from the ceremonial marker. Each year the marker is changed, and they keep the previous winning sculptures in a display case in the station. It disgusts me to think about it, but one year a visitor stole one of them, so now they are wary of allowing lay people into the station. What an honour it was, then, when Scott and I were invited in by the staff. Around 120 people live on the base in the summer, a number that drops to fifty over the winter. The staff were so welcoming. You don't end up in Antarctica

We've all got embarrassing pics from our youth . . . This was the least embarrassing I could find!

I guess the writing was on the wall from an early age. Loving the snow a little too much as a youngster.

Not quite Steve McQueen, but trying to play it cool, aged eight. 'I wanna go fast!'

All action for Pontypridd.

In the changing room
at Twickenham after
winning the Powergen
Cup with Leeds.

Earning my first Wales cap against the Springboks in Bloemfontein.

The game that changed everything. Playing for the Newport Gwent Dragons against the Scarlets in September 2008, the beginning of the end for my shoulder – and rugby career.

My amazing parents.

My sister Debbie and my brothers Graham and Andrew at my Dad's birthday party.

My training partner – Ben The Dog. If only he could ride a bike!

Cold water immersion testing at the University of Portsmouth.

The incredible 737 Challenge team at my leaving gala dinner in Cardiff. Yes, that is Gethin Jones muscling in on the left. No, he wasn't in the team. Ha!

Such a proud moment for me – completing the first leg of my 737 Challenge at the South Pole. I was already dreaming of returning, even back then.

Celebrating New Year's Eve at with some of the crew from the Amundsen-Scott Station.

Climbing to High Camp on Vinson, with the Ellsworth Mountains in the background.

The very early stages of this book. Writing my diary in the tent at High Camp on Vinson.

unless you're passionate about what you do, and that applies to everyone I met there, from the scientists to the chefs, the mechanics to the canteen staff. It's a mini metropolis in the middle of nowhere. They even have a DVD store and gift shop.

It was a crazy few days. The images I take from it whirl in my memory, as if they were out of time, which in a way they were. I had no idea what day it was. The sun never set, and looking at your watch serves only to confuse things further. The station operates on New Zealand time, which is GMT +13hrs, but we'd been operating on Chilean time, which is GMT -3hrs. Then there was GMT itself to factor in for the folks back home.

At least it meant I got to celebrate New Year's Eve three times. They held the most surreal party I have ever known to celebrate the New Year, local time (i.e. New Zealand). The operations manager at the station was a keen skier, so having Hermann Maier in the vicinity was a big deal for him. That may have been why they decided to throw the staff party outside and to invite all of us along. There was a general atmosphere of festivity. That year, 2011, would mark the 100th anniversary of Amundsen's expedition to the South Pole, so spirits were high already when a mad party struck up outside the base. The German team of celebrities had arrived now, and the race's support trucks, these massive six-wheeled jeeps, were commandeered as sound systems to blare out some Euro-beats. The Quiet Sector this was not. Some of the mechanics had carved a vodka luge out of a block of ice to better neck some shots. The scientists and staff at the station are cooped up for a long time, and they intended to make this count. I have a picture of myself with a guy in fancy dress cycling past the South Pole. It was insane. And then, as quickly as it had started, they packed up and disappeared back into the station, leaving Scott and me alone again outside. I still wonder if it ever really happened.

A few hours later, though, I was invited to take part in a more solemn ceremony. Another incredible privilege. The geographic South Pole lies under the polar ice sheet, which is constantly moving, displacing the marker by 10m every year. So they hold a marker moving ceremony each New Year to reposition it. A semi-circle is formed, and the marker is passed between everyone along the line to its new position over the exact location of the Pole. To have been there and held it in my hands is something that will live with me for ever.

But the dawn of the New Year also meant that, for me, it was game time. The clock had started ticking, and I had another eight landmarks to reach. Only a couple of hours after the marker ceremony, I was gathering my things, poo and pee included (you're not allowed to leave anything in the pristine wilderness), to be flown off the Pole back to Union Glacier, from where I would attempt to climb Mount Vinson, the highest mountain in Antarctica.

If the flight to the last degree is three and a half hours of staring out of the window at nothing, the flight from Union Glacier to Mount Vinson Base Camp is quite different. It's forty minutes of staring in wonder at mountains – about a hundred miles of them. The effect is much the same, though. I was in awe, mesmerised by each of the peaks that loomed large in the sunlight. Our little plane was not for flying at high altitude, so the mountains were right there, almost beside us, as if we could reach out and touch them. But the thought that so few, if any, had ever been touched by human hand or boot made a deep impression on me.

Union Glacier is tucked in at the start of the Ellsworth Mountains, which extend away from the South Pole towards the Antarctic Peninsula, gathering height as they go, until they build into the Vinson Massif, with Mount Vinson at its heart, 4897m above sea level. It is not the highest mountain of the Seven Summits – indeed, only Carstensz Pyramid, which is a technical rock climb, is lower, and that only just – but the weather is always the chief concern, as you might expect.

I was lucky. From the moment we touched down on the ice runway at Vinson Base Camp, the sun shone. At times during the climb I was uncomfortably hot! The wind picked up on day three, which meant we dug in at High Camp for an extra day before attempting the summit, but on 8 January we made it to the top of Vinson, leg number two. And, again, if the pristine vastness of the polar plateau is something to behold, the views of Antarctica from the top of its highest mountain are no less arresting. Miles and miles of peaks and shimmering terrain, almost all of it untouched.

I was climbing with two others – an Aussie and our American leader, Joey – and it was one of the strongest teams I would climb with. We climbed from High Camp to the summit in four hours fifty minutes. Joey told us six to eight hours is the norm. However strong you are, though, it is a tough summit day. Operating in twenty-four-hour sunlight takes a lot out of you. It doesn't mean you work any longer, necessarily, or even that you sleep any less, but the absence of darkness rocks your body's diurnal rhythm. It sucks energy from you. Still, it was another leg down, and one that has halted many attempts of the Seven Summits. I was grateful that it had passed without incident.

Antarctica wasn't finished with me yet – far from it. In fact, it turned out I was only halfway through my stay! I had completed the first two legs and was ready to fly back to Chile for the next, Aconcagua, but fate had other plans. It was my first taste (and certainly not the last) of the kind of thing that can derail a project with as many moving parts as mine. The physical challenge of climbing, trekking and sweating is only the half of it. I was to be marooned at Union Glacier for the next two weeks, along with around seventy others. And there was nothing any of us could do about it.

It would be a naked lie for me to turn it into a sob story. Truth be told, I had a lot of fun out there, although it would have created the wrong impression to have broadcasted that at the time! I passed the time climbing, skidooing and meeting some amazing people, some of them climbers and scientists, some of them ALE staff. They say that everyone in the kitchen at Union Glacier has a Ph.D., and I can well believe it. I even got to have a shower for the first time in a month, which back then was a luxury afforded only to members of staff (there's a client shower block now). It costs a fortune to spend a fortnight at Union Glacier on holiday, which some people do, and I effectively got one for free. They joked that I was the only person there who didn't want the Ilyushin to come, and they weren't far wrong. It's true that I was becoming a little twitchy in week two, but we had factored in unforeseen delays to my itinerary, and the Challenge had so far progressed without hitch.

The problem first of all was the weather. For a big, heavy Ilyushin to take off and land you need safe conditions at both ends – in Punta Arenas and at Union Glacier. At the latter, the balance is delicate. The wind and visibility have to be within safe margins to effect a landing on the blue-ice runway. It means such weather delays are common.

That accounted for the first few days' waiting. Then the weather cleared, but a fuel strike in Chile closed the airport at Punta Arenas for a few more. At the end of the first week, ALE managed to bypass the blockades to fuel the Ilyushin, which touched down at Union Glacier to much rejoicing. The weather was good at both ends. We were all set. And that was when they discovered that the fuel line on the plane was broken. You couldn't script it. Ordering new parts to Antarctica via Chile takes time – another three days.

People were becoming desperate. By definition, some of the paying clients in Antarctica are seriously rich. They simply don't understand that they are no longer in control. It's hilarious. In Antarctica the hierarchy of the universe is reimposed – Mother Nature puts us back in our place. Rich people are used to paying their way out of any situation, but that doesn't work in Antarctica. Not that it stops them trying.

'I need to fly out of here' was a common refrain.

'I'm sorry, sir. We can't at the moment. It's the weather.'

'I'll pay $200,000 if you can fly me out tomorrow.'

'I'm sure you would, but none of the planes can fly.'

'I'll pay for another to come and pick us up.'

'No, sir. There are no planes that can come and get you.'

At one point, a Russian businessman ripped off his shirt and demanded to fight one of the staff for the right to leave. He just didn't get it. Or he wouldn't. It was insane.

In the second week, while we were waiting for the part to arrive, the weather improved enough for ALE to consider flying the Basler to Chile. A Basler DC-3 is a smaller passenger plane, like the one from *Where Eagles Dare*, which can take off and land in poorer conditions. Steve made an announcement, asking for a show of hands from those interested in buying a seat on the Basler, should it fly. As much as I was enjoying myself, I had a job to do elsewhere, so I rummaged through my belongings and managed to pool the equivalent of about $500. We gathered in the dining tent, where the whiteboard read: 'Day 28 in the Big Brother House at Union Glacier. Still no fucking plane today.' When it came to it, I put my hand up to offer the $500. And I was so out of the ballpark. The seats on that plane were going for around $14,000. Logistics in that corner of the planet are insanely expensive because of the cost of fuel, or more specifically the cost of transporting it there.

While the rest of us were waiting, a Norwegian called Christian Eide arrived at the camp in a blaze of glory. He had just smashed the world record for travelling solo, unassisted (no non-human propulsion) and unsupported (no resupplies) across the 1140km (715 miles) from Hercules Inlet to the South Pole. The record had stood at thirty-nine days; he managed it in twenty-four. Every morning at Union Glacier they would update the progress of expeditions out on the ice. It became a ritual to gather round and see how far Christian had skied yesterday. 'He's broken forty kilometres!' they would

mutter in wonder at his daily progress, which would ultimately average out at 47km. It was no different from people
marvelling at a Shane Williams try, or a Lionel Messi goal.
Having just found out what it took to travel around 19km a
day, I shared in the general astonishment, captivated by the
reaction his achievements were inspiring, almost as much as
by the achievements themselves. The weather had been as
good as could be expected, but this was an extraordinary feat.
That record will never be broken, they said at the camp, and
I could believe it.

The vital part for the Ilyushin's fuel line arrived on 19
January, but it was not all good news. We were told that more
bad weather was closing in – another three to five days' delay.
Things were becoming serious now, but I was making the
most of the time. One of the many extraordinary people I met
out there was Victor Saunders, among Britain's most respected
mountaineers. It was while he and I were climbing that the
news finally came through, on 21 January, that we could fly. A
weather window had unexpectedly appeared. We were on
Mount Rossman at the time, a small mountain overlooking
Union Glacier. It was a new route we had broken, which
meant that somebody had to give it a name. Victor passed that
honour to me.

I called it 'Gratitude'.

In the end, it wasn't much of a weather window. We took off
in poor visibility, which was scary enough, even without any
windows in the hold of the Ilyushin. Then we landed at Punta
Arenas at 3 a.m. in more of the same. Let's just say that I
know now why they don't like doing it. And it was dark in

Punta. I found it really disorientating. 'Hello Darkness, my old friend.' I haven't seen you for more than a month. Nor you, Stifling Heat. After a flight to Santiago and a night bus across the Andes to Mendoza, my body was reeling in the Argentine summer. Sleep was hard to come by, the combination of heat and a conventional bed completely throwing me. I was already starting to yearn for a tent again.

My plan had been to climb Aconcagua with my friend from Cardiff, Paul Donovan, who is one of Jagged Globe's leaders. I had been looking forward to it, but the delays in Antarctica meant I'd missed his team. They also meant there was no margin for error on Aconcagua – and the weather on the mountain hadn't been good. That had been of some consolation while I was stranded on the ice, but now I needed it to change. It was the end of January, which meant I had two months to summit Aconcagua, Kilimanjaro and Carstensz Pyramid before the season opened on the North Pole on 1 April. All doable, but we couldn't accommodate any more delays.

A cameraman was accompanying me on this leg of the trip – a guy called Diego Sosa. We met up in Mendoza before taking the bus to Los Penitentes, from where we would trek to Plaza de Mulas, which is base camp. Diego was crazy. He spoke barely any English, and his vocabulary was largely made up of swear words, although I'm not sure he realised it. He'd picked up most of his English from our mutual friend, Russell Isaac of Sports Media Services, the producer of the documentary on the Challenge, which would have explained the language! 'Fucking plastic chicken', he kept saying for the first few days, having eaten some chicken on the first night and developed a bad case of the shits. But he was a great guy, who had trained hard for our summit attempt, and we hit it off straightaway, even without much more than the odd swear word to communicate by.

Having missed Paul's group, we joined up with the next Jagged Globe team coming through. They were a funny bunch, although not for the same reasons that Diego was funny. Because Aconcagua is the highest mountain in the world outside the Himalaya, and an accessible climb from a technical point of view, I find it attracts a lot of people who are looking to tick off a big mountain and get the T-shirt. What I found really difficult was when some of them started complaining about the food. Really? I'm sure they lived like kings at home, but you don't set out to conquer a mountain of 6959m and expect haute cuisine all the way up. Jagged Globe's food is as good as you'll find among adventure companies – not that any are trying to win a rosette – and, besides, we actually ate Argentine steak one day. As far as mountain expeditions go, we *were* living like kings!

The going was slow. Aconcagua is like that. If you take what is known as the normal route, as we were, there are just so many people on it. I hesitate to say this, because I wouldn't want to spoil it, but the following year I climbed Aconcagua again from the Vacas Valley, up what's known as the Polish Glacier route, and it is so peaceful and beautiful. The route is longer, so your loads are heavier, but it's the difference between having two tents at a camp and forty.

Although technically accessible, relative to the world's other big mountains Aconcagua remains a very dangerous proposition due to its altitude. Only a few days earlier, a German climber had fallen to his death from the Canaleta, the infamous 500m scramble over rocks and snow that leads to the summit. The weather is always a threat and, true to form, there were high winds at the summit and two avalanches near Plaza de Mulas.

When we reached Nido de Cóndores, or Condor's Nest (Camp 2), at 5500m, we had a decision to make. The group were absolutely shattered, with the altitude taking its toll, but the news was that the weather was set to deteriorate again. Not many people had been summiting that year, and if we wanted to do so before the next weather system we had to strike out soon.

Whatever the technical tariff, summit day on Aconcagua is tough. Most people would ascend to Camp 3 at 6000m, acclimatise to the altitude for a night and set off from there, but, with bad weather on its way, we would not have that luxury. I discussed tactics at length with the expedition leaders, Tore and Gianni. We decided that Diego and I would attempt the summit directly from Camp 2. This would make for a brutal summit day, climbing a kilometre and a half in vertical terms, but would maximise our chances of success without further delays. We were prepared to leave the group, but after the consultation was broadened they too decided to take it on. It was likely to be their only chance to summit as well.

We set off at 3 a.m. It's a relentless trudge, even after the sun's come up. At least then there is consolation to be derived from the views, which on Aconcagua are as spectacular as any. On a clear day they stretch to the Pacific Ocean, around ninety miles away. Aconcagua towers over its surrounding peaks, and when you're traversing at the top of the Gran Acarrero, the north-west face of the higher slopes, which falls away dramatically beneath you, it looks as if you could tumble all the way back down to Plaza de Mulas, some 2500m below. Not that you spend much time on the views. Your lungs are desperate in the thin air, the temperatures are below zero and the winds fierce. One foot in front of the other is the only policy.

The clouds were starting to gather as we reached the base of the Canaleta. Our group had thinned out by now, with only two still in the game, Brett and Andy, as well as Gianni. (Brett, in particular, was serious about the mountains and has since attempted all of the Seven Summits.) I was anxious about the deteriorating conditions. Gianni agreed that we should leave them and push on over the stones of the Canaleta on our own to maximise our chances of summiting.

I was feeling relatively comfortable at that point, but don't let anyone tell you the Canaleta is easy. You might not need an ice axe and ropes, but after more than eleven hours of climbing, at nearly 7000m above sea level, it's a final hurdle to be reckoned with. There wasn't much usable footage from it – just a very shaky camera, Diego's heavy breathing and more than a few interjections of 'fucking Russell'.

At 2.54 p.m. local time, on 5 February, Diego and I reached the summit of Aconcagua, nearly twelve hours after leaving Nido de Cóndores. The skies were still blue, but the first wisps of cloud were encroaching, and, within minutes, we were standing in a snow-flecked swirl of grey. Brett and Andy joined us half an hour later, which made the moment complete, and five hours after that Diego and I were back at Nido de Cóndores, sharing my luxury item for this trip. A hip flask of whisky.

Three legs down – and I was feeling great. Aconcagua was a real boost to my confidence. At the start of the 737 Challenge

I was in the shape of my life, physically, but I was still not much more than a novice as a mountaineer. Aconcagua was the first time I'd faced a serious tactical decision. Not only was I able to make the right choice, but I *was* in the sort of physical shape to see it through. And it was the right choice, as it turned out. The weather did close in after us, and there were no more summits of Aconcagua for more than a week. Had we been forced to wait as long as that, I would have missed the next leg, Kilimanjaro, which would have meant climbing it after Elbrus – and threatening my target of seven months.

Regardless of that, though, missing out on the scheduled Kili leg would have been a personal blow, because this was the mountain I was climbing with friends and family. The trip, which had been in everyone's diary for months, had already been postponed a week because of the delay in Antarctica. If I'd been delayed again they would have had to go without me. That would have been a great shame. I'd been looking forward to this leg for so long, and it wouldn't disappoint. There's no way to measure the boost to morale that I derived from that experience, but I know it served me well in the treacherous legs to come. I hadn't seen any loved ones for two months at that point, so just the few days I spent at home between Aconcagua and Kili were invaluable. A lot of laundry, mind.

Kilimanjaro is the most accessible of the Seven Summits. Ironically, its relative ease also makes it one of the world's deadliest mountains, simply because so many give it a go. They say around ten a year die in the attempt. And only 40 per cent of climbers actually make it to the top. Again, this might be attributed to its reputation as an easy mountain. What with all the celebrity climbs and operators offering dangerously short acclimatisation itineraries, some people think they just have to sling a rucksack over their shoulder and skip up it. Then they discover the realities of life at nearly 6000m and of the long days trekking through the mountain's various layers of equatorial rainforest, moorland, desert and snow. No, Kilimanjaro – at 5895m – is a mountain to respect. All mountains should be respected, in my opinion. Even a Brecon Beacon.

Our team of twelve included Dai Parks, my cousin. His dad, my Uncle Terry, had died of cancer when we were young. Dai and I had sort of lost touch since then, but this trip brought us back together. Climbing a mountain is a spiritual experience. Bonds are formed quickly between those who share the experience, and when those bonds are there already they are strengthened immeasurably. I'd embarked on this whole venture as a way of escaping rugby, pretending it had never existed, but the values I learned from rugby about the ethic of the team were constantly revisited, reinforced and reaffirmed. Climbing mountains pulls people together – the sheer hardship that you endure together, but also the outlandishness of it, the sense of being lifted out of routine, comfort and the everyday. And just the beauty. If this book is to avoid repetition I'm going to have to stop trying to describe the views from each mountain, but Kili … maybe it's the most beautiful of all. Maybe. It's a free-standing mountain, the highest on Earth, so the sense that you're on top of the world is particularly strong, as the African plains stretch away into the distance. And sunrise above the clouds on summit day … No. Words fail me.

Summit day on Kili is a big one by anyone's standards. The trip from Barafu Camp to Uhuru Peak and back down to

Karanga Camp takes around eighteen hours – that's longer than summit day on Everest. And the guys were struggling. We set off at midnight in temperatures well below freezing. Most summit attempts begin in darkness, and trudging along with only a head torch to light the way can be dispiriting. You have no sense of how far you have travelled or where you are going, so sunrises are all the more beautiful to a mountaineer for the relief they provide to the spirit, as much as to the body temperature. On the other hand, you could also argue that it serves only to illuminate your suffering. And there was suffering all right. Pinders was puking every twenty minutes for the best part of eight hours. If she'd been a horse, they'd have shot her. Dee was in tears. Jim shat himself.

I shouldn't laugh. The important thing is that everybody summited together, which in the context of that 40 per cent summit rate was one hell of an achievement by the team. And I had the time of my life with my friends and family. Forget any threat to the 737 Challenge – it would have been horrible if I'd missed this trip. I've never come off a mountain so energised and happy.

How that was about to change.

4

Another one of our team on Kilimanjaro was a guy called Rob James. Rob was a self-made millionaire, and I invited him to join the 737 Challenge team. He took up the role of team leader, with responsibility for commercial and legal matters, throwing himself into the project with as much passion as anyone, performing some invaluable services. The first £5000 donation came from him, which paid for the legal fees incurred in setting up the charity. He opened bank accounts, chaired meetings and so on. His entrepreneurial skill was a crucial dynamic among my incredible team, who had done so much to get this adventure up and running and who asked for nothing in return but the reward of involvement.

I suppose it was unrealistic to think that everyone would see it through.

Rob was so up for it all that he leaped at the chance to

climb Kilimanjaro. He and Tracy were the two members of the 737 Challenge 'executive' who wanted to sample a piece of the action first-hand on Kili.

One of the reasons I love mountains so much is the way they strip you of all make-up and bullshit. As with Antarctica and the angry oligarchs, a mountain holds you out naked before Mother Nature. It's an unsettling juxtaposition, to have your insignificance exposed to you like that, especially for the first time. Or maybe it's nothing to do with that at all. Maybe it's just that you are working, physically and then emotionally, so far outside your comfort zone. Maybe it's both. It *is* both. Regardless, the veneer that we hide behind in day-to-day life is scoured clean away.

I shared a tent with Rob on Kili, and a side of him emerged up there that I hadn't noticed before. It was clear from the start that he was going to adopt a forthright, self-made-man approach to this escapade. Fair enough – you don't become as successful an entrepreneur as he has without a certain edge, and this was consistent with that. It's only natural it should come out when you take on any challenge, whether commercial or recreational. Besides, I'm from a background in professional sport, so I am well acquainted with the spirit. It's called competitiveness.

But the higher we went, the stranger his attitude became. He'd developed a headache but he refused to take any advice about it, or even to accept that it was a problem. He was obviously in a fair amount of discomfort and suffering from the early signs of altitude sickness. He was in his late forties, I'd guess, and had achieved a lot in his chosen field, so maybe this mountain represented a new challenge to test himself by, which is also fair enough and similar in many ways to what the 737 Challenge was to me.

It was in the tent the night before summit day that I started to notice that something was not right. Rob asked me if I wanted to break away from the rest of the team. He was agitating to go faster, to reach the summit first. I was quite shocked by this. For one thing, going any faster was the last thing he needed. His headaches had not improved. He was in no fit state to go galloping up to 6000m. But that was neither here nor there. What really bothered me was that he wanted to leave the group. He had identified Tracy as the weakest link – Tracy, who had sat in the same meetings for months. Although I considered him a close friend at this point, this was a new side to him and a development, in view of the crucial role he was playing in the venture, that disturbed me.

I told him I wasn't going to be breaking away from the rest of the team. There was no reason for it. Anyway, I didn't want to go any faster. The Challenge was about to move up a gear in its brutality. This leg was meant to be a rest for me (and I did end up putting on a few pounds on Kili). But, most of all, we were among friends. We were having fun (at least I was). Everyone on that trip was supporting my quest to raise funds in aid of Marie Curie – Janet Suart, a Marie Curie nurse and wonderful woman, was among our group. We were all going to summit, and we were going to summit together.

Rob kept pushing it, though, and I told him that the only circumstance in which I would leave the group was if, as on Aconcagua, not doing so might jeopardise my chances of summiting. This was not the case here. There was nothing to be gained from it.

On summit day itself, progress was slow, as it has to be. 'Pole, pole,' say the local guides. It's Swahili for 'slowly, slowly', and it is something of a catchphrase on Kilimanjaro. Most people on the mountain have never been at that altitude before – to move too fast would be dangerous. And, yes, Pinders was really struggling. She might not have made it without the support of every one of the team, but she was not alone. Everybody was struggling, including Rob. Everybody was helping everybody else make it through.

None of us is perfect, but if Rob whispered it in my ear once, he whispered it a thousand times. 'Is the summit jeopardised yet? Is the summit jeopardised?'

A few hours in I snapped. 'Look, Rob, if you want to fuck off up the mountain, then off you go! I'm staying here.'

I think it's the last time we ever really spoke. Properly, at any rate, like friends, albeit friends in a mini argument.

My parents' fortitude and patience have been central to this project, as they have been to my life. Never have these qualities proved more telling than in this phase of the Challenge. I knew the fundraising – in terms of securing sponsorship – had not been going well. The economy was in a terrible state in 2010/11. Investors were not exactly clamouring to get involved. I was working my way from mountain to mountain now, with all of these concerns out of sight and out of mind. It was the rest of the team who were wrestling with them, with my parents suffering from the added stress that their son was risking his life on these mountains without a penny to his name.

They had been shielding me from the worst of it, but when

I returned home for a few days before my next leg, to Carstensz Pyramid in Indonesia, they broke it to me that Rob was leaving the team. I was stunned. He and I had just shared a tent together for a week, and although he had talked about wanting to leave the team on the mountain I had no idea he had this in mind. He had not mentioned it to me once, or, as far as I can recall, even hinted at it.

We had approached a couple of fundraising professionals to advise us on our commercial operations. At a meeting in those few days back in Wales, they assured us that our income profile so far was perfectly normal. This reaffirmed the advice we had been receiving elsewhere. Most of the funds raised for projects such as this are done so retrospectively, once the feat has been accomplished and the media surrounding it has increased. They actually commended us on the funds we had raised so far and said they'd consider taking part in the challenge themselves.

But Rob wasn't convinced. In his world, perhaps the business models are more conventional. As far as he was concerned, there were a lot of costs still to be endured, financial and otherwise, before the Challenge could succeed. Before we knew it, we were witnessing an unfortunate scenario in which he and I were arguing about the prospects of the enterprise in front of the very people we had hoped to involve. He started to argue that the Challenge should be shut down. The meeting became heated.

I thanked him for what he had done for us. It was sad that he was leaving, but perfectly understandable. This was not for everyone, far from it. I couldn't promise him that I would succeed, although after Kili I was as confident of my prospects as

I'd ever been. Nothing had changed on that front, but if his resolve was wavering it was right he should go. We would find someone to replace him. What I could not accept, however, was any move to have us closed down.

I wish I could say that was the end of it. Any trustee of a charity, as his wife had been to this, has to file a report when they leave. Hers was scathing, to the extent that we ended up having to file a counter statement to justify our decisions.

The two fundraising professionals decided against joining the team. Worse than that, Rob's prognosis for the Challenge's future was so bleak that Gareth Thomas, the Challenge accountant, decided to leave as well. Gazzy was an old family friend, particularly dear to my parents. As chief executive at Pontypridd, he'd offered me my first proper contract as a rugby player. This was where, for all the stress and hard work that I was asking of everyone, I suddenly started to question whether it was worth it. I'd wanted to shield my parents from too much involvement with the Challenge, which is laughable, because of course they would become involved – so much so *they* were now shielding *me* from some of the realities of the Challenge's circumstances; so much so they would go on to keep the entire operation afloat. But stress and hard work is one thing; the falling apart of old friendships another. Suddenly, the demon I'd imprisoned in a corner of my head, who wanted to scream at me that this whole escapade was an obscene indulgence, started to shout its piece loudly. How could I justify this mission I was on, now that the collateral damage was spreading into areas that should be sacrosanct?

I'm pleased to say that my parents are now (some years

later) reconciled with Gazzy, but they were really upset when he followed Rob out the door. I was devastated. What a sudden, vicious turnaround in mood! One minute I was coming off Kilimanjaro full of the joys, the next I was tossing and turning, unable to sleep at night. There were painful logistics to sort out before I flew to Indonesia for Carstensz Pyramid. I had to pack a drum to be sent on to Everest Base Camp, a bag for the North Pole and another for the trek to Everest Base Camp. And then, of course, there was the kit for Carstensz.

On 5 March, after a crushing four days in Wales, I was flying to Bali with a sick feeling in my belly. I might climb Carstensz Pyramid, then have to call off the Challenge for a failing as dull as a lack of income. I stepped off the plane in Denpasar. It was suffocatingly hot and humid, but what an idyllic place! And I didn't want to be there. Ahead of me lay the Indiana Jones leg of the Challenge, the one that most conjured up a spirit of adventure, jungles, ravines, sheer rock faces. And I didn't want to be there. I checked into the hotel, introduced myself to the four other team members at the bar, went upstairs and sunk to the bathroom floor of my room, weeping uncontrollably.

In the days that followed, Rob would extricate himself from proceedings. I'll never understand why he wanted to close us down. Wanting to leave I could appreciate. He'd been as heroic, as passionate and enthused, as anyone in the team up to that point (or, presumably, sometime before it), but now he had lost faith. Fair enough. He'd just struggled on the easiest leg – perhaps he thought the Challenge was beyond me. He certainly thought it was beyond us to meet the financial demands. Maybe he just didn't want to be associated with a project that he was certain would fail.

At a meeting while I was in Indonesia Simon assured the rest of the team that the Challenge was not over until such time as his company, Jagged Globe, called in the bills we owed. And they would defer that moment as much as they possibly could. In the meantime, they would manage their cash flow to meet the upfront costs of the Challenge and then trust that sponsorship would be forthcoming later. This was a huge gamble. If I didn't finish the Challenge, or if I did but we couldn't raise the funds, Simon's company would have been out of pocket. Simon would have been out of business. My father pledged that, somehow, he would be paid.

They shook hands like gentlemen.

My parents remortgaged their house.

Carstensz Pyramid, or Puncak Jaya, as the locals know it, looks like something out of Middle Earth – a vicious, jagged fin of rock rising sharply out of the Papuan mountains. It is named after the seventeenth-century Dutch explorer Jan Carstenszoon, who first saw it. They laughed at him when he returned to Europe and insisted he'd seen snow so close to the Equator. But it was not until 1962 that it was first conquered. It's the least climbed of the Seven Summits, because its mountain range is set amid the dense New Guinea jungle and the region has long suffered from political instability. In short, it's very difficult to get to.

There is some debate about whether it should be included among the Seven Summits at all. Politically speaking, it is part of Asia; geographically, it is on the continent of

Australasia. Or is it Oceania? The definitions are bewildering. I don't want to get into it. Suffice it to say, the alternative to Carstensz is the highest mountain on the Australian mainland, Mount Kosciusko, which is not much more than a hill with a car park. Any self-respecting mountaineer would choose Carstensz every time.

At 4884m, it is the lowest of the Seven Summits (albeit more than twice the height of Kosciusko), but technically it is the trickiest. It is proper rock-climbing. No walking up this one. But that's the least of your worries, because there is a hell of a lot of walking just to get to it.

It is possible to take a helicopter to base camp. That is undoubtedly the easiest option. But neither Simon nor I approved of it from a spiritual point of view. It's not the honourable way to do it. And we certainly didn't approve of it from a financial point of view. It costs a lot of money, and the last story I'd heard was about a team who were dropped off at base camp, in one of the most remote regions of the world, and held to ransom by the helicopter pilot, who wouldn't pick them up until they'd paid some hideous five-figure sum each, over and above the one they'd already paid. So the helicopter route is not without its perils.

In theory, the most direct route by land is to the south-east. Tight up against the mountain lies the Grasberg mine, which is the largest gold mine in the world and the third largest copper. It's a vast, circular pit, 4km in diameter, and contributes handsomely to the apocalyptic feel of the place. It also has a road. Commercial teams have been known to sneak through the mine at night in order to get to base camp, but for every story of ransom by helicopter pilot there's one of hostage in the gold mine. Again, I don't want to get into it, literally and metaphorically.

Which leaves the long route in, 90km through the jungle from the north, and you're not much safer from being held to ransom that way. The Papuan people are lovely, but if one of your porters doesn't want to carry on he won't hesitate to let you know, or demand more money before he'll pick up his bag again. You have to take them with you. It's part of the deal if you want to travel safely in the area.

We flew from Bali to Timika, a city in Papua. Papua is the greater part of the western half of the island of New Guinea. The eastern half is the nation of Papua New Guinea, but Papua is part of the nation of Indonesia, which spreads west across an archipelago of other islands. The region is fraught with political instability and afflicted with the most insane amount of rainfall. When we arrived at Timika airport, the place was teeming with local miners who were being flown to Grasberg because the rains had washed away the road. My luxury item for this trip was an umbrella. I've never seen rain like it – and I'm from Wales. We were stranded in Timika for two days because of it. That's two days of non-stop rain. With temperatures in the thirties (centigrade). It was not the sort of environment to boost my morale.

But what an amazing country. When we finally took off, it was across jungles and mountains to Ilaga, whose airport is basically a strip of concrete on the edge of the jungle, pitted and mossy and scary to land on. From there we trekked for a few hours to the village, where we stayed at the chief's house, a kind of wooden pavilion. We slept on the floorboards upstairs. Downstairs it was almost as spartan, with just a few amenities to enhance what was nevertheless luxurious accommodation compared to the thatched huts that the locals lived in. The chief sat cross-legged on the bare floor in his robes, headgear, bangles and a wristwatch. He called a meeting of the villagers in the morning to decide who would act as our porters. The chaos of it woke us up. We came downstairs, and there were scores of people, young and old, male and female, some with bags of potatoes, others with machetes. I imagine there was some kind of order to proceedings, but I couldn't make it out. People stood around in groups shouting and gesticulating at each other. I'm a big people-watcher, and this was extreme people-watching. It was mesmerising.

Our guide was Indonesian. Ethnically, he was different from the locals, South East Asian in appearance, where the villagers looked more like Aboriginal Australians. He was a hard man, who could handle himself among the negotiations. He explained what was going on. To be selected as porters was a big deal, as it meant they would be paid. The chief made sure we had porters from each of the tribes in the mountains, so that we could safely cross tribal boundaries on the way. When the negotiations/arguments were settled, we set off on a five-day trek to base camp, a train of about twenty of us snaking through the jungle.

It was brutal. On day one we climbed 1300m, sometimes having to force our way through the foliage. No two footsteps were the same, as the terrain twisted and climbed, but all were unified by the thick, pervasive mud, which was shin-deep in places. To begin with I tried to keep my feet out of it, picking my way round the deepest parts, nipping from rock to tree to branch, but it was too much. I soon gave up and just waded through.

That meant wet feet for the entire trip. Feet? I was wet all over, non-stop. It was so debilitating. Our clothes were soaked in the evening and still damp in the morning. The heat, the humidity, the insects, the endless sweat and rain, the knowledge that it might all be in vain anyway – I had to dig deeper over those few days than I ever had before.

There was some relief on day two, when we broke out of the jungle and began to cross the plateau on rocky terrain, but the rain was so heavy when we pitched camp that the porters chose to sleep in a cave a hundred metres overhead, where they normally bury their dead. They didn't want to sleep anywhere near the rivers, which were full to bursting and in places tumbled over ravines to form spectacular waterfalls. We, on the other hand, didn't want to sleep among skeletons.

On day three the terrain turned wet again, and we had to effect five river crossings. Our head porter was a terrifying dude – moody, muscular, purple anorak, combat shorts, wellington boots, cigarette in one hand, machete in the other. At midday, he put down his bag, struck up a fire and refused to go on without a pay rise. Our Indonesian guide was a tough man, who handled the porters really well, but there's not much rousing a Papuan with a machete if he doesn't want to move. More money was the only solution. One of the other porters, meanwhile, had contracted malaria and turned back. It was as if the Challenge were falling apart around me, both here and at home. Have you had enough yet? Have you had enough?

There's only one answer. Grit your teeth and plough on, no

matter what is thrown at you. And day four was the hardest yet. Ten hours of trekking up and down valleys, wading through swamps and rivers, scrambling over rocks. The night before, I'd tried to dry my clothes by the fire but managed only to melt a hole in one of my boots. I'd repaired it with glue and duct tape, but this was a test of its waterproofness – a test it failed. I'd been told to take wellington boots with me before-hand, but chose not to. It's all about weight, and, anyway, I had these state-of-the-art waterproof walking boots. Should have taken the wellies.

The porters would set off ahead of us each morning. At midday, just like the day before, we saw smoke in the distance. Here we go again. We knew what it meant – another porter strike, a bad one this time. They'd all sat down and lit a fire, refusing to move. Another pay rise was negotiated.

The impression that none of this could really be happening was heightened when one of the Papuan kids produced a slingshot later that afternoon and killed a bird with a rock, before calmly ripping its wings off and cooking it up for tea. A black dog, just like the one our neighbours had in Newport, had been following us all the way from Ilaga. We would cross raging rivers, four abreast carrying a tree as ballast to guard against being swept away. Still the dog would appear at our side. He was to follow us to base camp.

They were surreal times. We were in the mountains now and finally reached base camp on 14 March, after a seven-hour scramble over rocks in the pouring rain. The clouds swirling round the angry peaks lent the place an otherworldly look, as did the mini turquoise lakes (or were they just pud-dles?) that were scattered among the crags, almost luminous, as if they were of acid. We were at 4300m, but the weather had been so bad I still hadn't caught a glimpse of the top of Carstensz Pyramid. There she was, though, a sheer rock face before us disappearing up into the clouds.

We were forced to sit it out at base camp for another day. The rain was too heavy to climb safely, and it was snowing at the peak, but I was grateful for a chance to rest and try, at least, to dry out some of my gear.

The weather was clear in the small hours of 16 March. We set off at 2 a.m., head torches on. It's a technical climb, but I'm not going to pretend that it was the north face of the Eiger. There are plenty of foot and handholds to pick your way through, even if they were dripping wet. Most of the sections of the climb are protected with fixed lines, which are supposed to act as safety measures. Some lazier climbers are tempted to use a Jumar, which is an ascender device, to haul themselves up the ropes, but you never know on a mountain like Carstensz how long the ropes have been there, or how meticulously they've been fixed, so it's not wise – and, besides, it's nowhere near as rewarding. Why would you not want to use your hands and feet, anyway? Rock-climbing is probably the weakest technique in my tool box, but it's so much fun. I loved every minute of that climb.

Just before the top there is a breach in the mountain's summit ridge, about 20m wide, which requires you to perform a Tyrolean traverse from one needle of rock to the next over a drop of 50m or so to the ridge – and from there a few hundred more to the base of the rock face. The sun was up by now, to illuminate another edge-of-the-world moment. The mountains of the Sudirman Range spread out around us, speckled with these brilliant turquoise lakes, and straight ahead rose the summit of Carstensz Pyramid from out of a rock tethered loosely to the one we were standing on by a bundle of fixed ropes. These ropes were not just for safety. These ones we would use to pull ourselves along to cross the chasm beneath. You clip your harness on to the ropes and hang from them, then simply haul yourself across, one hand over the other. It's one of the few mountains in the world where a Tyrolean traverse is permanently in use.

One of our group was a Frenchman who had actually climbed Carstensz a couple of years before and panicked at this same point, abandoning his climb. Fair play to him, he loved the mountain – not many climb Carstensz once, let alone twice – and was a nice guy, although he did complain that there was no jam on the trip, or peanut butter. I forget which. So this was a big deal for him. And he panicked again. It made for one of the most gruesomely comic scenes. The rest of us were in tears of laughter as he gasped and wailed his way across. Mind you, we stopped laughing when he lost his grip on the rope and found himself dangling upside down over the drop. He was in serious danger then, because he could have fallen out of his harness. Thankfully he pulled himself together and made it across.

The summit itself was another hour or so from there, an hour of clambering our way up through the snowy wet rock. At 8.28 a.m. we reached it. And it really is a peak. There wasn't room for all of us to stand on it at the same time. From a distance, Carstensz looks like a blade rising out of the earth. When you're on it, it's a ridge and extremely narrow in places. It's not a place to be if you suffer from vertigo. Not that we could see how high we were now. The cloud had closed in around us since the Tyrolean traverse. It was cold, it was snowy, it was grey.

But what a feeling to have made it! You really feel as if you've earned the right to be at the summit of Carstensz. It was an inspired decision to trek in. To have flown in by helicopter, climbed it and flown straight out again would have felt so lame. Why not go the whole hog and get the chopper to drop you at the summit?

A side effect of trekking in, though, is that the summit of Carstensz Pyramid, more than on most mountains, feels less like an end to your journey and more like the halfway mark. There was no virtue in hanging around, nor was it feasible with so little space up there. Within minutes we were on the way down again, the rainwater now cascading over the rocks like mini waterfalls. We knew only too well the jungle that lay ahead of us.

I am so grateful now for the Carstensz Pyramid experience, but as with all the best trials by endurance the gratitude deepens the more the passage of time puts distance between you and the pain of it. All endurance athletes are well acquainted with the term 'hitting the wall', as well as the experience itself. I'd always known I would hit the wall at some point on the 737 Challenge. Carstensz Pyramid proved to be it, appropriately enough, given the mountain's appearance.

The journey back was brutal, just as bad as the way in, only I was more tired now and in more pain. And the rain. I'm not sure it stopped at all on the way back. My whole body was screaming out for relief, but my knees were a serious cause for concern. I had history with them from injuries and the wear and tear of a career in rugby. There'd been precious little respite on the wear and tear front over the previous couple of years I'd spent preparing for the Challenge and certainly none of it over the previous three months of the Challenge itself. To compound matters, I twisted my right knee when I caught my foot in a tree root submerged in mud.

The rivers were now so full from all the rain that they were waist-high. The casualty list of my equipment was mounting – a pair of boots, gloves, two pairs of socks, three cameras, a jacket, a pair of trousers, some trainers, a pole and a part of my sanity.

We trekked back to the chief's house in Ilaga in four days. I was finding it harder to be with the group. We all had different reasons for being there, and the other three were understandably demob happy at the end of their ordeal. One of the most interesting aspects of some of these expeditions is the amount of time you spend with people you've never met before. It's like meeting someone in a pub, then going off to live with them for a week or two – except it's not, because you're going off to live with them while pushing the boundaries of comfort and endurance. By definition, you meet some incredible people, but there are always times when you need your own headspace. Remain polite at all times is my one non-negotiable (at least, do your best to – I hope I always succeed), but here was such a time when I needed to break away.

Because this was not the end for me. Far from it. In terms of destinations ticked off, I was past the halfway mark now (five out of nine), but you could say that the Challenge was only just about to begin. Certainly, it was make or break time.

The North Pole, Everest and Denali – no one had ever attempted all three in the same season, and I was not exactly the most experienced mountaineer in the world, nor in the best condition. I couldn't afford to dawdle and joke.

On the last day, I pushed on alone. Then got lost in the jungle. The rain had washed away the trails, or at least turned everything into a quagmire. Thankfully, I picked up a couple of sets of footprints. Knowing that there was only one settlement in the vicinity I followed them. It turned out they belonged to a couple of Papuan boys who were carving guitars out of wood. How else could this leg of the Challenge end but with an escort home by two bare-foot boys in T-shirts carrying the skeleton of a guitar each. Or perhaps I should end it with the experience of the Canadian guy in our team, who went for a pee in the chief's house that night and walked in on a circle of Papuans sitting round a steaming pot with some kind of animal in it. I loved the Papuans, and no less for the surreal trip they led me on out there.

But it had come at some cost. When I returned to Bali, I weighed just over 13st (85kg), which meant I'd lost nearly a stone and a half. I was battered, physically and psychologically. The humidity had seeped into my bones. My knees hurt, my back ached. I didn't know where we were financially.

And so began the *Apocalypse Now* episode of the Challenge, when I spent two days solid in a Bali hotel room, smashing vitamin C into me, trying to recuperate for the North Pole. I had developed a fever and the beginnings of a chest infection. These were a serious concern. Skiing to the North Pole with a sweaty temperature would add a further layer of complication to my moisture management and render that leg even more dangerous. Who knows what state I would be in, come Everest. As for Denali ...

In an ideal world, of course, we would have been able to organise a different itinerary, alternating the tougher legs with the simpler ones, all building up to a grand finale on Everest, whereupon I could crawl under a duvet and sleep for a year. Unfortunately, this world is not ideal, but it is the only one we've got. And it has a very particular layout, geographically, as well as a particular orbit and rotation. So the Antarctica and North Pole legs were fixed in the calendar, as were to a lesser extent the Everest and Denali legs. The others had to fall in line around those.

The operational season for the North and South Poles is during their respective summers, because in their winters you can't see anything in the perpetual night and there's every chance you'll perish in a polar storm. So the South Pole and Vinson have to be undertaken around about the New Year, and while you're down there it makes sense to climb Aconcagua as well, which is also enjoying its summer. We could have taken on Aconcagua in December, before the Antarctica legs, but we wanted everything in the same calendar year. Kilimanjaro, Carstensz Pyramid and Elbrus have more flexibility when it comes to climbing seasons, so you attempt two of those in the couple of months between Aconcagua and the start of the new season on the North Pole, which is 1 April.

But, however you manoeuvre the pieces, there is no way to complete such a challenge in seven months without the more than inconvenient running order of the North Pole (at sea level), followed by Everest (as far removed from that as it is possible to be), followed by Denali (just as demanding). There's a reason it had never been attempted before.

The North Pole's is the least flexible of all the seasons. You have about a month from the start of April, when the sun is up, until the melting of the sea ice renders the journey impossible. Everest has to be tackled in May, or, more specifically, once you've spent six weeks acclimatising, the end of May. Then you have about a month in which to try your luck on Denali. This was unavoidable. This was always going to be the crux of the Challenge.

I flew to London and spent a couple of days in Wales. It was a whirlwind. Cortisone injections for my knee, vitamins and antibiotics for my chest infection, tears and gratitude for my parents. Rob officially left the Challenge just before I returned, and in stepped Nick Jones, Hefin Archer-Williams and Vida Greaux – more gratitude. Nevertheless, the stress the episode had inflicted on my mum and dad became all too clear. They were now leading the team and the project, they had remortgaged their house, and their son was about to continue his journey on the proceeds of it all to the most extreme places on the planet. Fundraising efforts were continuing. The website and blog were being maintained. What a family I had! What a team! It meant the Challenge was still up and running. It meant that failure was unthinkable.

One other crucial member of the team entered the game at this point. Steve Williams and I had been put together by a mutual friend. We had clicked immediately. Both of us had recently retired from our respective sports. Steve had won Olympic gold in 2004 and 2008 in the coxless fours. He is humble, hard-working and passionate about the environment, Everest in particular. During training the year before, we prepared together on the sea ice in Greenland and climbed Cho Oyu. He would be joining me for the North Pole and Everest.

We didn't know each other that well, but I really liked Steve. His mere presence came as a huge boost to my morale at the most crucial time. These things can't be measured, but I often wonder how things would have gone without him over the next two legs. I was already profoundly galvanised by a sense of responsibility to the rest of the team at home, but to have a team-mate with me, here in the flesh, set me on the balls of my feet again, just as I was at my very weakest.

We flew to Oslo and then on to Svalbard, an archipelago of islands in the Arctic Ocean that is the northernmost part of Norway, albeit way north of the mainland. It's the sort of place you are surprised to see on a map. We imagine Norway and Lapland and the like to be as northerly as things get. Wrong. Svalbard is another five hundred miles beyond that. If Punta Arenas felt like the end of the world, this place is something else again. Oslo is actually further north than Punta is south. Svalbard's 'capital', the settlement of Longyearbyen (population 2000), is the northernmost town in the world. At 78 degrees north, it is on a par with Union Glacier. It sits on the coast of the largest island in the archipelago, Spitsbergen, where there are more polar bears than humans, they say. This is where Steve and I were to be based as we waited for a runway to be opened on the Arctic ice.

Longyearbyen is my kind of town – a valiant effort by humankind to gain a foothold in a place they are not supposed to be. Colourful but simple dwellings huddle together in a valley by an inlet of the Greenland Sea. When we arrived, it was snowy and −28°C, around a 60° difference from Papua, but I was getting used to temperature swings by now. There had been a storm at the North Pole and its repercussions were being felt in Svalbard.

We stayed at the Spitsbergen Guesthouse, which used to be miners' quarters. Longyearbyen started life as a coal-mining community, although the focus has shifted since to research (there's a university) and tourism. Low on humans the place may be, but the community of 'adventurers' is well represented. (Incidentally, I'm not a fan of the words 'adventurer' and 'explorer', which are used too lightly by too many people who are not pushing boundaries, geographical or otherwise, and who cheapen the memory of genuine heroes from a time when so much of the world was unexplored. I call us athletes. I hope no one takes offence at this, particularly the 'athletes' themselves.) I was constantly bumping into people I'd met in Antarctica. There were other unlikely faces, too – Ben Fogle in a café, for example, or Prince Harry and the Walking With The Wounded team.

We were all waiting for this runway on the ice to open, but that polar storm was delaying things. This was good and bad. The reason that the North Pole and Everest are so hard to do in the same season is that the opening of the North Pole, scheduled for 1 April each year, when you lose the last of the darkness, coincides with when Everest expeditions leave for the Himalaya. Every moment we spent in the Arctic was time we should have been spending in Nepal acclimatising to the altitude. The longer this leg went on, the more our chances of summiting Everest were narrowing. A storm on the ice was not what the doctor ordered. Luckily, though, a week's rest in a hostel was. I kept knocking back the Berocca and antibiotics, so that by the time the ice was ready for us I was feeling much better.

Barneo Ice Camp is the base from which expeditions are launched to the North Pole. Each year, they identify a suitable ice floe for the runway. This they do by flying over the ocean. They need a floe with a minimum thickness of 1.3m, which doesn't seem much when you consider the size of the Antonov An-72 they will need to land on it. The Antonov is not as big as the Ilyushin of Antarctica, but it has a huge jet on either wing, which means it can take off and land on very short runways. It sounds like a space rocket when it does.

Once the scouts are happy, a couple of former Russian Special Service sky-divers are dropped out of a plane, along with this heavy-duty bulldozer on parachutes. These guys will machine the runway, so that an Antonov can land on it with the equipment to set up the camp. It's a hell of an operation, and it all took the best part of that week we spent waiting.

On 6 April we were flown to Barneo. The delay had meant that a lot of people, who had other commitments, were forced to shorten their expeditions to the Pole. Steve and I had commitments, too, on Everest, but we were adamant we would ski the last degree. The upshot was that our group was reduced in size and, best of all, we would be led by Alain Hubert, a legend of the polar community. He is a civil engineer by training, who designed the Belgian scientific base in Antarctica. I learned so much from him, which I still draw from today. In so many ways that week's delay was a godsend.

The other two guys in our team, a Frenchman and French Canadian, were strong, so we were set fair to make a swift journey. But there is so much that can go wrong on the Arctic ice. Other than weather, the biggest threat is negative drift. There is no *terra firma* up there, so the ice is always moving, depending on the wind and the ocean currents. It is perfectly common, when the drift is against you, to ski for a day, go to sleep and wake up back where you started. Then there are all the types of ice you must negotiate. Judging them is an art. Some floes are decades old and metres thick. Further down the spectrum, you have single-year ice, which can be brittle, or sometimes saggy and elastic. Next comes porridge ice, which is exactly what it sounds like and, according to the consistency, can be skied if you're quick and smooth with your action. Then, of course, you have the open water between the floes, known as 'leads'. We had planned to nego-tiate these is by donning an immersion suit and swimming them. These suits are expensive and heavy, though. As an alternative, Alain had recently designed buoyant pulks, which is what we used. The terrain under your feet is constantly changing along this spectrum from thick ice to water and all points in between. It is like an ever-moving jigsaw. The floes can split at any time, or collide with each other. Where they collide, they push up pressure ridges, which have to be climbed and in places are head high.

Finally, there's the relentless, inescapable cold. At that time of year, the sun has only recently established itself. There is no night, although there is a twilight, but neither is there a midday glare. At its highest point, the sun casts long shadows, as it would late on a summer evening. It is stunningly beautiful, and I encountered my first quad helix on this leg. It's a kind of rainbow around the sun, the rays refracted through ice crystals in the atmosphere. At times the sun can appear like an eye in the sky with a rainbow iris. But it makes for a deathly cold environment. At least on a clear day in an Antarctic summer you can pitch your tent in the sunshine and benefit from a greenhouse effect to warm you up. There's none of that in an Arctic spring. What solar energy there is bounces away across the ice. Inside your tent, you must pack all your clothes away, or they will freeze in the moist air. The humidity from your breath gathers on your sleeping bag as ice, joined by the humidity from your body, which permeates the fabric. Another film of ice from your breath forms on the inside of the tent. Melting snow on your stove is another activity that has to be managed. Any carelessness can compromise your equipment, with dangerous consequences. The discipline required is mentally draining.

What a relief it was, then, when this leg went just about as well as it could. Alain had a lot to do with that, judging which ice floes to pitch our tent on, constantly offering tips. He used his watch and the shadow of his pole to navigate. Thankfully, the general drift for the first few days was to the east. Some nights we actually managed to catch some action northwards!

The days were brutally hard work. Everyone took a tumble or two, climbing over the pressure ridges in their skis. Often such falls would be followed up with a clout from your 50kg pulk following on behind you: I was quite heavily dazed by a blow to the head on the penultimate day. On the same day, we were all nearly caught in a collision between two floes. Somebody had just fallen, and the rest of us were busy laughing at him. I am conscious that it may sound as if we spend our time laughing at each other's mishaps on these expeditions, and it is true, to an extent. Humour is as important a survival tool as any. But comedy can quickly change to something more serious, and here was another case. A profound groan could be heard rumbling beneath our feet. Water started to bubble across the surface, and these huge, several ton blocks of ice we'd just clambered over started to tumble like building blocks. There was about a hundred metres of it shifting and collapsing in front of our eyes. If it had happened a few minutes earlier we'd have been in the middle of it. One sheet of ice pushed upwards; the other – the one we were standing on – disappeared into the water. We moved swiftly on, but it was another sobering demonstration of the power of Nature.

As we approached the North Pole, the currents under the ice became more changeable. We suffered some negative drift on our last night – about three kilometres' worth – but the closer we came to the Pole the more the ice seemed to change its direction. The geographic North Pole these days is marked by a Russian flag in the seabed, but that's no use to you on the surface. If you'd watched our final half-hour from above and speeded it up, it would have looked like something out of *The Benny Hill Show*, five grown men running this way then that, trying to work out which patch of ice was above the Pole, knowing that the honour was constantly being passed on to the next patch. Alain finally located it with his GPS unit, but by the time the rest of us had pulled out our cameras and flags, wrestling with mitts in a temperature of −40°C, we had drifted ten metres off it. When we relocated again to have our moment, at 2.20 p.m. on 11 April, on the North Pole, we knew it would be gone again within a few seconds.

It was a bizarre experience. My sixth leg had been completed, but we might have been anywhere. This was not an obvious landmark, like the top of a mountain. All we had to confirm our destination was the electronic device in our hand. I was relieved more than anything else. So much could have gone wrong with this leg. Although the earlier delay meant we were now two weeks behind the other expeditions on Everest, this leg had gone as well as could be expected. There were the usual photos and man hugs, but it was the next day, back at Longyearbyen, that the satisfaction properly sank in.

This was the most businesslike of the Challenge's legs for me. It was all about getting there and away in one piece in a minimal amount of time. On every leg I wanted to be quick and safe, of course, but I also tried to breathe it all in. Steve and I had discussed our careers as sportsmen on earlier training expeditions. Both had flashed by too quickly; neither of us felt he had looked over the fence enough, as I put it, or out of the window, as he does. I think that common regret was a source of friendship between us. I was absolutely determined to make sure I lived in the moment on the Challenge. I believe I achieved that, and, naturally, the whole experience continues to develop the more I reflect on it afterwards. There were some wonderful times on that Arctic leg. Steve and I turned the Top 5 game into an art form while huddled around the stove in our tent. But, more than on the others, this one felt like a job that had to be done.

It was somewhat overshadowed, I guess, by the highest mountain on Earth.

5

The thing about these extreme environments, which I hope I am making clear, is that the norms of everyday life are suspended when you visit them. The world you're operating in just seems, well, abnormal. But Everest is the daddy of them all. Take what applies to all the others and magnify it again when you come to Everest. Everything is heightened – the apprehension, the exhaustion, the delirium and, of course, the mountain itself.

The airport at Lukla is a fitting introduction to it all. Its runway is nestled among the foothills of the Himalaya (for foothills in the Himalaya, read full-on 5000m mountains anywhere else). It is short, sloping, hard up against a mountain at one end, hanging over a precipice at the other. If you're a nervous flier, it's not for you; if you love the spectacular, it most certainly is. I was getting pretty hardened to this kind of thing, anyway. Compared to the mossy tarmac of Ilaga or a block of ice on the Arctic, Lukla was practically Heathrow.

There is a certain type of mountaineer – hard-bitten, steely-eyed – who looks on Everest with disdain. I can see where they're coming from, I suppose. In the same way that Kilimanjaro's reputation suffers from all the celebrities who go up it, so Everest is often derided among the fourteen 'eight-thousanders' in the world (all of them in the Himalaya), for the traffic it attracts. As eight-thousanders go, it's a tourist trap. You see photos of what looks like gridlock on the Hillary Step, as a long line of climbers try to reach the top. The highest it may be, but it's not the toughest technically, and besides there are companies who will pretty much haul you up. It's phenomenally irresponsible. People on any mountain without the full, or in fact minimum, skill set to be self-sufficient are dangerous.

But I'm not one of those cynical mountaineers. Although the idea of cowboy climbers chasing a trophy makes me sick and represents everything I aspire not to be, I am as in thrall to Everest as any of them. This was my first time, after all – and everyone remembers their first time.

It was my second time in the Himalaya, after our training expedition to Cho Oyu the year before, but I don't think it matters how many times you go to the Himalaya – it's just a magical, magical place. The trek from Lukla to Everest Base Camp is a little less than forty miles, rising in altitude from 2860m to 5360m. Again, if you're contemptuous of tourists, this trek may offend you – it is a well-trodden route – but if you can see past that it is surely worth it. To be surrounded by mountains seven or eight thousand metres high is a stunning experience. At this stage, the altitude and scale of everything is uplifting, rather than mind-twisting, as it will become. If you can bring yourself to look into the eyes of the other pilgrims (let's not call them tourists), you will see the wonder reflected again and again. There's a very special vibe on the way to base camp, facilitated by the beautiful Nepalese people. A tourist trail it may be, but it means a lot to them, and they take such pride in it.

As with the Kilimanjaro leg, we were supposed to be trekking to base camp with some friends of the Challenge, but our delays on the North Pole meant they had left without us. And the Jagged Globe expedition we were supposed to be climbing the actual mountain with had been out there for three weeks when we landed at Lukla. There was no way we could summit with them now, but we had plans to meet up with the expedition leader, David Hamilton, on the approach to base camp.

Steve and I left Lukla on 18 April. Steve's dad, David, and a cameraman for the documentary, Dai Williams, or Dai Camera, as we called him, trekked with us to base camp. It was a well-paced twelve-day trek, wending our way through the villages and monasteries, taking regular rest days to acclimatise to the altitude and feeding up for the challenge ahead on the cakes of the local bakeries and dal baht (a local dish of rice and soup I took a shine to) in the lodges. It was imperative we conserved energy and arrived at base camp in the best health possible. Many fail to get there at all. This was when Steve and I could really make good on that pledge to look out of the window and breathe it all in. Even if we were behind time, we had to take it slow after what we'd been through only a few days earlier on the North Pole – and we had to eat cake – lots of it. Steve and his dad played game after game of extreme Scrabble (the altitude was already getting to them, judging by some of the words they were coming up with), while Dai and I … well, we ate cake. We met many people along the way, too, including an extraordinary man called Shailendra Kumar Upadhyay. He was a former Nepalese Foreign Minister and was aiming to become the oldest person to summit Everest – at the age of eighty-two. Incredible audacity and a lovely man.

Idyllic though it may sound – and the memories are idyllic when I recall them now – I also remember a constant battle with the flip side of such beauty. I had wobbled over the Carstensz Pyramid leg, with team members coming and going. I'd wobbled, but, like a Moto GP rider coming out of a corner, I was still on it. I never forgot why I was there – how could I, with mountains everywhere we looked, so beautiful, but there, always there, waiting. My systems were as tight as ever. We were not rushing; I was meticulous with my hygiene, careful with what I ate, constantly taking advice from Ramesh, our sirdar, about the local produce. I remember when we stopped off at the Everest View Hotel. The name should be self-explanatory, and people spent hours there taking photos of the mountain. I came away with two, as opposed to ten, of Ama Dablam, one of the most spectacular peaks I've ever seen. I shied away from the main attraction. As a player, I never dwelt too much on my opposite number before a big game, not wanting to empower him or be beaten before the game had started. So it was here. The excitement and buzz of the crowds was all around, but I had to focus to avoid being disarmed by it. These mountains take on personalities as you approach them. They sit there doing nothing, but their motionless aura can start to unnerve you before you've even set foot on them. And the thinner the air becomes, the more your mind bends and twists in the face of it.

The tension increased as we approached. It was important for Steve and me to spend some time above base camp altitude, so he, Dai and I took one detour over the Kongma la Pass, at 5500m. The snow was heavy, and we lost the trail, taking ten hours to reach Lobuche. Dai, who is a surfer, and fit, had been another to climb the Kilimanjaro leg, but he considered this tougher still. Then, on the approach to Gorak Shep, last stop before base camp, we caught our first sight of the Khumbu Icefall, an ever-shifting cascade of ice, more escalator than glacier, which is the first proposition Everest puts to a climber leaving base camp.

At Gorak Shep, we finally hooked up with David Hamilton. I'd first met him on Vinson, and we have since become great friends. If mountains can unnerve, experienced leaders, not to mention friendly faces, work wonders for the spirit. We had tactics to discuss. The adrenaline surged as we sat in a window seat overlooking the mountains and talked it through. We really were cutting it fine. The Jagged Globe team had been acclimatising on the mountain for three weeks now. In another week or so they would be ready to push for the summit, weather permitting. David suggested 26 May as the latest we could leave it to attempt a summit ourselves, but if the weather didn't oblige there would be no second chance. Everest is so high it penetrates the jet stream, which means it is normally buffeted by winds of more than 100mph. For the month of May, though, the jet stream moves north, before it returns with the monsoon season in June. That, for obvious reasons, is when the climbing season ends. Either we joined his team on their acclimatisation programme, which would have been very dangerous, as they were more than halfway through it, or we pursued an aggressive and not much less risky programme of our own. We settled on the latter. It was a strategy that would place us under a lot of pressure. The Sherpas did not approve, but David knew us better and was prepared to endorse it.

The good news was that the Khumbu Icefall was well compressed and stable this year, with minimal ladder crossings over crevasses. The bad news was that the temperature was rising dramatically, so all of that could change as the glacier started to increase its movement. Even as we spoke, the ominous thunderclaps of avalanches were sounding in the distance. The mountain was raising her game.

Base camp was deserted when we arrived there on 30 April. All the other teams were on the mountain acclimatising and working through manoeuvres. It was eerily quiet. The tents sat in neat colour-coded groups, and the snow fell softly. We took the opportunity to have a quick look round. Everest Base Camp is an incredible place, a mini metropolis among the boulders of rock and ice with more amenities than you could hope for in so wild an environment – kitchen tents, mess tents (complete with Monopoly and Scrabble, so that was Steve and David sorted), toilet tents, medical tents and a comms tent (with pretty basic internet, but internet all the same).

As is traditional, the following day we attended a puja ceremony, in which the Lama blessed us and our climbing gear for the weeks ahead. Beautiful and moving, it lasted around an hour in the open air. Then Steve and I ventured out on to the ice for the first time. I was grateful for the activity. We could no longer see our ultimate destination, but the Khumbu Icefall was right in front of us and no less forbidding. It had looked almost benign from Gorak Shep, but the sheer scale of it was all too apparent now, an otherworldly landscape, rising hundreds of metres high, vast knuckles of ice interlocking chaotically, so big you can't imagine a way through them – and all of it on the move. They estimate the Icefall travels around three to four feet down the mountain every day. The temperature was noticeably rising over those three days we spent resting at base camp. You could hear the ice rumbling as it made its way down the mountain. Every now and then a chunk the size of a van would break off and fall in on itself. The boom of avalanches continued around the valley. News of the first death of the season filtered down to us. Someone had suffered a heart attack at 7400m. Someone else, heroically, had tried to perform CPR for an hour and a half. At that altitude, exertion, even breathing, over and above that required to climb is an investment that could prove ruinous in itself.

I was discovering what people meant by the mental challenge of climbing Everest. In my opinion, Denali is tougher physically, but mentally there is no comparison between Everest and any of the others. Perhaps it's the legend of the place, perhaps it's the drip-feed of deaths (a function, of course, of the number of climbers on the mountain at any one time), most certainly it's the altitude, but everything up there seems perfectly choreographed to come together and derail the climber. You don't sleep well, which is an altitude thing, but even without the physiological disturbances it is tough to settle under that kind of psychological stress.

On the fourth day, Steve and I made our first foray on to the Icefall with Pasang, our Sherpa. At 4.30 in the morning with our head torches on, the seracs and boulders that towered around us looked no less sinister than they had from a distance. The crevasses were still manageable, although widening all the time, as they would continue to over the next few weeks, but some of them required ladders to cross. These are laid down by a team of Sherpas called the Icefall Doctors, who maintain the route through the Icefall. If a crevasse is too wide to negotiate, an aluminium ladder, similar to the kind you might buy at B&Q, is put down across it, lashed to the ice with climbing rope at either end and usually flanked by more rope along its length, which acts as something to hold on to. You're grateful for it as you inch your way across, the ladders wobbling with each step you take. Sometimes the spikes on your crampons just won't fit snugly around each rung; sometimes they will, but then you run the risk of catching a crampon on the ladder. When that happens, you have to force it out as gently as possible, while teetering over a crevasse. Most of the crevasses were small at this stage, only one-ladder crossings, which are straightforward, but a crevasse is a crevasse and not a thing to fall into, however narrow. They would grow bigger in the weeks to come, requiring more than one ladder to traverse, lashed together with rope, end to end. One crevasse we would encounter later in the month, just above the Icefall at the start of the Western Cwm required five ladders roped together. As you would expect, it sagged alarmingly before anyone had even set foot on it. Crossing that one was genuinely scary. If only you could adopt the old adage of not looking down, but you are constantly looking down to place each foot on a rung. You just have to focus on those rungs and not on what lies beneath. It is exhausting mentally.

When the sun came up on that first day in the Icefall, it was to reveal terrain unlike any I have encountered. It's as if a bomb has gone off beneath the glacier, leaving behind vast piles of blasted wreckage. They call the most chaotic section the Popcorn Field, which is a neat image for what it looks like from a distance; but when you're a mite in the middle of it all, the dusky, blueish ice and snow crowds round and high over you. As the sun rises in the sky, the glacier beneath accelerates its progress down the mountain, creaking and groaning beneath your feet. You can see and hear seracs and boulders collapsing. The Icefall Doctors are careful to keep the route away from the most treacherous parts, so such collapses usually take place nearby as opposed to right beneath or above you, but there are no guarantees. The glacier is so fluid that not even the Icefall Doctors can second-guess the effect its progress will have on the piles of 'popcorn' sitting on top of it. The air is heavy with threat. Speed is the best policy. All you want to do is get through it as quickly as you can. We were lucky because most climbers were higher up the mountain on their acclimatisation programmes, so we could move swiftly. When it's busy, I think it would be horrific. More people die in the Icefall than anywhere else on the Nepalese side of the mountain.

All of which contributes to the assault on the psyche. On that first venture into the Icefall, we climbed halfway up and were back in time for our second breakfast of the day and to say goodbye to Dai Camera, who was heading home. Having him and Steve's dad around had helped to ease the tension. They brought a lightness of mood, a bit of banter. They weren't there to climb a mountain. Now Steve and I were being left to it, and we, too, were to go our separate ways in a few days' time. After another day and a half of rest, we climbed through the Icefall and spent a night at Camp 1, which sits just above it at a little over 6000m, then returned again to base camp the day after that. The rest of the Jagged Globe team were back down from their acclimatisation programmes and were preparing for their summit bid. The season was now officially open. The day before, a team of Sherpas had become the first to reach the summit, fixing the season's ropes as they did so.

David Hamilton was also at base camp, and we sat down with him to draw up the finer details of our acclimatisation strategy.

You can't just climb up Everest in one go. The thinness of the air at the top is deadly, which is what separates Everest from the rest of the Seven Summits, the next highest of which stops at just shy of 7000m. Everest is almost another two kilometres higher. It lies in the so-called Death Zone, which is generally classified as anything over 8000m. The atmospheric pressure is around a third of that at sea level, which means there is around a third of the oxygen available to breathe. If there were any way of being transported from sea level straight to its summit you would have only a couple of minutes before you lost consciousness. This is why a conventional attempt on Everest takes the best part of two months. The body has to adapt to life at that altitude. It must be coaxed into its acclimatisation by incremental shuttle climbs, or 'rotations', up and down the mountain. Once you are ready, the actual climbing of Everest may take only four days, if the weather obliges.

There are all sorts of physiological processes going on when the body acclimatises. Basically, the aim is to generate more red blood cells, thus increasing the blood's capacity to carry oxygen. This is usually done by the established practice of 'climbing high, sleeping low'. You climb high to trigger the demand for red blood cells, then retreat to a lower altitude, where the thicker air facilitates their production. Rest days in between are crucial to allow the various processes to take place, as is hydration, which counteracts the thickening of your blood plasma and maintains circulation through the finer capillaries.

The trouble was, neither Steve nor I could afford to observe a long acclimatisation programme without missing the end of the season. The prospect of meticulously following the protocols only to be denied by the weather didn't bear thinking about. So far we were negotiating the altitude well. I was having trouble with my sinuses, which are a problem even at sea level, but I was avoiding the infamous 'Khumbu cough'. This is caused by a drying out of the membranes in your lungs from heavy breathing in the dry, freezing air.

What I did have, though, that no one else on the mountain faced, was the prospect of an ascent of Denali the next month, as well as any toll that might have been taken by the four other peaks and two poles I'd journeyed to in the past four. We held a meeting with David and his assistant, Andy Chapman, Mingma Sherpa (our climbing sirdar) and Nima Sherpar (our camp sirdar). I was far from convinced that climbing up and down the side of the world's highest mountain was time well spent for someone in my situation. Again, David was in agreement, but Mingma and Nima did not approve of the plan we drew up. Steve was going to follow a more traditional acclimatisation programme, albeit speeded up, but I was going to minimise rotations up and down the mountain in order to conserve energy. The main points of contention in my plan were the decision not to spend a night at Camp 3 (7100m) until the summit push itself and the tactic of spending six consecutive nights above 6000m, five of them at Camp 2 (6500m), without returning to base camp. Mingma and Nima felt this was risky. Not even the Sherpas stay as long as that at Camp 2. Would my body be able to acclimatise properly at such altitude?

There was no way to be sure. All the indications from my training so far had suggested I acclimatised well, but, as discussed elsewhere, when it comes to handling altitude, past performance is no guarantee of future results. Still, I felt it was a gamble worth taking. With Denali and Elbrus still to come, summiting Everest was not the end of the game for me. I didn't want to be climbing any more than I had to be. Rather than shuttle backwards and forwards between base camp and the other camps, including a night at Camp 3, I would compromise by basing myself at Camp 2 throughout. The other advantage of staying at Camp 2, rather than base camp, is that any manoeuvres from there are up the Lhotse Face, the western flank of Lhotse, the world's fourth highest mountain. The Lhotse Face is a brutally steep sheet of ice, more than a kilometre high and punctuated by a couple of bands of rock higher up, but at least it's not the Khumbu Icefall, which greets you first up out of base camp. The Icefall may be at a relatively low altitude, but, pound for pound, O_2 molecule for O_2 molecule, I considered it the most energy-sapping section of the mountain, as well as the most dangerous. And it was getting worse. It never ceased to amaze me how much the terrain changed each time you passed through it. Crevasses you had been able to step over one day you had to jump over the next; ladders that had spanned a crevasse had now fallen in; parts of the route had collapsed or been altered by a fallen block of ice. It was constantly on the move, threatening and unpredictable. Every one of your senses was heightened as you travelled through it.

We set off from base camp once more at 3 a.m. on 8 May, the last time I would have to negotiate the Icefall for another week. Steve and I climbed to Camp 1 with Andy, the assistant leader, arriving there at 7.25 a.m. in high winds. A few poorly secured tents had been destroyed. We each found a Jagged Globe tent and crawled into it. This is when the thoughts start to thicken in your mind. It's one thing to rest down at base camp, with a DVD or Monopoly to occupy you – or, in the case of Jagged Globe clients, Gav the Chef's culinary genius – but at the higher camps there is nothing to do but sit in a tent.

At six o'clock the next morning we climbed to Camp 2 across the Western Cwm, a broad, undulating valley at the foot of Nuptse, another of the Himalayan giants. The Western Cwm links the Khumbu Icefall with the foot of the Lhotse Face. It took us a little over two hours to reach Camp 2, about two-thirds of the way along. At the start of the Western Cwm lay the five-ladder crossing mentioned earlier. At that altitude (more than 6000m), with a 90-litre rucksack on your back, it takes great mental focus to cross a thing like that, which wobbles, twists and tilts with every step. It's an analogy for life on the mountain in general. Just a simple reflex action like placing one foot in front of the other becomes an operation up there, a decision that has to be weighed and executed with minute care – or at least it feels as if it does. The relevance of everything seems magnified on Everest, every thought, decision and action. Taken together with the long stretches of inactivity, it is a draining environment.

By now, Everest itself is towering over you. You can't see it from base camp, or from the Khumbu Icefall, but it emerges from behind its West Shoulder round about Camp 1. Camp 2 sits between Nuptse on one side, Lhotse straight ahead and, to the left, the sheer, giant south face of Everest, two and a half kilometres tall. From here, the mountaineer's conundrum looms large. Just how much time do you spend looking up at the summit? You want to be able to judge your progress; you want something to aim at; but you don't want to be overwhelmed by the magnitude of the obstacle. This is no longer the nervous glance at a mountain far away. Now the mountain is right above you, the scale of it real and vivid.

I find the best policy is to focus on the minutiae of the tasks at hand, which, if repeated consistently and efficiently, will result eventually in the greater goal. I guess it's the mountaineering equivalent of taking one game at a time. But it is another dynamic to wrestle with. Those six days based at Camp 2 were tough. Steve and I climbed to the foot of the Lhotse Face after our first night at Camp 2, and when we returned to camp the main Jagged Globe team arrived on their bid for the summit. They brought with them news of Shailendra Kumar Upadhyay, the eighty-two-year-old we had befriended on the trek to base camp. He had died on the Icefall the day before from altitude sickness. You often hear of deaths on a mountain, but this was the first time I'd had a connection with one. What an incredible man he was. I can't tell you anything about his life as a politician or diplomat, although I can say that he charmed me the moment we met, but to have even considered a thing like this at his age speaks of a man with something extraordinary in him. His death made me very sad. And it did nothing to ease the tension. That afternoon, there was heavy snow at Camp 2. Each soft flake seemed full of menace.

Steve headed back to base camp the next day on his acclimatisation programme. It was the last I would see of him for a few days. I headed up to Camp 3 on the Lhotse Face with Pasang Sherpa and felt strong. Pasang was one of seven brothers who had summited Everest forty-three times between them! At twenty-seven, he was considered a bright young talent of Nepalese mountaineering. It was a privilege to climb with him. These forays were the highlights of my six days in Camp 2, but everything gravitated back to rest and the inside of a tent. After the first night, I moved into the communal tent, just for the sake of variety, but anyone passing through has the same heavy concerns on their mind.

On day four at Camp 2, the Jagged Globe team left for the summit. I was finding it hard to be around them. They were great people, but we had different agendas. Which is another way of saying I wanted to go with them. I felt ready. You can never be sure, especially when they were climbing higher than you've ever been before, but I just felt I could have gone with them. I still think it. Here was another decision, the dilemmas of which were magnified by the environment into a source of acute stress. In reality, I would never have gone, because I was climbing the mountain with Steve, and Steve was down at base camp, but you can't stop playing through the scenarios in your head. The attraction of attempting a summit now, rather than waiting another week before leaving from base camp, as planned, was powerful. The threat of altitude sickness would be more significant, but the threat of being denied by the weather would be greatly reduced. I never mentioned the idea to anyone. That doesn't mean it didn't dog me. But I had a plan and faith in that plan, so I stuck with it.

The days were long in Camp 2. There really is nothing to do. It's important to stay active, so I walked about camp every now and then, but your body enters a strange kind of suspension where activity itself is an act of will. We are not designed to operate up there. No one lives above 6000m. *In extremis*, the body prioritises its tasks. When you spend time at that altitude, all resources are diverted towards the acclimatisation process and away from your stomach, or your digestive tract, or your brain. Appetite is a good indicator of how acclimatisation is going. Mine held up OK. There is a kitchen tent at Camp 2. It's pretty basic by any normal standards, but up there a bowl of noodles or rice served up by a Sherpa feels the height of luxury. My digestive tract, on the other hand, pretty much shut down. When I returned to base camp a few days later, I was back and forth to the toilet as it cranked itself up again.

Then there's the brain and how it seems to bend. I'd love to be able to say that the thought of failure never even occurred to me. It's a well-practised mantra of sportsmen the world over. How often do you hear someone from the bottom-placed club saying, 'We've never even thought about relegation'? Well, I've been in a relegation fight as a player, and of course you have! You may not accept it until it's mathematically confirmed, but if you're rational the idea haunts you every day.

But at least it haunts you while you're smashing seven bells out of each other in training. At sea level. In a tent at 6500m, the fear closes in. What if I didn't make it to the top of Everest? The 737 Challenge would be over. Whether it be through the shortcomings of my own body or through forces beyond my control, the idea of failure was harrowing. To have come this far ... After a rugby career that had ended too soon, to be a nearly man again ...

When I thought of what others had invested in the Challenge. Jagged Globe had let me run up bills that, if they weren't paid, could ruin them. Tracy was working all the hours outside her job to keep the blog updated and the PR proactive. The whole team were stretching every sinew to raise funds. My mum and dad were managing it all and worrying themselves sick. They had remortgaged their home so it could go on.

If I failed ...

And that was just the bigger picture. On a micro-level, the self-doubts nag away at you, constantly asking whether you're doing the right thing, whether you've made the right calls. Do I push it, do I rest, do I go back down? I might wake up with a headache and acute lethargy. You know it's perfectly normal, but immediately the questions crowd round. Am I spending too long up here? At times your head wants to explode. That same day the team left for Camp 3, they came back down again in the evening. Contrary to the forecast, the winds at the summit were too high. They would try again in a couple of days. What if that happened on our summit push? There might not be time for another attempt.

In the end, the very process that was trying to wear me down ended up reinforcing me. Mountains strip away the layers we hide behind in everyday life. They can expose weaknesses, but they can also reveal strengths. Ultimately, my greatest strength lay in my preparation. Without that cornerstone of confidence in your own body, a mountain like Everest is a treacherous place to be. But it is a spiritual place, too. I am a man of faith, even if I don't always have the time and headspace to show it in the real world. Up there in the thin air among the mountains, you feel much closer to whatever it is that is bigger than us. And I do believe there is something. If ever I came close to panicking, to running out of the tent and up the mountain screaming in a deranged attempt to get it over and done with, I fell back on the simple conviction of faith. That window would open for me, I knew it would. I would be given an opportunity. I don't believe in all that macho bullshit about conquering mountains, man versus Nature. For me it's about conquering yourself, or at least reaching peace with yourself, and then working with the mountain to reach your goal.

In the end, I simply believed. She would give me my chance. Then it would be up to me to take it.

The Jagged Globe team left Camp 2 for their second summit attempt on day six, and I left for base camp. I'd passed Steve, who had gone up to Camp 3 with the team, where he spent a night, before descending for another at Camp 2. The word was that he was looking strong. He returned to base camp on 16 May, the same day as the team reached the summit. It was another 100 per cent success rate for a Jagged Globe expedition. God willing, we would maintain that record for 2011 in just a few days' time.

Actually, it wasn't quite a 100 per cent record, insofar as there was one person, Adam Potter, still at base camp (other than me), and another, Mark Pinnock, who had turned back at Camp 4, feeling unwell. Both would be trying again with Steve and me. Adam had stayed behind at base camp, suffering from a bad case of the Khumbu cough. He'd been in the news, apparently, earlier in the year (I was on Aconcagua), when he slipped on one of the Scottish Munros and fell 1000ft, over three cliffs, and walked away, having broken a couple of small bones in his back and taken some skin off his nose. He reckons the cooking pans and chocolate in his rucksack saved his life by breaking his fall. It was a miracle. Fair play to him – here he was on Everest, unperturbed, less than four months later.

On 18 May the rest of the team arrived at base camp after their successful summit. That was another difficult time. Naturally, they were in a very different frame of mind from ours – some elated, some exhausted, some muttering how it was the scariest experience of their lives. Steve and I formed part of the welcome party for them, but we spent most of the rest of that day in our tents. Worse still, we had planned to leave for the summit ourselves the next day, but heavy snow meant we would have to wait another. We were the last team in base camp. The Icefall Doctors were saying they would be taking up the ladders and closing the Icefall on 27 May, only a week later.

Even the longest waits eventually end, and so did ours, on 20 May, just three weeks after we had arrived at base camp. Steve, Adam, Mark and I left base camp at 2 a.m. after a quick puja ceremony. The rest of the team got up to see us off. The Icefall was different again, and the sound of a couple of avalanches in the vicinity kept us on our toes. The five-ladder crossing just after Camp 1 didn't disappoint, and we were on to the Western Cwm just as the sun was starting to flood the valley, turning it into an inferno. The temperature changes on Everest are violent. If the transition from Papua to the North Pole was a bit of a shock to the system, you can experience similar swings on Everest in the space of a few hours. The Western Cwm is a suntrap, and temperatures in the valley rise into the mid-thirties. You just have to manage your body temperature. I like to wear as few layers as possible and manage my body temperature through exertion. When it's hot, though, you need to slow up. It's a bit like when you're at a wedding on a really hot day. Well, a bit. You're not so worried on Everest about sweat patches appearing on your salmon shirt, but the idea of taking everything slowly with no sudden movements is similar. If you're dripping with sweat and the sun goes in, the consequences could be serious, as the temperature plummets.

It had been a tough eight-hour climb, but we spent the rest of the day in our tents, hydrating and eating and waiting for weather reports from base camp. The news was not good. The winds at the summit were forecast to remain high over the next three days, gusting to more than 45mph, but they were at least due to drop on 24 May, which became our new summit target. It meant another day at Camp 2, which was starting to crumble. Avalanches and rock slides were booming and rumbling throughout the valley, and cracks were appearing in the ice around us. It was obvious the end of the season was fast approaching. We were relieved to push on from Camp 2 on 22 May – at 5 a.m. so as to avoid the sun on the Lhotse Face.

We had to pass a dead climber in a body bag at the foot of it, the third victim of the season, which, sadly, made it quite a good one (although, unbeknown to us, another had been taken higher up the day before). The following year the death toll would reach double figures. Andy left us to help evacuate the body to Camp 2, and we continued up to Camp 3.

The Lhotse Face is a wall of ice and windswept snow that climbers must scale before turning left for the south-east ridge of Everest. It is steep and unforgiving. You are constantly on your toes, kicking your crampons into the ice, or climbing with feet splayed. There is nowhere to stop and rest until you reach Camp 3, which sits on a narrow ledge about two hours' climb from where the terrain steepens at the foot of the face. With the gales and recent snow, we spent it climbing into spindrift kicked up by the winds sweeping down from the South Col.

At Camp 3 we dug in again, spending the day melting snow and testing our O_2 equipment. From here on up, it is established practice to use supplementary oxygen. A tiny elite of climbers have managed to reach the summit without it. For obvious reasons that is considered by some to be the purest way to climb the mountain, but, for equally obvious reasons, it is extremely dangerous. Doing so was never an option for me as I had a bigger picture to consider, but Steve was adamant that he was going to climb to Camp 4 without oxygen. It was a risk I was not prepared to take – my directive was to get to the summit, come what may.

It's difficult to know what to say in that situation. Camp 4 is on the South Col at 7950m, in other words on the edge of the Death Zone. If anyone could make it there without oxygen on his first exposure to that kind of altitude, Steve was the man. He's an incredibly strong guy, mentally and physically. No one needs me to tell them that – he's a double Olympic champion and one of Britain's most successful athletes in a sport whose very essence is strength and endurance. He's humble and respectful and had trained hard for this. If he wanted to climb to Camp 4 without oxygen, who were any of the rest of us to urge otherwise? Besides, there's no way anyone would have dissuaded him. That mental strength includes an iron will. Everyone respected his decision and the confidence he had in himself to make it, but I don't think there was one of us who didn't have misgivings.

We left Camp 3 on 23 May at 7 a.m., later than usual in order to try to avoid the high winds forecast that day on the South Col. The climb to Camp 4 involves another three hours on the steep ice of the Lhotse Face, before you scale a seam of distinctive rock known as the Yellow Band, the first rock a climber encounters on Everest. The next significant obstacle is a rocky outcrop called the Geneva Spur, which becomes the pass between Lhotse and Everest, known as the South Col. The winds were high for us up there. Sometimes I had to plant

The most beautiful siesta, overlooking the Andes from Canada Camp, 4877m, on Aconcagua.

A Welsh sunset from Nido de Cóndores Camp, 5500m, on Aconcagua.

A very happy Kili summit with the wonderful group of friends that helped me fundraise on this leg.

My first sight of the elusive Carstensz Pyramid after a week of trekking to get to there.

The Tyrolean traverse on Carstensz's summit ridge is pretty spectacular, although not the place to savour the views.

I've never been happier to meet two Papuan kids in the jungle, holding the wooden carcasses of the guitars they were making! My guides home.

The 'pressure ridges' of The North Pole leg, but never far from the cold Arctic waters underneath.

The low Arctic sun doesn't provide much heat to warm the tent. Steve and I savouring every mouthful of a hot bowl of super noodles!

Some of the world's biggest mountains in the distance behind me as I climb Everest's summit ridge up to the very top of the world.

The incredible Mingma and I on the summit. I'm holding a 'It's a girl' message of congratulations for my mates Gemma and Ian!

A lot of gear to load into a not very big plane in Talkeetna. Time for a quick tweet! If Matt and I only knew what the first day on Denali had in store for us!

A sore but healing frostbitten toe made every step and foothold painful. Matt and I made a rule after this pic that toe-bandage dressing was for after dinner!

The top of 'Pig Hill' at the foot of Denali's summit ridge. 'No matter how brutal today has been, I would go through every second again for these views.' I meant that with every part of me.

Standing on the summit of Elbrus, the final leg of my 737 Challenge completed, the moment I climbed into the history books. No tears this time – just smiles!

Matt, Dai Camera and I back in Elbrus Base Camp. The lull before the storm – I can still remember this pic!

Being received at the Senedd, National Assembly for Wales, on my return, greeted by so many and with the Cardiff Arms Park Male Voice Choir singing, will live with me for ever. Thank you.

Sunrise on Elbrus. For me, proof that we are all part of something bigger.

my feet and brace myself while a particularly strong gust rushed by. But when you've cleared the Geneva Spur, everything changes. You're up and over the Khumbu Valley, above the clouds, close to the gods, Tibet one way, Nepal the other, the tops of mountains ranged below, everywhere you look. And straight ahead, another vertical kilometre into the sky, the biggest of them all. It's spiritual.

More immediately, the South Col, which is the low point of the ridge to Everest, is where Camp 4 is set. It's how I would imagine the Moon to look, little rocks strewn across a wasteland, only here it was littered with food, rubbish and broken tents. The weather had been so bad that teams had just abandoned camp. One Italian team had left everything, including some excellent chocolate. I went from tent to tent gathering food. Mind you, food is only of so much use to you up there. In the Death Zone, your body's ability to take on nutrients is severely compromised, which is why you can't stay there for more than a few days. Mingma and Chongbi, two of our Sherpas, erected a couple of Jagged Globe's tents, which had been collapsed by the first team to protect them from the weather, and it was some relief to dive into one and out of the weather.

It is hard to explain how exhausted you feel up there. You just don't want to do anything and whatever tasks you do have, from melting snow to putting on a pair of socks, just stretch out before you as seemingly impossible chores. You have oxygen, but people imagine that makes it seem like sea level again. These are not the sealed units used by divers. The reason it's called supplementary oxygen is that you're still breathing the air around you, but it's mixed with extra oxygen. They say that with a full flow (you can adjust the rate) it is the equivalent of climbing 1000m lower. Either way, it's a savage environment that takes it out of you. As soon as we'd got there (and mineswept a few chocolate bars), I put on my mask and went to sleep.

A couple of hours later I woke up, and Steve was sitting on his sleeping bag, shivering uncontrollably. He had changed colour, a sort of bluey-purple, and he was struggling to communicate. To have made it as far as this without oxygen was a feat that seemed all the more remarkable now I'd tried it myself with some, but it was becoming obvious that it had taken its toll. I'd seen what sort of state a person had to be in to be airlifted from base camp with serious altitude sickness. This was like that. I was worried that he had the symptoms of a dangerous case of hypoxia. His coordination had deteriorated. He kept trying to put his oxygen mask on, but to no avail. Somehow, the strap had become twisted. He couldn't work out what was wrong. I untwisted it for him and put it over his head, turning the flow rate up to full blast. I helped him into his sleeping bag, but his condition was a genuine concern to me now. I went to Mingma's tent and warned him we needed to keep an eye on him.

The good news, although it wouldn't have seemed it a few hours earlier, was that the winds were too high for our planned summit bid that night. Camp 4 is not meant to be more than a shelter to rest up for a few hours on the way through to the summit, but we were forced to stay there for another twenty-four (the first of what would be nearly three days in the Death Zone). I believe that delay saved Steve's summit attempt. The wind was battering our tent and flecks of snow were whizzing

122

past outside. I didn't get much sleep that night. The winds were supposed to subside the next day, but as our tent rattled and shook I couldn't imagine it ever being calm again. And was my climbing partner fit to carry on? We were so close to the summit now, and still it seemed so far away.

Supplementary oxygen and warm drinks were all it took to bring Steve back to something resembling his normal self. His colour and coherence returned with every hour he had his mask on. The man really is a phenomenon. I don't know how many others could have clawed it back from where he was at that altitude. The fact that he left with us at all was an achievement. The Sherpas passed him fit, as we prepared for our 9.30 p.m. departure on 24 May, but summit day was tough for him. Luckily, we were climbing with such a reputable company, so we had enough Sherpas to allow us to separate. David Hamilton on the radio at base camp and Simon Lowe in Sheffield were monitoring Steve's progress anxiously. They were worried he wasn't going to make the summit in the timeframe. But there was no way Steve was ever going to give up, because he's as strong as an ox, and his Sherpa, Pasang, was a good man to have with him. The two of them stuck at it.

I climbed with Mingma, an extraordinary Sherpa. He had summited Everest sixteen times at this point. Incredibly, one of them had been with the rest of the Jagged Globe team barely a week ago. We were at the front of the group, climbing the south-east ridge to the Balcony, breaking a trail through the fresh snow, which was knee-deep in places. The wind had dropped, but at that time of night it is bitterly cold. Whatever temperature it was (I'm guessing −25°C), it feels much colder at such altitude. Your body burns oxygen to generate heat, but up there it can only burn so much.

I was wearing my big Rab down jacket, with its huge furry hood. I was comfortable, and I love that feeling – when you are in a hostile environment like that, yet you feel ... cosy is the wrong word, obviously, but comfortable. It's ridiculous, really. Thanks to nothing more substantial than some insulated clothing, you feel protected, but it's a wonderful bubble to be in. The mountaineering equivalent of sitting by the fire while a storm rages outside.

The Balcony is the start of a ridge that runs onwards up to the South Summit. It becomes very narrow in places. With thick, unbroken snow, it is exhausting. We paused on the Balcony to adjust our clothing and masks and were on the way up to the South Summit when the first rays of light emerged over Tibet, that special moment on any summit attempt, but on the way to the highest of them all even more magical. The temperature picked up as we plodded on, and I remember thinking, this Balcony's not that bad. You hear stories about all the features on the mountain, with their colourful names. The fixed lines were a bit loose at this point, so you couldn't use them to stabilise yourself, and I was aware that we were edging along an exposed section, with a sheer drop on either side, but with the sun rising and my blood warming I was feeling pretty good about things. Exhausted but good. It was so warm, in fact, that I pulled back my hood ...

I swear the world reeled around me. In pulling back my hood, I was pulling back that protection, pulling back the blinkers. My brain was suddenly exposed to the vastness of where I was. To my left, the world fell away kilometres into

Nepal; to my right it was into Tibet. If Adam, just behind me, were to slip on this one, no amount of chocolate in his ruck-sack would save him. We were at the top of the world, teetering along what felt like a tightrope to the platform at the very top. I'd known it – seen it, even – but from out of my furry hood it all seemed manageable. Suddenly, with the hood pulled back, it felt too much to take in – the vastness of it, the peril, the beauty. I pulled my hood up again.

That did the trick. I carried on with a steady heart, as if pulling up that hood had made it all go away. I laughed at myself into my oxygen mask. How illogical! Hood up – safe; hood down – in mortal danger. It made no sense.

Within a few minutes, I was gasping for air. The climb up to the South Summit was brutally steep, and the fresh snow only made it harder. I was shattered, but now something seemed to be restricting my oxygen. I took off my mask to look more carefully. You can normally hear the flow. I knew immediately my mask had blocked. The technology is evolving, but for now these masks climbers use are designed for fighter pilots and therefore enclosed spaces, the very opposite of the one we were in. The condensation from my breath, perhaps from all that laughing, had frozen and blocked the airway. I spoke with Mingma, but we were on a steep, exposed section of rock, so we couldn't stop for long. He managed to take off his mask and attach it to my cylinder. Mingma continued on without supplementary oxygen another couple of hundred vertical metres, I would say, to the South Summit. There we were able to stop on a rock about the size of a snooker table and unblock my mask. I will be forever indebted to Mingma: he not only saved the Challenge but quite possibly much more.

The sun was up now. The shadow of Everest stretched on for miles into Nepal, swallowing up entire mountains. And there, just the other side of a ridge so familiar from countless photos, lay the highest point in the world. My energy surged now that I could see how close we were. It's easy to be tricked by apparent summits, which can prove false, like mirages in a desert, but from here I could see the ridge lead to the ultimate peak. Still, my focus remained on the next step. The game was not over, with maybe a couple of hours to go, another precipitous ridge called the Cornice Traverse and the inconvenient 15m high rock that is the Hillary Step, but the end was in sight.

We were blessed with the most perfect summit day. You see photographs of this final ridge with hundreds of people back to back, queuing to climb up or down the Hillary Step. It's lethal and another image to make your stomach turn, but if there's a weather window and hundreds of climbers who have paid a lot of money for their one shot at the summit, it's an inevitable consequence. We were in the last-chance saloon, though, at the end of the season, so we had it to ourselves. There was an Indian team a couple of hours behind us, who had climbed up from Tibet, but, because of the recent weather, we were the first to summit for four days. The snow was deep and unbroken, which made it harder work and pretty scary at times, but it felt so much purer. And the visibility was perfect. Along the Cornice Traverse I couldn't quite shake off the powerful, primitive instinct that screams to a human *you're not supposed to be up here*, but neither could I imagine a more beautiful, breathtaking place in the world.

At 7.42 a.m. on 25 May, I finally reached the summit, just

126

behind Mingma. It was unlike any exhaustion I'd felt yet, but unlike any altitude either! One heavy, slow footstep followed another until, after who knows how many hundreds and thousands of paces, the last brought me to the mound of snow at the top. I knelt and placed my hands upon it, among the colourful prayer flags that fluttered in the breeze, and, delirious with relief, gratitude and exhaustion, I wept. Imagine the climax of a clichéd film, and you wouldn't be far off.

But clichés become clichés because they are so true. If I could have stopped myself crying I would have done. There's a purity of experience up there, which cannot be smothered by the coolness we defend ourselves with down here. This was Parksy in the raw. Adam and Mark joined me a minute or two later – at the top of Everest and in floods of tears. Even the Sherpas were at it, and it's not often you see the Nepalese emotional. Adam's Sherpa, Chongbi, was summiting for the first time, so Mingma (on his seventeenth) and Pema joined him in shedding a few tears. Then Adam produced a Tupperware container and asked me to take a picture. My brain wasn't working properly – my oxygen mask had been off for a while – and I couldn't understand why he wanted me to take a picture of him eating soup. What I hadn't realised was that his wife, with whom he'd pledged to climb Everest, had been killed in a car crash the year before. He was scattering her ashes. Having just composed ourselves, we all fell apart again. I just hope I caught the moment on camera.

To be there in perfect visibility, without hordes of others, was the most incredible privilege. The gratitude was overwhelming. The only time I've felt the same rush is with love. There are a handful of people in this world for whom I have an overwhelming love – a handful of people and a dog. Sometimes I feel as if I can't contain it. I joke that sometimes I want to head-butt Ben the Dog, because I can't contain how much I love that little shit. Had he been up there, I probably would have!

For the same reason, Mum and Dad will be relieved they weren't with me, but I rang them, as always, from the summit, this time a sobbing, blubbering wreck. Tracy and Lindsey were with them, and Ben the Dog, of course, and Russell and Simon from SMS, the documentary makers. They have often regaled me since with stories of those ten hours at home in Newport. At least I was on it and active; they had to sit there listening to the tick-tock of the clock, working through the piles of sandwiches and cake my mum had prepared, waiting by the phone. Tracy describes Mum as a woman in anguish, her son in the Death Zone and not a thing to be done about it – other than churn out sandwiches. When I told them in between sobs, at three o'clock in the morning, how much I loved them and how grateful I was to everyone who had made it possible, no man had ever spoken more truly. To illustrate the point, Tracy spent the next thirty hours on her laptop, writing press releases and handling phone calls.

If only Steve had been with us, but he was on his way. We probably spent about fifteen minutes at the top before we gathered ourselves for the descent, the most dangerous part of any climb. We passed Steve at the South Summit. That was another moment. He and I hugged. He congratulated me; I told him he was not far away. His tenacity was extraordinary, considering the state he'd been in the night before. He and Pasang made it to the summit at 10.10 a.m.

What a day! After weeks enduring the peculiar stress of life on Everest, we had achieved our goal. I was weak and emaciated, but I had summited safely. All three poles had been completed. Just Denali and Elbrus to go. Just. But this was a day to savour. Mark and I sat down at the Balcony and spent an hour looking out over the world, breathing it in. The air was freezing, but the sun was up and we were hot in our downy gear. Then – and the serious mountaineer in me is ashamed to confess this – we tobogganed into Camp 4 on our arses, using our ice axes to brake and steer.

I wanted to dive into a tent and collapse, but there are always jobs to do. The stoves barely work at that altitude, but you need to fire them up to melt snow. I ate some soup and, once in my tent, removed my socks. That was when I noticed that the big toe on my right foot was a dark shade of blue.

6

How quickly I came down. Two days later, I was at base camp. Two days later, the Challenge was in the balance again.

My toe was noticeably uncomfortable on the climb down to Camp 2, and then again the next day through the Icefall to base camp. I thought I must have bruised it against the inside of my boot. It hurt, but not particularly. Down at base camp, it had started to swell and there was plenty of that bluey-black discolouration you would associate with a bruise. The toenail looked as if it would fall off in the not too distant.

I was used to damaged toenails from my rugby days. As I would have done then, I went to the doctors, so that they might drill and drain the nail, but when I presented it at the medical tent they immediately flagged it up as frostbite. I stared at them, dumbly.

They told me there was no way I could climb Denali in the next few weeks. And, even if I managed it, the word from home was that recent terrorist activity on the mountain had led the Russian authorities to close down Elbrus, the final peak of the Challenge. Who knew when it would reopen? There were two months left before the seven were up. I sat in a daze, as if someone had ripped the life out of me.

How had it happened? I thought of that climb in the dead of night through the deep snow. I do remember my feet being cold – my hands had always been fine – but that's par for the course. I'd scrunched my toes every other step, always keeping them moving. When our bodies acclimatise up there, the extra red blood cells thicken the blood plasma, making it harder for the blood to flow through the smaller capillaries in our toes and feet. That's why our extremities are so vulnerable. That's why it is important to remain hydrated, to keep the plasma as fluid as possible. I had observed the protocols meticulously, but, equally, I'd been pushing harder than most would, both during my three weeks on the mountain and in the five months of the Challenge. I had been cold on summit day, but the situation had never felt unmanageable. At the summit, my feet felt fine.

The medics told me I had to be airlifted down to Kathmandu as soon as possible. The higher temperature and lower altitude in the city would help the toe's healing. This was organised for the next day by David Hamilton, who was brilliant in keeping me going over those crucial hours. I had a fifty-fifty chance, in the medics' opinion, of keeping my toe, regardless of whether I climbed Denali.

I emailed photos of the toe to Dr David Hillebrandt, one of

Jagged Globe's medical advisers. He responded before I'd even left base camp, corroborating the diagnosis of frostbite. It would take from six months to a year to heal properly. Should I climb Denali within a month? He outlined a few scenarios if I did, listing them by number: 1) Goes to Denali, contracts septicaemia and dies; 2) Goes to Denali, suffers further frostbite and loses toe; 3) Goes to Denali, suffers further frostbite and loses foot; 4) Goes to Denali, the toe's fine, but falls into a crevasse and dies.

In short, he didn't think I should go.

He reiterated that point of view when I met him for the first time a few days later. I was flown by helicopter from base camp down through the Khumbu Valley to Kathmandu, where I received hospital treatment before flying home. I wanted – I needed – David to see my toe immediately in the deep-yellow and dying flesh, which was beginning to separate from the skin on the rest of my foot, like an over-cooked cherry tomato. So the day after I landed in London, I went to visit him at the Bath and West Show. He was the medical officer for the show, and he was able to find time to see me in the back of his camper van. Forget the 737 Challenge, I can now also say that I am the first person to be treated for frostbite at the Bath and West Show. In a van.

David talked me through once more how the body adapts to altitude. Ever since I'd come down off Everest, my blood would have been thinning. The capillaries and tissue in my damaged toe, which would have been damaged when they froze, had since refilled with blood. Hence the swelling. But up on Denali, the process of acclimatisation would begin again. The red blood cells would proliferate; the blood thicken. This is bad enough, as we know, in the smaller capillaries, but in a toe that is already damaged with frostbite it is worse still. Then there was the prospect of the toe refreezing, which causes further damage. I would have been better off keeping my toe in a block of ice than to have let it start to thaw and then refreeze.

But the prospect that concerned me most was septicaemia. He and I knew Denali. I remembered my experience up there the year before. If I were stuck in another week-long storm in temperatures of 40°C, this time with septicaemia, it could be catastrophic. The last person David had treated for septicaemia on a mountain had lost both legs and an arm.

The doctor in him said stay at home. But the mountaineer appreciated it wasn't as simple as that.

At this point, I was a physical wreck, never mind the state of my toe. I had been climbing for six months now, to the exclusion of almost anything else. As a rugby player I had weighed 16st; as a mountaineer, my fighting weight was 14st. Coming off Everest, I weighed less than 12½lb (79kg).

But if I was physically weaker than I'd ever been, I was also mentally stronger. Before I started the Challenge, I was in the shape of my life, but I was terrified. Since then my strength in the two departments had travelled in opposite directions of the spectrum. I was empty from a physical point of view, but now I was so hardened by experience and the closeness of my goal that complete physical breakdown was the only setback, other than the weather or the threat of terrorism, that could stop me. That I might yet experience such a breakdown before the Challenge was over was a thought that tortured me throughout the three weeks I spent in the UK between Everest and Denali. I had embarked upon this mission as a way of wrestling with the demons of a rugby career cut short by injury. For this mission to be cut short in the same way would be too bitter an outcome. All those demons were there again, but now I was able to recognise them as such. They were over there, rather than here, and I went about my business in that fortnight with an intense focus. I was still in expedition mode. It was great to see friends and family, but there was a veneer in place. I didn't want to switch off, because if I did I might take that fateful step back and suddenly find myself unable to face what still lay ahead. And, anyway, you can't switch off and arrive at the mountain laughing and joking. That's how accidents happen. I knew what could be waiting on Denali, and I had to give myself the best shot of being fit to face it.

I had been due to fly out on 6 June, a week after my return from Nepal, but my flight was put on hold. I went to Sheffield to meet up with Simon Lowe and Matt Parkes, who were to be my two climbing partners on Denali. We needed to make a decision. What was the latest we could summit Denali? The climbing season closes in July, as the warmer weather opens up the risk of avalanches, crevasse falls and even more violent than usual weather changes. So late June, early July was our cut-off point for making it up there and back down. How long would it take to climb? The year before I'd done it in twenty-one days – this time we could go a bit quicker, so maybe fourteen. Working backwards we came up with 18 June as the latest we could leave the UK, and our flights were booked for that date.

Whether we would be on the plane remained in doubt. I

knew I couldn't attempt Denali carrying an injury. There could be no half-measures. You can't go on to the mountain thinking you won't kick quite so hard into the next foothold ...

But, equally, there was no way I could let the project end here in the UK. The only way out of this now was through the middle. The implications of failure, which had tormented me on the side of Everest, were no less real now I was back at sea level. There was too much riding on the Challenge for it to be abandoned. I had never embarked on it to make money, but neither had I to ruin myself – or my parents, or Jagged Globe. If I stopped at seven out of nine, the whole project would sink without a trace. So many people would be left out of pocket.

As compelling as the financial situation might have been, though, there was something deeper at work in me now as I considered the input of others, and it was an imperative that was fostered in me by my life in rugby: the sanctity of the team. The irony was that one of the main reasons for the Challenge was to retreat from rugby, push it away, draw a line under it, never speak to it again. Now, the values I had learned from the sport had become the Challenge's principal driving energy. When you're at the end of your tether you revert to type, and most of my life had been spent as part of a team – even when I raced bikes, I was in a team with Mum and Dad. It's not a conscious thought, it's a feeling. For all my tendencies to be an island, I have never felt more galvanised or inspired than when feeling part of something bigger. That spirit now possessed me more strongly than ever, as I thought of the people involved in the Challenge. The idea of letting them down was intolerable.

I saw so many specialists over that period – surgeons,

doctors, chiropodists, podiatrists, nurses, mountaineers. I wanted all the information laid out on a table. None of it was good. I was lucky to be able to grab a coffee with Simon, Matt and Alan Hinkes in Sheffield. Alan is the first Briton to have climbed all fourteen of the eight-thousanders. It was a privilege to hear his advice. But he didn't think I should go, either.

I was put in touch with the South Wales Multiple Sclerosis Therapy Centre in Swansea, who kindly let me use their hyperbaric chamber. I had no money now, but they subsidised my sessions. The support I received from them and so many other professionals in this time was humbling and kept the whole Challenge on course. A hyperbaric chamber allows you to breathe pure oxygen under pressurised conditions, increasing the amount of oxygen absorbed into your tissues. It's not clinically proven yet, but there is powerful evidence to suggest that it promotes healing and wellbeing. I had nothing to lose. The worst-case scenario was that it made me feel stronger but left the toe unaffected. I spent an hour and a half in there, which is the maximum, sometimes twice a day, staring at the inside wall, with the air pressure turned up to maximum (the equivalent of 30m under the sea). I believe it helped, but we'll never know for sure. I'm a good healer anyway.

It certainly helped me restore a little energy after Everest. I came off the mountain so weak. Most people spend years planning for an assault of Everest and months recovering. I'd lost more than a stone in weight, down now to my lightest yet, but within ten days of arriving back in Britain I'd put it back on again, so that I was back up to 14st. I was on a feeding frenzy, ordering two main courses if I was out for a meal. I would wake in the night craving something to eat. When you come down from extreme altitude you recover your lost appetite with a vengeance.

All of which played havoc with my choice of suit for a bonus event during my stay. I had broken the news to Kev Morgan that the delay in my flight to Denali meant I could attend his and Ella's wedding on 11 June after all, an invitation to which I had previously declined. At the start of the week I'd bought a suit to fit my wasted frame. Come the day itself, I'd piled the pounds back on and I turned up at my mate's wedding a frost-bitten, bushy bearded wilderness man in a new suit I had already outgrown. Grooming had not been high on my list of priorities lately, so I wasn't exactly a picture-book wedding guest, but I wanted to be there. It was great to see friends and to be in such a warm and positive environment. I didn't stay for the dancing, though. There's no protocol on that for a frost-bitten toe, as far as I know, but instinctively I felt it wouldn't help. Besides, someone had trod on it at the bar.

The toe was now agonisingly painful, but that was good. The more pain I felt, the more it was healing. Again, rugby helped – or at least the kind of person rugby had required me to be – as I embraced the pain, willing it to course through me. The nerves started to fire up again. The best way I can describe it is like someone sticking a needle into the end of your toe and pushing it all the way in. It came in fits and starts, but I was visited by it continually for a long time. Even after the Challenge was finished, I would be walking down the street and it would strike, forcing me to sit down and zone out.

When I spoke to the various specialists, I would tell them about the pain with a kind of boyish enthusiasm, almost pleading the agony of it. I must have been convincing, because as the days ticked down to departure the verdict began to change. The vascular surgeon who'd been helping me was Mr Ian Williams at the Heath Hospital in Cardiff. He and I sat around the toe the Tuesday before I was set to leave and pored over it.

'It's *really* starting to hurt now,' I said joyfully.

Ian took my foot and held it up to the light, inspecting the toe so closely he could almost have removed the dead, black skin from it with his teeth.

'That is … That is *really* good, isn't it?' he gushed in reply.

He wasn't the only one gushing. The dead flesh in my toe had now started to separate from the living tissue, causing open wounds that wept into the bandages. The swelling had gone down, but the dead skin was fragile and hard, like a natural plaster protecting the regenerating tissue underneath. There was a major concern over when this might break off. The exposure of raw flesh renders you vulnerable to septicaemia, and this stage would almost certainly happen to me up Denali. I spent this period between Everest and Denali, as always, meticulously preparing, and provision for my toe was as crucial a discipline as any. I practised for days with nurses, dressing my toe, testing every type of bandage, changing my sock and boot systems. Nothing was left to chance. It was for my psychological wellbeing as much as anything else.

Because I still had reservations. I was in turmoil over this decision. Everyone I had approached about it was coming from the same direction, as was I. The toe had to be saved. It's easy to be gung-ho about it, and, if you'd said to me in a rational moment some time in my past that I might have to sacrifice my toe in order to achieve something no other human

138

had, I might well have sanctioned the amputation for some indefinite point in the future. You can be blasé about the idea, but everything changes when you are confronted with the genuine possibility of losing a part of your body, or even dying. It's a reality we are protected from in today's society, where things are so sterile and without consequence. That's why I love the purity of these hostile environments. If I stopped the Challenge now it might ruin me financially, but my choice for a future after that was to return to these extreme wildernesses and hopefully one day to try to earn a living in them. Losing a big toe would compromise such a life. Everybody told me, as well, that I needed a big toe to run and to cycle – all the things I love doing would be affected.

The meeting that changed everything had nothing to do with medicine. Andy James at Ace Feet in Motion turned my perspective upside down. Ace are a company who have made all my orthotics for the Achilles tendonitis and knee issues I'd picked up from rugby. Mum drove me to see Andy about two days before departure to discuss the idea of electrically heated soles, which are often used in ski boots. Mum's presence at that meeting would turn out to be important. She didn't say a word (unusual for her!) but she, too, came out of it with a new perspective. She and Dad had a horrible seven months of worry and disturbed sleep during the Challenge. This meeting would help to put her mind at rest as much as it did mine.

Andy must have sensed I was troubled, because, after we'd discussed the new orthotics, he asked what was concerning me. Spontaneously and uncharacteristically, I opened up to him about my fears.

He shrugged. 'If you lose your toe, so what? I'll make you

a pair of boots you can climb in; I'll make you a pair of shoes you can cycle in.'

I knew that Andy works with elite athletes in disabled sport, so his casual claim was enough to give me pause. His attitude to my predicament was unlike any I had come across. I wouldn't call it blasé, because he's far too professional for that, but this was his field and it was not a big deal. No one else had said this to me.

'Not that long ago,' he went on, 'and I'm not talking Hillary/Tenzing time, I'm talking maybe ten years ago, they would have amputated your toe anyway. That was the treatment for frostbite. You would have got back to Kathmandu and they'd have cut it off! And in some ways it would have been better that way. It would have been cleaner.'

I decided there and then that, if I lost my toe or foot, I would strive to become a Paralympian. I went so far as to ask Andy if I would be eligible, should the worst happen. He confirmed I would.

'It's a risk, going to Denali,' he said, 'but if you were risk-averse, if you were afraid of injury, you would never even have started all this. You deal with risks every moment you're on a mountain.'

My world was starting to shift around this impromptu little conversation, and we went on to tackle my even greater fears of septicaemia up the mountain. Andy deals with diabetes and open wounds, so, again, this was his territory. After I'd unloaded on him once more, he paused to gather his thoughts.

'If you developed septicaemia here, how would you treat it?' he asked.

'I'd treat it with antibiotics,' I replied.

He nodded. 'And how long do you think you will be up the mountain?'

'We're aiming for two weeks, but if we get caught in a storm ...'

'Could you carry three, maybe four, weeks' worth of antibiotics, do you think?'

'Yeah, probably.'

'And, tell me, if you cut your finger on the cooking stove on the first day of the expedition, would you turn back?'

'Don't be ridiculous!' I laughed.

As my laughter subsided, Andy looked at me in a certain way. And, suddenly, all the pennies cascaded. So what if I lost my toe? Paralympics. Septicaemia? Carry more antibiotics. Risk? Ha!

We didn't even go for the electric soles in the end. They run on batteries that need to be kept warm, which is one thing in a ski resort but another in a snowstorm up Denali. Nevertheless, this meeting had proved the most decisive for the future of the Challenge. Up till then, I had sorted out all the logistics for Alaska on one side of my brain, but on the other there was a massive blockage over the consequences of continuing. Now, like a weather change on Denali, it had cleared in a moment. The synapses sparked into life, and, with two days to go, I was back on it, in it and climbing it. I had no doubt then that, as long as the mountain was kind to me, I would reach the top of Denali.

I'd always known that this would be the hardest leg of the journey. We were cramming the North Pole, Everest and now Denali into such a small window that the margin for error was tiny. Yet, after six months of continual climbing, I was so exhausted that the potential for error or mishap was high. I hadn't foreseen frostbite exactly, but in retrospect that was just the sort of complication I could have expected to add to the extreme exhaustion after Everest.

So much for exhaustion. Denali has no time for climbers complaining about that. And we had some big loads to pull up the side of her. The load limit for the alpine-style assault required on Denali is 125lb per person. We would be using up the full allowance. The reason we took so much was that 'we' was now only two of us. Because of the delay in our departure, Simon was unable to join us, which meant it was now just me and Matt Parkes from Jagged Globe – Parksy and Parkesy.

I'd known Matt just over a year, but he was already a good friend – and is all the more so now. He's the same age as I am, but he was a more experienced mountaineer. We'd climbed Cho Oyu the year before, so he knew what I was about. I was thankful to have him with me. I had prepared for the possibility that I might have to climb this leg alone by climbing Denali the year before, but, in view of recent developments, my continuing alone would have been extremely dangerous. Nevertheless, his decision to accompany me was a big one. When it became clear that it would be just the two of us, we sat down in Sheffield to talk it through. The dynamic changes dramatically when you climb as a pair. If you are in a team of three or four, the dangers are spread more thinly. As a pair, you rely implicitly on each other. And, if your climbing partner has a frostbitten toe that may yet turn septic, the cause for deliberation is greater still. I was honest with him and, I hope, level-headed. If I'd said, fuck it, I'm going up there whatever, I would have come across as too gung-ho, and I know Matt wouldn't have climbed with me. So too if I'd been too nervous or frightened. As it was, I was genuinely anxious, but I had mental composure and strength as I had never had before. Matt agreed to climb with me, for which I will always be grateful. It was a huge call. If I developed septicaemia up the mountain, Matt would have to manage the situation, were I not able to. And, if either of us fell into a crevasse, it would be much harder to get out with only one man at the other end of the rope.

Which brings us to another of the perils for which Denali is famous – its crevasses. A crevasse in a glacier is formed in a number of ways – sometimes when it splits open as it flows over convex undulations, sometimes when there are different flow rates in the ice and sometimes when two or more glaciers converge. When it snows, these chasms are then covered over by what we call snow bridges, which normally hold strong, especially in the colder months. But we had left our ascent so late that the snow on the lower glacier was now beginning to melt.

We flew to Anchorage on 18 June, which was the very latest we could leave it. Luckily, we were flying against the Earth's rotation – a twenty-four-hour journey, but at least it was still 18 June when we arrived. From there, we made the three-hour drive to Talkeetna, a small hippy town in the wilds of Alaska. It's like stepping back in time. There's a general store, a road-house and a tavern. And the airport, from which we flew to Denali Base Camp, is basically a log cabin.

As on Everest, base camp was pretty empty. We were late in

the season again. Most people were either up the mountain or had left altogether. We spoke to the ranger about the conditions. I remembered him from the year before. When I told him the date I'd summited then, he winced. The weather had been so bad, he remembered the very day.

That, though, was about it as far as confidence-building went. Nobody here, or in Talkeetna, had anything positive to say about the conditions now. This time, the opposite problem applied. It was too warm, scarily so. The snow bridges were melting, bringing those crevasses into play. There had been several 'incidents', as the ranger described them, in the past week or so, and he showed us on a map where each had occurred. Most had been on the lower reaches of the Kahiltna Glacier, between base camp and the first camp, just shy of 8000ft (we're back in America, so everything's in feet again). Beyond that the temperatures are colder and more stable, as are the snow bridges, but at base camp, which is 7200ft, around 2200m, the temperatures were about 5°C and the sun strong. At that time of year, there are around twenty hours of sunlight in Alaska and it is never completely dark, so you can't even rely on a nightly freeze. The ranger told us the temperature hadn't dropped below freezing for a couple of days.

Two other teams were preparing to leave at the same time. It was important that Matt and I were ahead of them. As a pair, we were likely to be moving faster, but it was also smart practice to have people coming up behind in the event of something going wrong.

We set off at 3 a.m. on 20 June. The sun had not quite risen, but there was a dawn and the mountain was at its coldest. The thermometers had just about touched freezing that night. Our techniques were sound, as they had to be in these uncertain conditions. In order to spread weight, I was carrying only 25lb or so on my back, with the rest pulled behind me on my pulk. I had a long pulk trace, or rope, of about 4m, to keep the weight of the pulk as far from me as possible, and we'd lengthened the rope between me and Matt, who was in front that day, to about 20m. It remained taut at all times. Our snowshoes were on, and even though the climb at this stage is gradual we each had our ice axes to hand.

There are different types of snow, and recognising them is an art I will always be learning, but when the snow is wet you know it's wet. And this snow was wet. We were about two hours out of base camp on a well-trodden route and had passed the first area the ranger had identified as the most unstable, when I suddenly fell through to my waist.

To punch through snow is not uncommon when it's warm. Normally, you put just your foot through. Dropping down to the waist was new to me, but after the initial shock I was quickly assessing my position. With my snowshoes on, the hole I'd punched was big, but the rucksack on my back and the tension of the rope between Matt and me had broken the fall. What concerned me – and was unusual – was that my feet were hanging freely, and, try as I might, I could find nothing against which to secure any purchase, even with big snowshoes on, even with my long legs. That was when I began to appreciate that the hole I was hanging over was big.

Matt had felt the tug on his rope and turned to see that I had fallen in to my waist. 'Come on, Parksy, stop fuckin' about!' he said, as anyone from Sheffield would.

'Mate, I'm struggling here,' I replied. 'I can't find anything with my feet.'

When he saw I wasn't coming out, he set about digging in a snow anchor.

I was starting to worry now, and the longer I spent investigating my situation the more worried I became. I had no choice but to reach forward and gently plant the spike of my axe into the snow.

As I prepared to try to haul myself out, the area of snow in front of me, about the size of a dining table, fell away.

There's no describing the feeling of terror as you free-fall into nothingness. It still visits me now from time to time. I watched a film with Liam Neeson in it nearly a year later, and there was a scene in which the snow gives way on him. It's brilliantly done and took me straight back there. Suddenly, I was more involved in the film than I wanted to be.

I remember that sickening, heart-in-mouth sensation, like when a roller-coaster begins its drop. Then the weightlessness and the unknown. What's going on? Where are you falling? How far will you go? It's a split second, but it leaves its mark. I don't like walking on wet snow any more.

My next memory is of lying on my back, looking up through broken snow at a sky the cool-blue colour of dawn. A million thoughts rushed through my head like trains. Fuck. Am I alive? How far down am I? Will I get out? Is this it? After a while – it could have been a couple of seconds, it could have been a couple of minutes – the thoughts started to gather into something more coherent. I was alive and seemed to be unhurt. I was pinned on my back. I was in a crevasse, about 7m beneath the surface. The rope leading to Matt was stretching taut towards the surface; the rope attached to my pulk, however, was down here with me. It was taut, too, and it was pulling me down.

I looked about me. A ledge had broken my fall. My pulk had continued on past the ledge, and it was buried in soft snow. It weighed 100lb, so there was no way I could sit up. I had been incredibly lucky to land on this ledge, unharmed. Had I fallen just slightly further to my right, I would have fallen into the soft snow myself, who knows how deep? Did the snow mark the bottom of the crevasse, or did it mask a greater drop beyond? My pulk was at the end of a rope 4m long, yet it wanted to keep falling. Even if it was already at the bottom of the crevasse, though, had I fallen into it I would have been packed into an all-embracing bed of snow more than 10m down into a deep-freezer. It wouldn't have given me very long to get out.

As it was, I was pinned on a ledge of ice 7m into that same freezer. I was tight against one wall of the crevasse to my left and to my right the other wall was too far away, across the soft snow below, for me to touch. So it was a big crevasse, and, unusually, the section I had fallen into was running in the same direction as the route we'd been climbing, as opposed to cutting across it. So the rope leading to Matt had sliced into the snow ceiling like a cheese wire as there was no hard lip. This meant I was not going to be able to climb out, nor was Matt going to be able to pull me to safety from where he was. It occurred to me that he might be standing over the same crevasse himself.

Matt. I fumbled in my jacket for my radio and tried to contact him. I knew he would be building a snow anchor and maybe even a pulley system. I also knew his radio was in his rucksack, so I wasn't alarmed when he didn't reply immediately. I started to wonder how I could help myself. I felt composed now. Eighteen months of training and meticulous preparation was paying off. I continued the assessment of my predicament, and the more I did the more the severity of it began to register. I was in trouble here. It was hard to imagine a worse start to an expedition. Humans are not meant to find themselves in crevasses. It's an alien environment, which chills you in more ways than one.

What terrified me most, though, when my eyes finally settled upon it, was what I saw off to the left beyond my legs.

Nothing.

It was darkness like I'd never known. For a moment it paralysed me. My composure deserted me, I confess. It's possible that in so alien an environment you are more prone to irrational thoughts, or perhaps you have to be in such a place to experience a blackness pure enough to stir up the sleeping terrors of your childhood. How big was the darkness? In interviews I've described that black cavern as the size of a cinema. In truth, I have no idea how big it was. My sense was that it was vast – the fact I couldn't see anything meant it had to be – but there was no way of knowing, such was the purity of darkness. Imagine if I'd fallen into that. I felt sick with relief that I hadn't.

More terrifying yet, though, was the question of what might lie in there. I thought monsters, dead bodies, ghosts. Those words seem so childish now that I conjure them up in a comfortable home built for humans, but alone pinned to a ledge in that frozen chamber the ideas carried weight. When it came to that darkness I was a boy again, seeing monsters in a shadow on my wall. Would I see something looking out at me from it? Like a child, my resolution was to turn away. Bury your head under the covers and it won't be there any more. I've since wondered whether allowing childish fears to dominate like that was not a coping mechanism to distract from the seriousness of my predicament. Who knows? Either way, for the rest of the hour and a half that I would spend in the crevasse I simply never looked to my left again.

It was a relief when my radio crackled into life with Matt's familiar voice. The reception was poor, but I managed to tell him I was OK and that I was investigating my prospects of getting out. There was not a lot he could do at his end but dig in. If I couldn't get out by myself, we would have to hope for an appearance from one of the two teams we knew were behind us.

The rope connecting me to Matt was not going to be of any use for climbing up or being pulled out by, because it was slicing into the snow bridge. I considered cutting my pulk loose, but that had to be a last option because it might disappear into the crevasse, which would mean the end of the Challenge. There was a treacherous balance to strike between escaping safely and not sacrificing the entire project. I was increasingly confident I could get out of there. If nothing else, I could abandon the pulk and free-climb out. I had two ice axes on me, and although there was technically no ice-climbing involved in the Challenge, Simon being Simon, my preparation had included it. Now I knew why. But without my pulk we would have to turn back, and, with Denali's climbing season about to end, the Challenge would be over. How long should I leave it

149

before resorting to that? Received wisdom is that after forty minutes in a crevasse you are into frostbite territory, and I didn't need any reminding about the vulnerability of my big toe.

Nevertheless, with plan Z in place I enjoyed a measure of confidence, at least. My mind started to fill with people's voices. I remembered David Hillebrandt's email and the last bullet point on it: 'falls into a crevasse and dies'. I do believe I laughed. Then I heard Tracy telling me to get this on film. As luck would have it (normally it would be Matt), I had been carrying the camera when I fell, and I reached into my jacket to pull it out.

Around about now, as the sun rose higher, the snow roof above me began to melt. I was directly under it and powerless to stop a steady drip of water compound my problems. I couldn't get out of its way and, even if I'd been able to, it would have been dangerous to move because I didn't know how stable my ledge was. The cold was taking its grip. Add in the wetness, and hypothermia was making a move on me, too. I'd taken my big mitts out and now focused on managing my extremities, constantly keeping my fingers and toes moving, but as the dripping continued and I grew wetter and wetter it wasn't long before I was shivering uncontrollably.

Suddenly – and I don't know precisely when any of this happened; I know only how long I was in there – snow started to tumble on to me. I looked up and saw a spade chipping away at the rim of the hole I'd fallen through. An American climbing party had arrived. My guess is that it was forty minutes after I'd fallen in. They were a commercial team, and the guy leading it called out to me.

'Am I on air here?' he said, blindly bashing his spade against the crevasse wall.

'No, that's solid where you are,' I called up to him.

Confident he was safe, he leaned over to talk to me and we were able to make eye contact. He was roped to the five people in his group. I was able to tell him that the path was directly over the crevasse. He waved his team off to the side and walked round to where Matt had built the anchor for me. As he approached Matt, one of his legs went through the snow up to the groin. Matt had to unclip himself from the anchor to pull the guy out by his other foot, but now Matt knew that he was sitting over the same network of crevasses. And they all knew they were walking on a minefield, knowledge that rendered the situation really serious. Matt tells me the other team came through just then and stood by the American's group. As Matt was helping him out of his hole the American lost his rag, screaming at this other party to get away from his team.

I was by now soaking wet and losing the feeling in my fingers and toes. Plan Z was still a possibility, but wouldn't be for too much longer if the feeling in my fingers continued to deteriorate. Should I rely on this American to help me out? He was under no obligation. On a mountain, you cannot expect any assistance. If this were above the South Col on Everest, nobody would help you. Bearing in mind the terrain here, this American and his team didn't have to. The other group he'd just screamed at chose to continue on their way. Thankfully, he chose to help, and he and his team started work on a pulley system off to the right of where I was lying.

This takes some time, and I was constantly fighting to keep up my circulation. The cold had sucked all but the last feeling from my extremities. Again, Simon's training programme was serving me well. After my stints in the cold-water tank, I was confident this was not hypothermia – yet. I didn't panic. I knew this could be endured. It probably saved my life to be able to stay rational down there, to be an ally to those up above, rather than a shrieking liability.

My arse was numb against the icy ledge. I had visions of a future bending over in front of nurses so they could dress and redress the frostbite on my backside. I had visions of having to say in public that the Challenge had failed because of my arse. I took to sitting on my hands. One hand would have a turn being flexed repeatedly until I could feel something in the fingers, then I would slip it under my bum to replace the other, which I'd then try to flex back to life.

My mind turned to home. Logistical considerations, such as how to get out of there, drifted away now. I thought of my friends, my dog, my parents. My life. Wouldn't it be appropriate for this single man to die here, alone, in a freezing hole in the Alaskan wilderness. I'd deserve that. How I longed now to be with all those people whose affections I might have kept at arm's length in the past. The warmth. I thought of people I'd pushed away and not given a chance. Life is so much better shared. How grateful I was to have the family and friends that I did. I wanted to get back to them.

I was losing the battle when a new rope was lowered to me. I remember it swinging towards me like a lazy pendulum. I pawed at it clumsily with my numb hands wrapped in heavy mitts. I missed and had to wait for the pendulum to swing at me again. At the third or fourth time of asking I managed to secure it and clip it into my harness. I unclipped Matt's rope, so he could come round safely to join the team at the end of the other one. Still tied to a pulk of 100lb, I was a heavy load. And I wasn't able to help much. I couldn't even grip the rope properly.

One of the most dangerous parts of such a rescue is when the climber is pulled up to the lip of the crevasse. If it's overhanging with snow, he or she can be crushed against it and suffocate. Thankfully, the American team leader was a professional and he had already cut away the overhanging snow with his shovel. Nevertheless, the rope they pulled me up with was attached to my harness, which was round my midriff. When my harness reached the top of the crevasse, because of the weight of the pulk pulling me down I became jammed against the wall. My top half was now above ground, and I could see the team pulling and pulling in an attempt to force me up and over the lip. But they were just pulling my legs and pelvis into the crevasse wall. My feet were already numb, and at one point during the struggle I lost feeling in my legs.

'Guys, you're going to have to stop,' I said with as much respect as I could muster. 'I'm stuck, and I'm losing my legs here.'

The American came over with a knife. He was going to cut my pulk loose. There might have been a small flicker of protest deep within me as he did, but it had gone beyond saving the Challenge now. This was about coming away alive.

The moment the pulk fell away they were able to pull me out, an hour and a half after I'd fallen in. I managed to get to my feet, but I was soaking wet and wobbling all over the place. I thanked them all sincerely, but I would have been a disturbing sight. Nobody wanted to know! As soon as they had undone the anchor and gathered their rope they were gone, for their own safety as much as anything. Matt and I were on our own again.

Shivery and numb, I changed into dry clothes. Matt was shaken, too. It had been a long hour and a half for him. We were both rocked by the speed with which things had turned for the worse.

But, if we wanted the Challenge to continue, we needed that pulk. When I was dry and had some measure of feeling back in my hands, I secured Matt to the anchor and he abseiled into the crevasse to try to retrieve it. Thankfully, it had not fallen to the bottom, but had stopped on a ridge a few metres down. Everything on the outside of it had been ripped off, but the bag and the pulk were intact. The fact that I had tied the trace to the bag as well as the pulk had saved it. Soon, Matt and the pulk were back on *terra infirma*.

I hadn't really had time to consider what to do next. We still had a day's climbing to reach the next camp and we were only two hours into our journey, so it would have been easy to turn back. But a defining moment of the Challenge and, for me, a defining moment in my life was fast approaching.

Matt and I looked at each other. I think we were both shell-shocked. I know I was. At the same time there was something else in his eyes, and I hope there was in mine. Shell-shocked but not beaten. It was one of those moments I'd known with team-mates in changing rooms after an epic match. Nothing needed to be said. No discussion; no rationalisation. Just a look.

'You all right?' he said.

'Yeah, I'm all right. You?'

'Yeah.'

We glanced up the mountain. Then at each other.

'Shall we crack on, then?'

I nodded. 'Let's crack on.'

7

The temptation to turn round had been strong. I look back now, rationally, from a distance, and there was only one decision, which was the one we took – to carry on up the mountain. But when you emerge from an experience like that it is not so easy to see the whole picture. In theory, I could have died down there. In practice, I was always likely to emerge somehow. Nevertheless, by the time they pulled me out I would say I was skirting hypothermia. I was past the point of being able to climb out on my own. The option of plan Z had expired.

I had let it expire because the American team had arrived. I'd always known there were two teams coming up behind us. Had they not appeared, I would probably have proceeded with plan Z (and, as it turned out, we may well have been able to salvage the pulk anyway). Once they had turned up, though, it took another half an hour or so to pull me out, by which time I was in a bad way. So, I never seriously thought at any stage I was going to die, but by the time I emerged I wasn't far off the sort of condition from which I might have spiralled. Another half-hour down there would probably have done it.

Either way, it was a disconcerting – and you might say chilling – reminder of who was boss round here. It was the mountain. If she wanted to end the Challenge, she could do it whenever she chose. Our job was to persevere for as long as a chink remained open. Already we were pushing our luck. As on Everest, we were in the last-chance saloon. The end of the season is not quite so cut and dried here – we're not talking the reliable return of a jet stream to close the mountain – but, knowing what we do now, if we'd turned back then to regroup and try again we wouldn't have summited. It would have been failure, derailed on leg eight out of nine. I would be looking back now, rationally, from a distance, and tearing my hair out. It's a lesson for life, I think. Courage is not being immune to fear but confronting it and pushing on regardless. Certainly, that moment when we decided to continue has resonated in my life.

Let's not overlook, though, all the other moments in the six hours that followed. I will never forget the rest of that day. It was one of the most horrific of the Challenge. With every step I was reliving the moment I fell through. I don't think either of us had any confidence in the ground we were treading on. This section of the climb was supposed to have been incident-free, but I'd fallen into one crevasse on it already. We were on our own again, and now nobody was coming up behind. The

157

snow was so wet, it actually sounded different in the deathly silent air. Intellectually, I knew no one had punched through here, but it was a slow walk of anguish over the next few hours. Every time I put my foot down, it felt as if I were pulling the trigger in a game of Russian roulette.

And then we came to the second section of the glacier that had been flagged up as dangerous by the ranger at base camp. This one was visibly treacherous. You could see the snow sagging in places and ominous shadows lurking among the whiteness. We hadn't stopped at all since the fall – we didn't think it safe to – but now we chose to take a break, pulling into the side of the route. Coming down the mountain, at the far end of this crevasse field, were three teams of climbers. We had been climbing alone for hours, so this was a timely arrival, just as we reached the most dangerous section. It was almost as if Denali were throwing us a bone. We didn't say so, but I'm sure Matt felt just as much as I did that it would be wise to stand aside and let these teams go through first. That sounds a horribly cynical tactic. Actually, it's quite sensible.

The dynamic for five-man teams, as these were, is completely different from that for a two-man. Everyone is roped up. If one falls in, the others can easily take the strain or pull the fallen out. It was sound practice for us to hold back and not add our weight to the crossing unnecessarily. Not that the other teams were for stopping anyway.

What followed was like something out of a sick, twisted comedy, slapstick at its most sinister and threatening. I'm not sure any of these teams realised how unstable the terrain was, because they stomped across it.

First team, first person, bang! She falls straight through.

Disappears. It's called a header. Gone, out of sight, under the snow. Like in a cartoon. Her team-mates back up in tug-of-war fashion and pull her out. That's how easy it is in a team of that number. Nevertheless, they're spooked now. The air is alive with hollers and cries and arms waving with emotion. Then team two come on down. They don't wait for team one: they carry on past. Until one of the guys in the middle falls through to his armpits. The front of the team pull one way, the back the other, and he scrambles clear. Everyone's freaking out. My jaw is dropping, my head exploding. What the fuck? We're next on this.

Next but one. Team three come down. The guide of this group is a tiny woman. She's at the back. They have pretty much made it across, so that she's level with Matt, who is watching it all just ahead of me. But she's pulling a heavy pulk with most of the team's gear on it. It's heavier than she is. The pulk goes through, and it pulls her with it. She is dragged back to the lip of the hole. She can't stand up or help herself, so she has to talk her clients through the procedure to get her back on her feet.

We offered them help from our vantage point, but we'd seen enough.

'We need to get out of here,' said Matt.

On the far side, the snow looked more stable. It was off the main climbing route, where there are no guarantees, but there were clearly no guarantees on it either, so we headed over there.

It took us half an hour to move around 200m. Every time we approached a snow bridge, I would dig a snow anchor and secure Matt as he crossed to the other side – it's a climber's technique called belaying. Once Matt was on firm snow he would dig in and belay me across.

You're never totally sure whether you're over a crevasse or not, but these ones were as clear to see as any. The most obvious indicator is a hole in the snow. Sometimes these can be huge.

'Don't go falling into that one, Parksy,' said Parkesy a bit later as we gazed at a void the size of a tennis court.

A hole like that will indicate the presence of a crevasse, but it won't always tell you where the crevasse runs under the snow. Sags and shadows in the snow are more accurate indicators, but the truth is you could be above a crevasse at any time in an area like that without realising.

Geography helps. You know there won't be any at the foot of a steep section, because the glacier is compressed in on itself there. Conversely, where the terrain flattens out at the top of a steep slope, the glacier bends away and cracks, as when you break a chocolate bar in two, which is when crevasses do open up. Normally, they run laterally across a route up the mountain. Where I fell through, though, and where we witnessed 'Carry On Crevasse' a few hours later, two glaciers were coming together, which is when the crevasses can run in any direction. In other words, you could be walking *along* a crevasse, not across it.

As in the Khumbu Icefall, your only aspiration is to get through it all quickly. We knew where we wanted to be, come the end of our day's climbing, which was just above 8 Camp. On Denali, the camp numbers refer to the height above sea level of each in thousands of feet. Eight Camp (actually, it's a little under 8000ft at around 2400m) is the first of them, 600ft above base camp and about a five and a half-mile walk. We saw there the team who had rescued me. We thanked them again and told them we were pushing on to higher ground. They didn't seem too impressed. They probably thought we were cowboys.

For the next three days the weather remained clear and sunny, but we were frazzled, physically and psychologically. We slept for thirteen hours, before moving up to 11 Camp in excellent conditions. There were some huge crevasses to cross at the start of the day, but it was much colder now, the snow much firmer. We had highlighted the fact that we needed to be up and off this mountain as quickly as possible, pushing at every opportunity the weather gave us.

From 11 Camp, we climbed to 13,500ft, just past Windy Corner, where we cached a load. Caching is a routine mountaineering procedure, part acclimatisation strategy, part weight management. It's a chance to break up the loads you've been hauling. Besides, the higher up the mountain, the less practical it is to pull a pulk. So you set up camp and climb ahead of yourself with a load on your back, then bury it at a strategic point en route to the next camp, before returning to the previous one. Normally, once you're established at that next camp you return to pick it up, but we were collecting ours on the way through to save days. This process of shuttling up and down the mountain also serves as a standard acclimatisation programme, so you benefit in that regard as well. Unfortunately, I had to acclimatise all over again. Not only had my delay in the UK undone the gains on Everest, but I had actually spent a good deal of that time in the hyperbaric chamber, at the equivalent of 30m below sea level! I was back to square one on the red blood cell count.

By 24 June, though, we were solidly dug in at 14 Camp, about halfway up the mountain – dug in being the operative phrase. All the forecasts were pointing to the sort of storm out of nowhere that Denali is famous for. It was due the next day and they said the low-pressure system would linger for four or five days. All we could do was prepare to sit it out. We spent a couple of hours building a snow wall round our tent. This is a sensible precaution on Denali anyway. Camps 14 and 17 resemble suburban communities, each tent enclosed by its own garden wall. We'd built one at 11 Camp, too, because they said the weather was coming down there, but it had never materialised.

This time it did. We woke to a raging snowstorm the next day, our tent sagging under two feet of snow. The day after that, it was even worse in the morning, gusting past 50mph, then clear as a bell in the afternoon. You just don't know what Denali is going to do next. All you can do is sit tight and get digging during any lulls in the weather. At 17 Camp – the last before the summit – they'd had a metre of snow in 70mph winds. The last person to leave for the summit had gone missing. The helicopter would find him three days later. It appears he'd fallen off the summit ridge.

My toe was now falling apart. It was entering that delicate stage, when the dead skin, which had been acting as a modest film of protection, was now starting to come away from the sides and front. The nail was little more than a lid that could be lifted to reveal the flesh beneath. Do you pull it off or do you leave it on? I wanted to pull it off – it just seemed neater – but to do so would have meant cutting the skin it was flapping from at the top of the toe. That seemed unwise. We hadn't got a clue, really. Parksy and Parkesy will *not* be setting up a surgery in later life. We eventually decided I should leave it on. I found the toenail and flap of skin in my sock a few days later.

But I'd been meticulous with hygiene. I would keep my socks in my sleeping bag overnight, so that when I put them on in the morning they were warm and dry. The inners to my boots would also be kept either in the bag or just inside the tent, depending on the temperature. It's not so much the layers that keep you and your parts insulated, it's the air between the layers. If you start the day with that air inside your boots warm and dry, you are giving yourself a better chance. Then it's down to wiggling your toes and managing your body temperature by how hard you work. And drinking – lots of drinking – to keep the blood thin and on the move. My toe went through a lot on that mountain from the crevasse fall to the climb through heavy snow after the storm. It never refroze; indeed, it continued to heal – something I'm hugely proud of.

Otherwise, there is not much to be done during storms like that but sit in your tent, or in someone else's, passing the time over coffee, soup and the stove. Matt and I had a lot of food with us, and the Parksy and Parkesy Cook-off quickly became a daily routine. An American company had been commissioned by Jagged Globe to source our food for us – and they'd sourced enough for three, because Simon was supposed to have come, too. When we had sorted through our kit at Talkeetna, Matt and I had picked out the best bits. We chose to take a lot, more than three weeks' worth. We were strong enough to carry it, and we knew we might have to hunker down for a long time if the weather didn't oblige. And what a stash we had! Americans have a different idea from the rest of us of what passes for expedition fodder. There were hamburgers in there! And only in America could they take the delicious, nutritious concept of the salmon fillet and market it, in big bold letters across the top of the packet, as 'Chicken of the Sea'. You practically had to read the small print to find out it was salmon. My chicken-of-the-sea pasta was the leader for much of the expedition, but, having thought I'd smashed it out of the park with a bumper breakfast on the morning we climbed above the Headwall to cache a load at 16,000ft, I later found myself with stomach cramps and a desperate urge to shit just 20m from the top of the fixed lines. We were roped together at that point, so I had to urge Matt on in desperation. Naturally, he was beside himself with laughter, and all the more so when we finally made it and I emptied myself on the other side of the ridge, out of sight of 14 Camp and the other climbers below. Then, clinging to an axe planted in the ice above a drop that has claimed its fair share of lives, and with the wind and snow whipping my exposed behind, I had to ask him to pass me the toilet paper from my rucksack. I lost the cook-off on a steward's enquiry after that.

Teams were returning from 17 Camp battered by the conditions. No one had been summiting. Having cached at the top of the Headwall, we were ready to push up to 17 Camp as soon as the weather would allow. Conditions had been marginal on the diarrhoea climb, as I will always remember it, but they were manageable. When the weather improved again the next day, those of us still at 14 Camp decided to make a dash for it.

One of the climbers we befriended on the mountain was Vern Tejas. The year before, for the second time in his life, he'd broken the record for the fastest ascent of the Seven Summits (134 days). It was the ninth time he'd completed the set (another record). And in 1988 he became the first man to succeed with a solo summit of Denali in winter and live to tell the tale. In short, he's another legend of the mountains, a guitar-strumming, harmonica-tooting, fiddle-bowing legend.

He was the guide for one of the commercial groups. There were around five teams at 17 Camp, some of which had been there for a few days and toughed out some appalling conditions, worse than we had at 14 Camp. No one had much of an appetite to continue. Lengthy debates were held about what to do next. The weather was pretty good now, on 29 June, but the snow would be thick, the risk of avalanche high and the forecast was for another storm. We were supposed to be in the middle of one even as we spoke. You could tell that some teams were trying to talk the others out of going up, because if one team went the others would feel obliged to follow.

No one was making a decision. Vern would have gone, obviously, but he had his clients to think about. Matt and I kept out of the general discussion, but when we returned to our tent we decided to go for it. It was understandable for the others to hesitate – they were on holiday, essentially – but we could handle more challenging conditions, and there was an urgency behind our attempt. This was exactly the kind of situation I needed to act on if I wanted to achieve a world first. Preparation and boldness. The sun was shining, which meant we should be moving. If the forecast was bad, it was important to take advantage of this window. If the weather turned, we would come back. If it turned too quickly, we would improvise with a bivy shelter and sleeping bag. We would take cooking equipment.

We talked to Vern over the snow wall between our tents, nattering as if we were suburban neighbours. I think our decision to strike out took him by surprise initially, but once we made it that was it – everyone else was in. Vern suggested we work together. The biggest hindrance for his clients and the other teams was the need for someone to break trail. No one had summited for a few days, in which time a lot of snow had fallen. If Matt and I broke trail, Vern would picket the route behind us, planting snow anchors on the steepest parts of the climb.

I would say it was my proudest day of the Challenge. Matt and I shared trail-breaking duties, but to be leading the way as we reopened the higher reaches of a mountain like Denali only two years after my rugby career had ended, with a legend like Vern behind us, was a big deal for me. The proudest day and the toughest, physically. Tougher than summit day on Everest (though it's a close call).

We left camp at about 12.30 in the afternoon. The first significant climb that greets you is the Autobahn. Normally, it's a steep face of hard snow and ice. The Americans refer to it as the fastest route off the mountain and named it the Autobahn after a group of German climbers who slipped to their deaths from it. Such an end was unlikely to greet any of us that day, because the snow was so deep, but the threat of avalanches was heightened. To be roped up to Vern's team provided a significant measure of security.

What the snow meant most of all, though, was hard work – and lots of it. In places it was waist-deep. I couldn't lift my leg to make the next step; I had to use my hand to drag it up and over the snow.

And then there was the toe. If summit day on Denali was tougher than that on Everest, the toe may have had something to do with it. I had been getting used to the pain by now. Down on the lower slopes, in the crevasse fields, every step might have felt like an invitation to disaster, but every other step came with the guarantee of a shot of pain as well. I was treading gingerly then anyway, and the toe was still relatively dead, so the worst of it could be avoided. Now, though, there was no hiding. Every step had to be kicked in hard through a few feet of snow, then harder again for safe purchase on the ice or rock beneath; every other had to be kicked in with a peeled tomato for a big toe. The dead skin that had formed a protection of sorts had fallen off, exposing the raw flesh. The bloody thing was healing so well that the nerves were firing again, stimulating new sensation, transmitting unspeakable pain. And this wasn't like rugby, where adrenaline courses through you for eighty minutes and dulls the senses; this was cold, calculated infliction of pain on self, hour after hour of it, at altitude, in a state of exhaustion.

At the top of the Autobahn we took a break. The same discussions struck up about the wisdom or otherwise of carrying on. The helicopter found the lost climber that very day, and his fate was mentioned more than once. It had taken us four or five hours to get to this point, which is far slower than you would expect to travel on a well-worn route. But the skies were still clear. We were above the cloud line now, and higher up the mountain the snow might well be more consolidated. Matt and I struck on while the debate continued. A Chinese team chose to go with us, and after around half an hour the others followed.

Denali Pass, then across the Football Field to the last big climb on summit day. I don't know of any anecdote behind the naming of Pig Hill, and certainly no scientific explanation. It's just a pig of a hill in the last place you want to see one. Not that it's huge – about 200m in height – but at that altitude after the day you've had it is a big ask.

Matt and I were climbing alongside this Chinese team – a wealthy businessman, his Chinese guide, who talked a good game, and their Tibetan Sherpa, who did all the work. I was breaking trail up the hill on a conservative traverse, before Matt passed some comment questioning my age and whether we were ever going to get there. So I picked a more aggressive line, whereupon the Chinaman complained that it was too steep. While we were arguing the toss, Matt (and I don't know what possessed him) surged up the final 50m or so. I followed him, and the two of us collapsed at the top, giggling and cursing ourselves for making such a gratuitous burst.

But what a feeling! There's none better than to be rewarded with views like that, having worked so hard. The conditions this high were perfect. Matt and I sat for a few minutes looking out over the clouds beneath us. No matter what you go through on these mountains – and this one had asked a lot – I'd do it all again, and I will keep doing it, for that feeling of spirituality at the top. When there are clouds beneath you, I find it even more moving – as if you've transcended something less than ideal below.

At 11.08 p.m. on 29 June, after a half-hour or so on Denali's summit ridge, we reached the top of North America. The sun was still up, but the shadows were beginning to lengthen. There were no tears this time, as on Everest. I kept my head amid the slightly thicker air. The sense of fulfilment, though, was every bit as powerful.

Leg eight complete. One more to go.

Except leg eight was not quite complete yet. As always, we had to make it down, which this time meant running the gauntlet through the crevasses again. We slept for around twenty hours at 17 Camp, before climbing straight down to 8 Camp, picking up our cached loads at 14 Camp. Eleven hours of toe-bashing in a cloud. The weather had closed in, as expected. We were the last people to summit for more than a week: our timing had been perfect.

When we dropped below Squirrel Hill, we were out of the cloud, then stopped at 8 Camp, just before the crevasses of the Kahiltna Glacier. It was around midnight at this point, with the sun below the horizon. We wanted to take on the crevasses in the twilight, before the temperature rose, so we ate and slept for three hours or so in the open air.

The other teams that had summited on the same day as we did were now alongside us, including Vern's, which meant we felt more confident travelling through the lower slopes. Generally speaking, people look out for each other on the mountains, if it's safe to do so. Nevertheless, there's a certain amount of 'chicken' played in situations like this. Who's going to go first? Who'll bring up the rear? It's amazing how long some people can take over that last cup of coffee. And then how quickly they can down it once someone else has headed off.

Once under way, you quickly suss out which teams to stick around, which to avoid. Nobody wanted to travel with the Chinese team, for example. They seemed blissfully unaware – or contemptuous – of the dangers, heavy-footed while travelling, standing around in a tight group, ropes slack, while taking a break. It was obvious they'd be going through. Sure enough, the Chinese guide fell in. Sure enough, the Tibetan Sherpa pulled him out.

Our friendship with Vern was now established after we'd teamed up on summit day, so we followed his group down. No one knows the mountain better than Vern. I hadn't realised this (you don't talk about these things on the mountain), but that was his fiftieth summit of Denali, almost certainly a record. No one alive can match it (I think Scott Woolums, my friend from the South Pole, is next, on about thirty), but they only began logging summits in 1995, so we can't be sure. Even so, members of his group were putting a foot through right, left and centre. That helped Matt and me to avoid the worst, and we made it through without incident, leaving us with just Heartbreak Hill to get over at the end. Again, not for nothing do they call it that. Of itself, the hill is a gradual incline of no consequence, but after the ordeal of a Denali summit it appears to a climber pulling a pulk as a long, agonising – yes, heart-breaking – obstacle before freedom.

When we finally pulled into base camp, I confess I let myself, for the first time, contemplate the idea that I might actually do this. The pivotal section of the 737 Challenge – North Pole, Everest and Denali – had now been completed.

From a technical point of view, the back of the Challenge had been broken. Everest had softened me up, then Denali had pinned me on my back. But she'd let me wriggle free, and now we'd sneaked up and away before she could change her mind.

Matt and I uncovered the bottle of bourbon we'd kept at base camp for this moment and within an hour we had necked it and gorged ourselves on what was left of our food, dreaming of the burger we'd be eating that night at the West Rib in Talkeetna. Big mistake. We were the second team in, which meant we were supposed to be on the second 'air taxi' out. Vern's team caught the first, but in the hour it took us to polish off our provisions the weather had turned from serviceable into snowstorm. No more air taxis for three days. No more food – or whisky. So close to civilisation, and yet so far.

But I've always believed that if you put happiness and positivity out there, it'll come back to you. We stayed grateful and upbeat for the three days at base camp. Vern had stayed behind. He shared out his team's excess food with us; he played his guitar and his fiddle. Then, when the clouds parted three days later, as suddenly as they had gathered, he managed to call in a sightseeing plane to pick us up. And so we caught the second half of this middle-aged couple's tour of Denali, swooping low over the mountain we had climbed just a few days earlier, en route to Talkeetna and burgers. It was a wonderful end to the leg.

Not yet, though, an end to the adventure. From America, we headed straight to Russia. From guitars and burgers in the Alaskan wilderness to Kalashnikovs and menace in the wartorn Caucasus. In February, three skiers had been shot dead by terrorists in Elbrus's ski resort, forcing the authorities to close the mountain. A gunfight between militants and the Russian army had led to further casualties on the slopes. In Britain the Foreign Office's advice was not to travel. 'There is a high level of threat from terrorism,' advised the Russian authorities. 'Attacks cannot be ruled out and could be indiscriminate, including in places frequented by expatriates and foreign travellers.'

It meant we were wary from the off.

Mount Elbrus is situated in the Caucasus range, just on the edge of Russia's border with Georgia. Chechnya is a couple of republics to the east, a hundred miles away. The mountain and surrounding area is thus at the heart of the trouble between Russia and some of the local ethnic and religious groups.

As with Carstensz Pyramid, there is some (although less) debate about its status as one of the Seven Summits, because some question whether it is even in Europe at all. Politically, Russia is not in the European Union (but then neither is Switzerland), and geographically the boundary between Europe and Asia in the Caucasus region is not categorically defined. Elbrus sits right on that border. Some therefore claim that Mont Blanc is the highest mountain in Europe, and at this stage of the game a trip to the Alps would not have gone amiss. But Elbrus (5642m) is higher than Mont Blanc (4810m), which I've climbed anyway. So that was good enough for me.

I've mentioned a few times the extreme swings in temperature on the Challenge. Arriving in Russia was the biggest culture shock. Matt was climbing Elbrus with me, too, and Dai Camera joined us at Heathrow. Even in Moscow, I was reeling. It was manic, swarming with people, everything written in Cyrillic. We hadn't a clue what we were doing, or how to find our connecting flight to Mineralnye Vody (it's easier to copy out that name than it is to say it, I can tell you). I'm black, so I stood out like a sore thumb anyway; throw in my bushy beard, and my discomfort level was soaring. Matt was bearded, too. We both had weird goggle marks round our eyes.

We eventually located the aircraft we understood to be flying to Mineralnye Vody. It was packed, and I swear the place fell silent when we finally boarded the plane, one of those rickety throw-backs to the days before customer satisfaction. Things reached another level when we stepped out at the other end.

Mineralnye Vody has a small airport, not much more than a building, a tired old carousel and some big Soviet-style signs. We walked through the airport, and I could just feel everyone's eyes on us. Sure enough, a month or two later, when we saw the footage for the documentary, we were able to confirm that everyone's eyes were. I imagine our modest little camera would have attracted some attention, but even so – if you're travelling through a region affected by religious terrorism, dark-skinned and bushy-bearded is not the best look. I couldn't have been more conspicuous. In the same footage, I saw myself walking with my head down and cap pulled low, which is consistent with how I remember feeling – as uncomfortable as I ever have. Scared, in fact.

Outside, we were thrown among the taxi drivers, like lambs among wolves. We knew only that we were supposed to be picked up by a car organised by our liaison, who was called Sergei. We had the name of our hotel written on a piece of paper.

One guy talking aggressively into a mobile phone came up to us and said with a heavy accent, 'American?'

Now, we were naive, but we knew enough about Russia and its history to feel strongly that the last thing we wanted to be in a rural outpost like this was American.

'No, no, no,' we said. 'British.'

Which, who knows, may have been just as bad.

'Taxi?' he replied.

'Sergei?' I said.

There was a pause. I didn't want to get into his car. He walked off again talking loudly into his phone.

More taxi drivers approached us, but we stood our ground. Somehow, we felt we would know which car was ours.

After a very long fifteen minutes or so, the first man came up to us again, still arguing into his phone. He looked very Russian – big and bald with a moustache.

'British?' he said to us this time.

We nodded uncertainly. We'd told him that much.

'Sergei?' he said.

We nodded again. Told him that, too.

'Yes, yes, yes,' he said. 'Come, come, come!'

Dai, Matt and I looked at each other. There were no other options presenting themselves, but this guy could have been anyone. We followed him – a light fifteen-minute jog, past the car park and on down a road, hauling our expedition gear in two large duffels, the Russian summer swelteringly hot. He seemed to be rushing us, as if we were in danger or something, all the while arguing on his phone. When we eventually climbed into his car, he sped along lanes, undertaking other cars, half on the road, half on the verge, still yelling into his phone. Maybe it was the anxious state I was in (it was, I'm sure), but the Russian language just sounded aggressive to me, and the people are large and demonstrative. For all I know, he could have been talking about how happy he was about his new-born child, or he could have been saying that he had these three guys in his car who would be great news for his terrorist organisation – but it sounded like an argument and one of the longest I have ever heard. Dai, Matt and I were exchanging glances as if this might be the last journey we ever took. We laughed about it as well, obviously, but we were genuinely scared.

No idea how far we were supposed to be going, no idea when we should start to worry that we were being kidnapped, about an hour later we finally pulled up at a hotel, much of that hour spent darting in and out of the traffic and back streets. It was in a town in the middle of nowhere, rural and rundown. Big statue of Lenin in the centre. The hotel had obviously once been a huge statement of opulence and power, but the big Cyrillic letters were now crooked and peeling. There were Bentleys and Mercedes with blacked-out windows parked outside.

And standing in the car park was a younger guy in climbing gear. I have never felt so relieved. Sergei greeted us warmly. Our driver helped fling our bags out of the boot of his car, then sped off again to who knows where. Still arguing into his phone.

With Sergei's help we checked into our rooms – and the first thing Matt and I did was to shave off our beards. I was sorry. There is something primitive and liberating about growing a beard. It was the first time I had grown one for as long as that and I had become quite proud of it. My heart was heavy as Matt's hair clippers did their work, refamiliarising me with my jaw. Dai insisted on filming it. He was worried about continuity; I was worried about getting out of there in one piece.

Early the next morning we piled into the back of this Cold War-era utility vehicle. Sergei kept calling it the Wazo. It was a retired military vehicle, kind of a cross between a minibus and a camper van with four-wheel drive, which it was going to need where we were going. Sergei had briefed us the night before over dinner. He had just returned from Elbrus. It was OK, but this was not the best time to be visiting. The south side of the mountain was still closed, which was where all the infrastructure was. The mountain could be accessed, though, from the north, but we would be off-roading as we approached base camp, which this year was pitched alongside a temporary Russian army base, set up to retrieve hardware from a military helicopter wreck on the side of the mountain. There would be checkpoints along the way. When we reached them we were not to say anything. Just remain calm, stay in the vehicle and try to act Russian – whatever that meant. As far as anyone was concerned we were three mates on a climbing holiday. No Challenge, no cameras, no sponsors' logos – no reason for anyone to think we had added value as potential hostages.

The journey to base camp was about six hours. As we progressed from the town, along the B roads through farmland, to the tracks and river crossings that led to the mountains, the evidence of the region's troubled past made itself increasingly clear. Big, abandoned buildings, burned out and in ruins; bullet holes in walls, bullet holes in the road signs, bullet holes everywhere.

With Producer Russell's voice in his head, Dai couldn't resist filming some of the scenes, despite Sergei's warnings. At one point, I was dozing in the back when I heard a sharp word from Sergei and a curse from Dai. Before I could open my eyes, something landed in my lap. It was the camera. Dai had thrown it into the back. Through the window I saw that we were at a roadblock. A man was approaching us with an AK-47 slung round his shoulder, one hand on the grip, one on the barrel. Could have been a soldier; could have been any old dude dressed in combats. Producer Russell was the last person on my mind when I flung the camera to the floor, as if it were burning hot, and kicked it under the chair in front of me. The Russians aren't afraid to look you in the eye, especially the ones with AK-47s, and this one faced off with me for a good few seconds. I can only assume he hadn't seen the camera, because he moved on to talk to Sergei, who got out of the Wazo. Again, I have no idea what was being said. They might have been inviting each other for a coffee later, but no conversation in Russian with a guy brandishing an AK-47 in a region riddled with bullet holes sounds anything other than extremely menacing. They walked round the Wazo together. The rest of us were frozen to the spot, trying to act Russian. I'm assuming Sergei paid this guy something – his brief as liaison was just to get us through – because soon he climbed back in and we were allowed to drive off. In silence. Complete silence. Looking straight ahead, not moving a muscle.

After about ten minutes Dai broke the ice. 'Russ is going to be so fucked off we didn't get that on film.'

'Yes,' I said, 'but he'll be pleased we're still alive.'

Base camp sits in green pastures, not unlike those back home. But at 2300m, more than twice the altitude of Snowdon, the similarities end there. Another point of difference was the military base that was pitched just the other side of a fence of plastic mesh. Again Sergei urged us not to film or take pictures. It was oppressive. Avalanches were not a risk here, but threat was constantly in the air all the same.

Barely a week after summiting Denali, Matt and I were already acclimatised to an altitude half a kilometre higher than the peak of Elbrus, so our game plan was simple. Go straight up the mountain, then come straight back down. Dai wanted to come with us – and I think the mountain would have been within his capability – but he wasn't acclimatised, so Simon wouldn't allow it. He trekked with us the next day to Camp 1 at 3800m, just on the snowline, and waited for us there. It's a 1500m altitude gain from the green hills to the rocky glacial moraine: a hard day's slog. My toe was red-raw – another reason to make this as quick as possible.

On the morning of 12 July, at three o'clock, we gathered for the final push. We had a long day ahead of us. Most people take a week and summit from a camp higher up the mountain. In fact, at around 1900m, this was to be the biggest single-day gain in altitude of the whole Challenge.

Emotions were swirling around within me, as they had been for much of the Challenge. I am a man who lives by his heart. At the top of Everest they overflowed for a moment, but mostly

I had kept them in check – part discipline, part defence mechanism. Focus on the processes; do not allow yourself to waver. But here, for the first time, I let myself run with them. I let myself savour the pride and think about what I had achieved. Because, barring some freak catastrophe, I was going to finish this now. A world first. There had been people, far more experienced than I was, who had said it couldn't be done. Well, it *could* be done – and it will be done again. No doubt someone will do it quicker one day. With a fair wind, I could do it quicker. But I will always be the one who broke the trail. I will always be the first. I struggled to get my head round the idea that morning. I struggle to get my head round it even now.

After seven months on the move, constantly exhausted, constantly pushing myself, the idea of an end to it, of a chance to spend time with family and friends, was one to relish. But I was sad, too. This *was* the end, the end of an extraordinary adventure, where the outlandish had become routine and the thrill of morning on summit day a regular drug. I thought of the white room in which I'd languished just two years earlier. Here I was now, ready for one last push, so far removed from that place.

I was reminded of it again, though, about three hours later. We'd stopped for a break when the dawn began to glow on the horizon. I love sunrises. You might say I'm addicted to them, which is funny when I think of the person I used to be – contemptuous of mornings, up at the last minute, blending a shake, smashing it down me on the way to rugby training. Now, I'm up for sunrises whenever the weather allows. It's a complete change of perspective. That ball of fire in the sky predates everything around us. Seeing it come up every day is an experience we share with all the creatures that went before us and all that are still to come. It is the fire that keeps the whole show moving, and never is its role as life-giver so keenly felt than when you are on a mountain on summit day. You're freezing cold, climbing through the night, and up comes the sun to warm your bones and your fingers and toes; all of a sudden the blood flows through you more easily. There's something primeval about that.

This whole project had begun in that white room with the words from my grandmother's funeral that I'd had tattooed on the inside of my left forearm, 'The horizon is only the limit of our sight'. The words run around a crucifix, from which I'd asked Kath, my tattooist, for rays of light to emerge. I don't know why.

There I sat, looking out at the horizon on the last morning of the Challenge, a project I had quietly dedicated to my nan. It began to glow. The sky above the horizon, like the mountains, snow and cloud beneath, was a pale, icy blue. We watched the orange spread and thicken, until the sun achieved some precarious balance with the clouds in its way. Not only did its rays burst forth, piercing the clouds beyond the horizon, but they did so, somehow, in exactly the same pattern as the rays on my arm, coherent, separate shafts streaking across the sky in yellows and oranges and reds. I've seen rays emanate from the sun in simplistic, idealised pictures, but never had I seen them do so as vividly as this in the real world. And I don't expect to again.

It was one of the most incredible moments of my life. Having allowed all those emotions to percolate through me earlier in the morning, to be so close to the end of this monumental project, which had been born of one of the bleakest, most frightening periods of my life ... to have it crowned with this moment felt like a blessing and the end of a thread that ran through the entire project, back to the despair of the white room, my grandmother's funeral, and on to who knows where. Whatever it is that's bigger than us.

We weren't any more tired than usual on that break, but we sat there in silence for a long time, just watching in awe. I don't know what Matt and Sergei were thinking. We were all lost in our own little worlds. Physically, I hadn't completed the Challenge yet, but I think, spiritually, that was it for me – the moment it all came together. It's funny when you approach an obvious climax, in this case the peak of a mountain – it sometimes doesn't quite live up to expectation. Maybe your defences are primed, you can see it coming, it's too obvious. In fact, the 'moment', the really powerful one, sneaks up on you. It has to take you by surprise. That sunrise was mine.

A few hours later, at 11.53 a.m. on 12 July 2011, I kissed the boulder at the top of Elbrus, six months, eleven days, seven hours and fifty-eight minutes after I had set off from the South Pole. Gratitude, as always, was the overriding emotion, gratitude for the team who had made it happen, gratitude for Mother Nature. When you climb a mountain you pray for that one weather window; to have been blessed with nine of them was something again.

But a peak is never the end. You always have to come down again. And in this case the work was nowhere near finished. I'd promised the team that, whatever happened, I would put as much into the fundraising when I returned as I had into the 737 Challenge itself. All that still lay ahead.

We posed for photos, and I called Mum and Dad from the top of a mountain for one last time. Their boy had done it! He was on his way home.

8

'm not a big drinker. In my line of work, as in my previous
career, I can't really afford to be. Nevertheless, having been
a rugby player and having known the buzz of a successful
summit, neither am I unfamiliar with the concept of the big
piss-up.

Certainly, as with most people, I know when I've been in
one the night before, although for the really big ones that realisation can take a while to sink in. First of all, you have to
work out where and who you are. The morning of 14 July
dawned on me by degrees in just such a way.

I was lying on the floor of a tent. Nothing unusual about
that, but this one was big, had a hard floor and people in it
wandering about getting themselves breakfast. I sat up, in
some pain. The breakfast-goers carried on with their business,
mostly ignoring me. There may have been one or two looking

in my direction, shaking their heads, but I'm not sure. They were all dressed up as if they had a mountain to climb. This, I now remembered, was the mess tent at base camp on Elbrus. I was half-naked in my sleeping bag. There was someone else in a sleeping bag nearby. It was Matt. I nudged him. He groaned.

What had happened to our tent? I picked up my bag and went outside. It was still standing. Not that it was our tent – it belonged to the base camp. I opened the flap, and a wave of the foulest smell imaginable hit me. Stench and heat. The sun had risen, and it was shaping up already to be another hot day. There was a human being in here. It was Dai Camera. I stepped into the tent and found a neat pile of poo on the grass in our vestibule. Venturing further inside, I found Dai lying on the floor like a stricken animal in a cartoon. There was vomit everywhere.

Cue flashback. I'd woken in the night to find Dai and Matt fighting each other, proper wrestling, with punches and swearing.

A croaky voice came from behind me. 'Dai, you vomited on me last night, you bastard.'

Matt had joined me in surveying the wreckage of our tent. We'd all been asleep in it that night. Dai had been in the middle when he'd suddenly sat up. There but for the grace of God ... He could have turned to the right, where I was sleeping, but instead he turned to the left, where Matt was. From a personal point of view that was a blessing to rank with the sunrise I'd experienced two days earlier.

Dai was prolific with his vomit. It could have been altitude sickness, but by now I knew that it was likely something else.

184

Matt was covered and attacked Dai, who, confused and unaware of what he had just done, defended himself with gusto. The two of them were rolling round in sick belting each other; that's when I thought it best to go and sleep in the mess tent.

I remembered that much now. And then I remembered the afternoon before, when we'd come down from Camp 1. I remembered reaching the peak of Elbrus the day before that. We'd stood around at the top for only a few minutes. I'd made a couple of phone calls, but Sergei had warned me that there were military patrols in the area who would confiscate a satellite phone as soon as look at one. At 5642m? Was there no escape? We'd descended to base camp in two days, passing the helicopter crash the military were salvaging along the way and picking up Dai at Camp 1. Once back at base camp, Sergei had produced a bottle of champagne. Then he'd brought out a crate of beers. Then, photographic evidence suggests, there were three bottles of Russian cognac. We had no idea where he was getting it all from, but we were happy to indulge.

More evidence came to light the next morning. Dai was detailed to clean the tent. There he was on his hands and knees, scouring the floor of a soiled tent that steamed in the hot Russian sun, retching with every other scrub of his hand. His sick was discovered in bags and in bags within bags – it was everywhere. To enhance his pain, I started to film the scene, when a thought occurred to him.

'Parksy?' he said. 'What time does the counter say on the camera?'

'Fifty-three,' I said.

If it had been possible for him to turn paler he would have. 'Oh, no. It was on twenty-five when I stopped filming yesterday.'

I rewound the camera to a random point. Dai, Matt and I watched the footage with our jaws on the floor. There he was, dancing topless with the base camp chef, a formidable woman with powerful forearms (who wasn't topless, I might add), to some deafening Russian techno music. We still don't know where the music came from. There was me jumping into shot for a moment, shirt off, too. Occasionally, the camera would turn to reveal a bare-chested Matt behind the controls. It was swooping and shuddering all over the place. We fast-forwarded to find some footage of me sitting in the mess tent with a bottle of cognac in my hand, shouting into the satellite phone to my friend Amy from Sheffield that I loved her. Drunk-dialling from Russia. There was more footage of the satellite phone (with the Russian army base just the other side of some flimsy plastic mesh) being passed around among all of us with Tracy on the other end. Media outlets were lining up to talk to me, but I couldn't string a sentence together. She had to tell them all that there was no reception where I was.

Dai panicked when we reviewed the footage the next day. He was afraid of what producer Russell might think (nothing to do with the fact he'd been caught on camera dancing half-naked with a Russian babushka). I told him Russ would love it. Dai shook his head and deleted the footage. I regret that decision to this day. They were some of the funniest scenes I've ever witnessed. It turned out Russ was gutted as well.

As for the mystery turd – it remained a mystery. We three denied all knowledge, and, although I doubt we'd have remembered anyway, I doubt as well the ability of any of us in that state to have laid one so neatly in the middle of our vestibule. We think it was probably one of the other climbers. Or maybe one of the soldiers from the army base (who, incidentally, had been really friendly). And why not? These people were here to climb a mountain, not be kept awake by drunken idiots at the end of their mission. If that's how they wanted to express their anger, I apologise for our behaviour and doff my cap.

It had been a big piss-up, all right.

But, however much we climb, however much we drink, we must come down eventually. I returned to Heathrow to be greeted by Mum and Dad, Simon and Tracy. I couldn't have wiped the smile from my face if I'd tried. Next, I was granted a reception at the Senedd, in Cardiff, from where I'd departed eight months earlier. It was there, amid all the excitement, that it started to sink in I'd achieved something that could capture the imagination. It was there that a whirlwind twelve months began, which ended up taxing me just as much as the 737 Challenge had.

I genuinely mean that. Not because what followed was of itself as much of an undertaking (although it was manic); more because it followed immediately on from a seven-month period (not to mention the eighteen months of prior training) that had pushed me to the limits of my physical capability, examined every last corner of my mind and thrown a near-death experience or two at me.

187

It had nearly cost me a part of my body, too. The toe, though, proved to be a miracle of natural science. Ian Williams, the vascular surgeon who treated me, wanted to write a paper on it. Most people thought it would refreeze on Denali, or that the altitude would halt the healing process. How the toe didn't refreeze down the crevasse I'll never know. The clinical evidence, from this and other incidents since, seems to suggest that my body simply heals well. The falling apart of the toe sounds gross – and it was – but it meant it was healing properly. That process continued for a long time. It was more than a year before I grew a toenail back. The pain was at times excruciating as the nerves regenerated. I wore flip-flops for the next few months after I returned, even when I was wearing a suit, because the toe was too swollen for shoes. Typically, having managed to climb two mountains without hurting it, I stubbed it against a table leg in one of the Challenge team meetings. The others were a little freaked out, as the blood oozed across my flip-flops. I did lose a corner of the toe, which never grew back properly, so it looks a little misshapen, but it's still there and fully operational. The main legacy of the frostbite is impaired circulation, which has to be managed. Even cycling in the UK, I can feel the toe getting cold.

The first time I wore a shoe, in fact, was for a black-tie gala dinner in mid-September at City Hall in Cardiff to welcome me home and raise funds – £52,000 that night. Fundraising was my business now. For the twelve months after I returned, when I wasn't away on expedition I was driving up and down the country on speaking engagements, school visits, corporate events and so on. Mon Motors Audi, one of my brilliant sponsors, not only donated an Audi A1 for us to raffle, they also gave me a car, and I racked up 40,000 miles in it, attending an average of four engagements a week. People imagine that I came back, went on holiday and rolled around in my new-found fame and fortune. That couldn't have been further from the truth. I had no money – indeed, there was a five-figure bill to pay. I had solemnly pledged to everyone – the team and Marie Curie – that I would invest as much energy into the fundraising as I had the Challenge itself, and God knows I meant it, but even if I hadn't there would have been no choice anyway. Those bills needed paying, and the Challenge had always been part exorcism, part new start, part (and it was at least as big a part) a chance to raise money in aid of a cause that was dear to my family's heart. This had to be done, and the nature of these things is that you have to strike while the iron's hot, which meant no holidays for me. In 2012, I did 'get away' to test equipment on expeditions up Aconcagua and Denali (the latter another brutal, near-death affair) and I guided a fundraising trek to Everest Base Camp for the Welsh Women Walking group, but the first actual holiday I took was a cycling trip to Sicily at the end of August 2012, over a year after the Challenge had ended.

We raised more than £300,000 in the end across a campaign that I'm told reached sixty-four million people and achieved a media value, for what it's worth, of more than £3 million. Our central office was my parents' house; the campaign was masterminded by Tracy Pinder (in her spare time), executed by Mum and me, with a support team of around seven or eight others. No one took a wage. I really do mean it when I say I am as proud of our fundraising as I am of the

Challenge itself. If driving on motorways and attending events were as dramatic as climbing mountains and trekking to poles, then that year of my life, in terms of effort expended, would be worth at least as big a spread in this book as the 737 Challenge.

But what next? I knew, more than ever, that this was the life I was supposed to lead. It was around then that Tracy and I came up with the term 'extreme-environment athlete' to describe what I was. The 737 Challenge had taken me to some of the most incredible places on Earth, while servicing in me the athletic inclinations that had led me to a life in sport in the first place.

I needed a new project, though, and my mind kept coming back to Antarctica. I'd fallen in love with the continent the moment I'd set foot on it. Maybe it's because it was the first leg of the 737 Challenge, the beginning of the adventure, but I think it's more to do with the epic scale of its wilderness and the role it played in the heroic age of exploration. The legend of Scott, Amundsen, Shackleton and other such pioneers is captivating, but, for all their heroism, the star of the show is Antarctica herself.

The truth is that in this overcrowded world of ours the opportunities for genuine geographical exploration have all but gone. Everest, the most extreme mountain on our planet, at least in terms of its height, has become a bit of a thoroughfare precisely because of that extremity. Humans seek out the extreme, constrained only by the level of technology at any given time. Once one has broken trail, others follow, all the more so as the technology improves. When you look at it from a distance, it is deeply depressing to see these wildernesses become overrun, bit by bit, as by an infestation of ants. Then again, you can't complain while contributing to it yourself. Everyone has their own reasons for being there.

Antarctica is beginning to suffer from the same phenomenon, but where Everest, Aconcagua and the like are single lumps of rock trying to accommodate hundreds of climbers, Antarctica is a vast continent. It is still possible to go there, to one of the world's most extreme environments, and be entirely alone. The call of that, to me, is irresistible.

I mulled over a few ideas, some of which are still live possibilities, but it was the Scott Memorial Service at St Paul's Cathedral in March 2012 that galvanised me to press on with one. There were so many proud days in those twelve months – invitations, awards and honours that I had never dreamed of. This is not the place to list them, but they all meant so much, and I hope my gratitude shone through on each occasion, because it was sincerely felt. But the Scott Memorial Service was a highlight.

I went with Amy. I'd made good on that drunken call from Russia, and we'd started dating. This was our first get-dressed-up-and-meet-people date, so it was special for that reason alone. But it was also one of the proudest days of my life. Sir David Attenborough read Scott's last entry in his journal, when Scott knew he was going to die. St Paul's was silent but for the wobble in his voice, as he read those last noble words. Later, the congregation stood to sing the National Anthem. It was the first time I'd sung it, the first time I'd even heard it as anything other than the anthem of the enemy before a game of rugby. To sing it as a Brit, in celebration of British heroism, was incredibly moving. Grown men were in tears; veterans of war too old to stand straight laboured to do so all the same. It was such an honour to be there – and yet I didn't feel as if I deserved to be among that company.

I'd already decided by then that my next big expedition would be to Antarctica, but that morning at St Paul's inspired me to set things in motion, to earn my place in the Cathedral, albeit retrospectively. I gave it the name Project X. The nature of it was a secret – and the precise details remain so – but I resolved to attempt the longest solo, unassisted and unsupported expedition in history from the coast of Antarctica to the South Pole.

There are so many barriers to such a project, but the physical and financial demands are two of the most formidable. With the latter in mind, Tracy introduced me to a few agents. The first one I met was Jonny McWilliams of Wasserman Media Group. I saw all the others, too, but Jonny and I clicked immediately. The others wanted to put me in their portfolio of rugby players; Jonny understood that, much though rugby had played such a crucial role in my life, I wanted to move on from it.

With someone like that behind me I felt more confident that we had a chance financially. Physically, though, it was up to me. I targeted the winter of 2013/14, which meant in the year building up to that I had a huge amount of work to do, preparing myself for a challenge that could test me even further than the 737 Challenge had. I also needed the best equipment available. In January and February, before the Scott Memorial Service, I had already tested a tent in another successful, but more difficult, summit of Aconcagua, this time from the less popular Polish Glacier. Then, in June, I tested clothing, dehydrated food and another tent on Denali.

Once again, Denali didn't disappoint. No problems with crevasses, because this time it was cold, really cold. I climbed it in a pair with Nikki Skinner from Rab, my clothing sponsor. The conditions were the worst I'd experienced yet on Denali, which is saying something. It took us ten days to reach 17 Camp, having been stuck at 14 Camp for five. Then the weather really closed in. We were marooned at 17 Camp for four days, battered by 70mph winds, temperatures nudging −40°C and a metre of snow in one twenty-four-hour period. Avalanches were going off right, left and centre. Couldn't go up, couldn't go down because of the winds. There had been talk of 'Magic Tuesday', a much-anticipated break in the weather, but it never materialised. We took advantage of a brief window on Tuesday evening to climb down to Camp 14, but by the time we reached the top of Washburn's Ridge, at the bottom of which I'd had my diarrhoea moment the year before, the winds were high again and the visibility zero. It was not safe to continue, so we turned back. The forecasts were proving unreliable, the weather vicious. The only sensible thing to do was to abort our summit attempt.

The following day, we left 17 Camp at lunchtime in better conditions and climbed for twenty-five hours straight to base camp. At 14 Camp, we learned of a team who had been with us the day before and hadn't turned back when we had at the top of Washburn's Ridge. They were caught in an avalanche on the Headwall. Thankfully they survived, but we saw their rucksacks strewn across the slopes. Then, in Anchorage, we learned of a Japanese team behind us who had not been so lucky. They were caught in an avalanche on Motorcycle Hill, twenty-four hours to the hour after we'd been on it. Four out of five of them died.

I don't mind admitting that I was shaken after that trip. When I returned to the UK, the public side of fundraising for the Challenge was about to end. We'd given ourselves a year to raise as much as we could. I'd wanted to raise £1 million, but I know now that that had been an unrealistic target with the resources available to us. There's a lot I know now from that time.

Since I'd emerged from the white room three years earlier, I hadn't stopped. I had another research and development expedition planned for Antarctica that winter. I was supposed to be training for it, but the doctors ordered me to take a break. When we wrapped up the fundraising in July, I started to spiral again with the kind of symptoms that I had wrestled with in the white room. It hit me like a ton of bricks. As much as anything else, because I just hadn't expected it.

They call it Olympic Syndrome, and it was to be in the news a few months later when the big party moved on from London 2012 to its next stop. I was as caught up in the Olympic fever as anyone – carrying the torch for the leg through Swansea, with my parents and team there, too, was another incredible highlight of my year after the Challenge. But such highs can't be sustained indefinitely. As from a mountain, we must come down.

While the party raged around me, my own personal Olympics had just moved on with the passing of July. Any one of the nine legs of the 737 Challenge might have been justification by itself for a good, long rest. Having spent the year since on the road, running on empty, then suffered Denali's latest combination of upper cuts, my body slumped in August and the demons returned to claim their due.

I couldn't help feeling that I was back where I'd started. This wasn't quite the white room, nor was I in a place from which I couldn't see a way forward, but familiar symptoms were returning – the despondency, the lethargy, the inability to face a world beyond the duvet. The questions swarmed round. Just what had the 737 Challenge done for me? In what way had I moved on? The room might not have been white, but three years on I was still a thirty-something-year-old with no income living with his mum and dad. I saw the world outside growing taller around me, support structures crumbling beneath. Normally, I would train through times like this, but I was physically spent.

I didn't feel as if I could talk to anyone about it. My parents had been through enough already with the Challenge. My relationship with Amy was still in its early stages, and I cared about her deeply. I didn't want to put pressure on us by coming across as some needy wreck. Jonny had suggested by then that I put together a submission to try to secure a book deal, so it was to the pages you are reading now that I turned. As a way of working through issues, I recommend the setting down of words.

But I don't want to come across to you, the reader, as a needy wreck, either, although I realise the damage may be done on that front. I suppose the point, which I hadn't appreciated in the white room or even three years later during the post-737 crash, is that this sort of crisis is normal in any life. I think an undertaking like the Challenge, or an expedition to Antarctica,

195

can intensify the microscope we all put ourselves under from time to time, but so, too, can any endeavour or life event of great personal significance. You have to be ready for the down-turn, or at least recognise it as natural when it strikes.

The 737 Challenge did a lot for my life. It opened the way to a future for me, but just as importantly it drew the line under my past. I watch rugby now as a fan, pure and simple. To have that joy returned to me is one of the greatest gifts. I didn't want to be that bitter guy at the bar saying, could have, should have, would have. By the time the Challenge started, I'd found that peace within myself. Then, when I stood on Elbrus, I saw new doors opening ahead of me. In terms of the white room, it may be that I had not dealt with my psycho-logical issues properly, just pushed them to one side and focused on something else, but it may also be that focusing on something else is precisely how you do deal with them. I don't know.

Either way, the Challenge helped me enormously, but it hadn't yet delivered its final lesson. I was learning it as I strug-gled that August. Happening upon a name for my condition, as the media discussed Olympic Syndrome in the wake of the Games, was a big step. I'm sure there are lots of other names for the phenomenon in different walks of life, but being able to assign a name of any kind helps to identify your foe and to know him the next time he calls.

I wasn't prepared for that crash after the 737 Challenge. When it struck I couldn't understand what was going on. I'd thought the Challenge had 'cured' me of all that. I tried to fight it, but that only made it worse. Now, though, I under-stand a bit better how the highs and lows work. I'd be lying if

I said I didn't suffer the demons any more, but at least I know now to expect them and how to recognise them.

That knowledge seems to me to be the last great gift the 737 Challenge left me.

9

As soon as I had decided to make Antarctica my next project, I set about making plans. The Aconcagua and Denali expeditions of 2012 were all part of it, testing gear and perfecting systems. But you can't even think about tackling the sort of thing I had in mind without having experienced Antarctica proper.

I knew Antarctica from the 737 Challenge, but, really, I had barely broached it. What I needed was a longer expedition. I decided to attempt a solo coast-to-pole expedition, and I gravitated towards the route along which the generally recognised speed records are judged – from Hercules Inlet. Christian Eide had smashed the world record when I'd been down there in January 2011, lowering the old record from thirty-nine days to an astonishing twenty-four. The distance between Hercules Inlet to the South Pole depends on the route you pick through the crevasse fields, sastrugi and inclines, but it is approximately 1140km (715 miles), give or take 20km. The last degree, on the other hand, is sixty nautical miles, or 111km (69 miles). So a very different proposition.

At the time, only fifteen people had ever skied solo, unassisted and unsupported from coast to pole, although a German was to complete a slightly shorter route that year from the Ronne Ice Shelf. Eight Brits had done it, the most remarkable being Hannah McKeand, who has completed the journey six times, more than anyone else in history. Her solo expedition in 2006 from Hercules Inlet to the South Pole set a new world record of thirty-nine days. Two years later, the American Todd Carmichael lowered it by an hour and a half, before Christian pulled off his incredible feat, a record they say will never be broken.

There's a reason it is so rarely attempted, as I was about to find out, even if I had a pretty good idea already. Slogging your way through the Antarctic wilderness for more than 1100km, climbing from sea level to the polar plateau at an altitude of 3000m, is a big ask at the best of times, but to qualify as solo you really must do it on your own, to qualify as unassisted you must use nothing but your own muscle power, and to qualify as unsupported you cannot receive any external material assistance, which means you must pull a pulk behind you carrying everything you need for a month or two. (Some people have the definitions of unassisted and unsupported the other way round, but this is the way I've always known them. It makes more sense to me.)

I was aiming to complete the journey in thirty-five to forty days. That would require me to cover 30km a day, uphill, on skis, hauling an 82kg pulk, which is not much lighter than I am. And that's before we've considered the weather. With the weather in mind, the advice was to travel late in the season, setting off in December, aiming for a mid-to-late-January arrival at the South Pole. Whatever happened, I had to be there by 25 January, when the last flight before winter left the Amundsen–Scott Station. If I missed that, the financial penalties would be huge – £40,000 a day to keep the plane on the ground, and if for any reason they needed it at Union Glacier in the meantime it would be another £200,000 to fly it back to the South Pole to pick me up. Jonny McWilliams had managed to secure me funding from some sponsors, which covered the costs of the trip, but shelling out that kind of money was obviously not an option.

Having such a cut-off to sharpen the mind was no bad thing, though, and would accentuate one of the realities of life on expedition in Antarctica, which is the way your existence is defined by quantities – how many kilometres travelled, on what bearing, in how many hours and calories. When things go wrong out there, those simple quantitative standards can take on a sinister qualitative aspect. And things do go wrong.

Witness the first problem to arise before I'd even set foot on the continent. My freight, including my specially designed pulk and all my gear, was supposed to have followed me to Punta Arenas via Miami and Santiago. I'd sent it the week before I'd left, but two days after my arrival it was still showing up as in Miami. Not that anyone had actually set eyes on it. When somebody tried, they discovered it wasn't even in Miami. Eyes were finally set on it back in London! So I had a week's delay to contend with before I'd even left Chile.

So many proud moments. Being received by the WRU to celebrate my world first with the fans at the Millennium Stadium before Wales v England. The flip-flop wasn't a fashion statement!

I proudly wore the gold and silver embroidered WRU feathers on my Rab expedition jacket. Presented to me by Wales's First Minister, Carwyn Jones, and WRU chief executive, Roger Lewis.

Although you can't see, I wasn't wearing the flip flop in this pic! Celebrating my Honorary Fellowship at the University of South Wales with Mum, Dad and Amy.

Some of the 737 Challenge team at the Senedd.

Simon and I at the Senedd.

Andy James of Ace Feet in Motion inspecting the toe on my return.

Working with kids at Casllwchwr Primary School as part of a sports literary project. They interviewed me all day, some amazing and insightful questions, and then produced a book on the 737 Challenge. Amazing!

A lovely letter written by Rebecca from Hereford Cathedral Junior School. 'When I'm allowed!' – I'm not sure I'm actually 'allowed' even now! Ha!

Hereford Cathedral Junior
28 Castle Street
Hereford
HR1 2NW
Telephone 01432 363511
www.hcjs.org
enquiry@hcjs.org

16th June 20

Dear Richard Parks,

Thank you very much for coming to our assembly and talking about your 73 challenge, it was very inspirational.

I think your determination is amazing.

I think when I'm older I might try and do somet like that, when I'm allowe

Best wishes
Rebecca
McKay

Registered in Cardiff No 2082261 (Limited by Guarantee)
Registered Charity No 518889

Being voted by the public to be an Olympic Torchbearer for the London games was such a huge honour for me, my family and all the 737 Challenge team. We had such an awesome day in Swansea.

The Welsh Women Walking group that I led to Everest Base Camp raised an incredible £30,000.

Harriet, owner of Cardiff's iconic New York Deli, supported the 737 Challenge by naming my favourite sandwich the 'Richie Parks Special' and donating a percentage of all sales of it.

Richard from the World of Groggs with my broken crampons from Everest, which I donated to their rugby museum. The limited edition '737 beard' Grogg they made sold out in days and raised over £6,000.

Howard and Wayne, who were amazing supporters of the 737 Challenge, organised a 'man v horse' race and this 'Parks and ride' event. They even trekked to Everest Base Camp.

The Ten2Ten Cycle Challenge, organised by Laura and Phil Thomas, inspired by and in support of the 737 Challenge. Ten rugby clubs and two valleys in ten hours! The event is still going strong.

One of the 737 Challenge's main sponsors, Mon Motors Audi, kindly donated an Audi A1 for a fundraising raffle campaign we ran.

Keith Casey, owner of Arch Engineering in Newport, discussing the modifications I asked him to make to the cooking system that I had designed with my dad, which saved me carrying about 3kg of fuel.

Pensive, and a little nervous, at the drop-off for my first solo expedition to the South Pole in 2012. Looking out at the Wilson Nunataks from Hercules Inlet.

There's nothing unusual about lost luggage, but the likelihood of these things happening ratchets up the more extreme your final destination.

That week was actually invaluable in fostering my relationship with ALE, the logistics company for all things Antarctic, who worked wonders with the freight company to track down my gear. In the end, Tracy picked up the gear and flew out with it in person, leaving my new pulk behind. Instead, I borrowed one of ALE's. Mike Sharpe and David Rootes, two of the owners of ALE, became good friends, and we had crossed all the t's of the expedition and dotted the i's by the time the gear arrived and I flew out to Union Glacier. When I made it on to the ice, there was even less margin for error. If I took forty days now, I would miss that last plane off the South Pole. In other words, I was going to have to match or break the previous world record just to catch it.

Hercules Inlet is a short – but dangerous – hop on a Twin Otter from Union Glacier, and as soon as I landed at ALE's base I was off to the start line. On the coast it may be, but this is Antarctica, so everything lies under the pervasive ice. It's not quite right to say you start at sea level, because you're standing on that ice, which is 200m thick. There is a sharp incline of around 10m where the glacier from the continent meets the water beneath the ice, which changes according to the tide, but otherwise you would have no idea you were by the sea. You would have no idea where you were, full stop. Actually, at Hercules Inlet, you can see the Wilson Nunataks (a nunatak is the tip of a mountain emerging from a glacier), but it is a rare landmark on the route to the South Pole. The default landscape I would have to get used to moving through was a featureless expanse of white. The Thiel Mountains would provide some relief around halfway, but otherwise the best I could hope for in the way of variety was the infamous sastrugi, which are usually at their most vicious in the 87th and 88th degrees. We shall come to those. Hercules Inlet sits at the start of the 80th.

I'm always apprehensive before expeditions, but this one was different. I would be facing a new hardship – solitude. One of Antarctica's attractions is the prospect of being totally alone. There can't be many on this earth who have never known the urge to get away from it all. Solitude appeals to every one of us at some stage or other in our lives, but you can have too much of a good thing as well. One of the most important resources on any expedition is the company of other people, and not just, say, to pull you out of a crevasse you might have fallen into. When you're exhausted and hungry, demoralised and battered by the weather, the psychological vultures circling, a simple look or word of encouragement from a team-mate suffering the same thing can work wonders. There is no such support on a solo expedition in Antarctica.

I set off at 1 p.m., Chilean time, on 18 December 2012. There are lots of crevasses in Antarctica, and they're big – much bigger than those on Denali. The start of the route from Hercules Inlet is one of the danger spots, but on a pair of skis the threat is reduced and skiing round the worst areas is easier in Antarctica than it is on a mountain. It took me a few days to find my rhythm (it always does), but by day six I was hitting 30km-plus a day, a rate I maintained for three and a half weeks. By the end of day twenty-five, I was well into the 86th degree, having covered 762.72km at a rate of 30.5km a day. (See what I mean about the quantitative measures you judge yourself by?) That meant I was operating at the level of the very best polar athletes. I was on course to catch the plane and to set the second fastest time in history, albeit much closer to Todd Carmichael's and Hannah's old records than the one Christian had set two years earlier. Not bad for what was essentially a research and development trip.

But that makes it sound as if I was breezing through. Those three and a half weeks were absolutely vital preparation, but my morale went on a roller-coaster. As for my body, that just took a pounding from start to finish. I've spoken elsewhere about the importance of minimising the loads you carry on expedition, how every last gram takes its toll. Nowhere is that ethos felt more keenly than on a solo expedition in Antarctica. One of the products I was testing was a new cooking system my dad had designed with Arch Engineering, a company in Newport. He had adapted an MSR stove and a pot to increase efficiency. It worked brilliantly. So well, in fact, that I used a lot less fuel than anticipated. The implications of such efficiency for any future expeditions were very positive, but for this one I was paying for it by having to lug much more fuel than I needed.

Then there was the poo I was packing up in bags and stockpiling on my pulk. I swear some of it weighed more than the food I had eaten that day. It is soul-destroying to have to load new items on to your pulk each morning (poo or otherwise), when all you want to do is to be free of the weight behind you.

In addition to the food, the clothes and the equipment I was testing, I was also trialling a tent, my third that year, having not particularly agreed with those I'd taken on Aconcagua and Denali. This one was a great success. Your tent becomes your home. In Antarctica, you come to rely on it – and value it – even more than you do your actual home, your bricks and mortar. The erecting and packing away of your tent is actually the most dangerous part of your day. If the wind is up, which it usually is, one moment of carelessness can cost you your shelter. If it's not secured, your tent will be gone in an instant, whisked away across the ice. End of expedition. And if you're in heavy sastrugi, for example, far away from anywhere a plane can land to pick you up, it could be the end of more than that.

The significance of every seemingly trivial detail is magnified enormously. The combination of the fatigue, which is constant, the cold, the loneliness and the monotony warp the mind. I remember New Year's Day on this expedition, in particular. I woke up, for some reason, missing everyone back home far more that morning than I had on Christmas Day.

I was skiing in two-hour stints, or tabs, as I called them, four or five of them a day, and for the first of the New Year it was into a moderate but bitter headwind, which grew in intensity. I could see dark clouds on the horizon. I watched them approach until they were overhead, and within five minutes the light had become totally flat – no shadows, no features. The wind picked up next, hurling spindrift into my face. There may even have been snow, although it rarely snows that far into the continent.

I was in a total whiteout now, battling into a howling wind, straight from the South Pole. Progress was painfully slow. Skiing in a whiteout is savage. You may as well be skiing inside a ping-pong ball. There is no horizon, nor a single shadow to navigate by. You have to slow right down, because you can't make out any details even beneath your feet. Every time you take a step, it might be into a drop. Your ski might break, or you might sprain an ankle, twist a knee. The going was so slow that I decided not to take a break after my first tab and carried on for another two hours like this. With every step I just wanted to pull the plug, but those numbers are always taunting at you. How many kilometres? How many hours? In the middle of it all, I developed vertigo, as I tried to manoeuvre through the sastrugi, up and over, up and over, no horizon, no detail. For half an hour I was Bambi on skis, the ground seeming to lurch beneath me.

But this was New Year's Day. I'm a big believer in starting a year strong, so I pressed on and on. Then I looked at my GPS to discover I'd travelled 3km in two hours. Enough was enough, New Year's Day or not.

Just as I was about to call it quits, I saw a tiny speck of blue in the distance. I skied on to see if it was a break in the weather system. The blue grew bigger and bigger, the wind dropped, and I enjoyed the most glorious afternoon of perfect conditions. After six more hours, I finished the day on 33km.

I saw it as a purging. The New Year had found me in a melancholic frame of mind and sent this two-hour stint from hell to test me. I persevered and, when the skies cleared, I was rewarded with a rush of optimism and joy for the day and year ahead. It felt as if something had cleared me out. Something bigger than us, something bigger. Antarctica is like that. A break in the weather lifts us all in everyday life; in Antarctica, as on a mountain, the effect is magnified until it becomes spiritual.

This can work the other way as well, though. I wouldn't care to dwell too long on my reaction to dropping a couple of Jelly Bellies at the end of my day about a week later. Jelly Bellies are my special treat. I love them so much. I had them meticulously rationed out, fourteen to a portion. Each morning I would put a portion in my pocket to look forward to at the end of the day. The skies had been blue on day twenty-three, but I was at 1600m altitude and starting to feel really cold. It might have been the altitude making me feel that way, but it was more likely a combination of the actual temperature, fatigue and my fast-disappearing fat reserves. The calorific deficit I was operating on was wide. My average day would put me through around 8000 calories of work, but I was eating a little over 5000 – 3000 of them at dinner and 1300 at breakfast and the balance between. You tread a fine line. You can't carry, or for that matter eat, enough food to match what you burn on an expedition like that, so a deficit is unavoidable. Nevertheless, my food strategy was one system that would need reviewing.

It made those Jelly Bellies at the end of the day seem extra sweet. When I stopped at the end of this one (nine hours twenty minutes; 32.2km; 1627m above sea level; on the edge of the 86th degree), I dropped my Jelly Bellies into the snow. I wanted to burst into tears. I had the presence of mind to stop myself, just about, but the irrational was starting to take hold. I dropped to the ground and ate them one by one off the snow.

The word was that the sastrugi this season were the biggest anyone had seen for around ten years. As mentioned earlier, sastrugi are irregular features in the terrain, caused by the wind scouring the surface, piling up the snow into ridges and humps and gouging out troughs. They come in all shapes and sizes and in a photograph from above can look quite beautiful. When you're among them, though, they become a brutal series of obstacles to fast, efficient progress.

They can be found all over Antarctica but on the western side are at their worst in the 87th degree, where the winds roll off the top of the polar plateau. This year they were said to begin in the 86th degree. On 12 January, day twenty-six, as I continued through the 86th for the third day, I'd hoped I'd navigated to the west of them. But I hadn't. There they were in the distance, like some grotesque scene in a film. Normally, sastrugi are ankle-to-knee high; some of these were taller than I am. There was just no way to go up and over; you had to go round, playing havoc with your navigation. And this, just as the incline up to the plateau reaches its steepest.

'Every day stronger, every day closer.' Repeat to self, over and over again.

For the first time since day six, I dipped below 30km. I knew these sastrugi were coming, but knowing about them and experiencing them are very different things. Another example of why these preparatory expeditions are so essential. I might have been expecting these sastrugi, but I wasn't properly prepared.

Day twenty-seven was even worse, my distance travelled dropping further to 27km in an eleven-hour wrestle-athon with my pulk, body and mind, the sastrugi, a headwind and the ever-sharpening incline. I was feeling colder and colder, unable to establish any speed, unable to generate body heat. Every situation is different, according to your levels of fatigue, hypoxia, even sweat, but generally I have found my comfort threshold to be −20°C. Below −28 is when it becomes challenging to manage. This seemed well on the way to the latter.

At least I'd crossed into the 87th degree. Such milestones take on huge psychological significance. I tore into day twenty-eight with determination and sailed through the first four hours, until, bang, Antarctica sat me on my arse again, literally this time. I took a fall, which is quite common, but this one shook me amid sastrugi so big that even the smaller ones I was picking my way over were big enough to ski down. I felt fine physically, but the headwind ripping down from the polar plateau (I was at 2300m now) was vicious. Constantly having to flex your fingers and toes is almost as much of an impairment to progress as these monstrous sastrugi. The more you have to do it, the slower you move, the colder you become, the more you have to do it. It's a vicious circle, which is the second time I've used the word vicious this paragraph, and I don't care. Viciousness was everywhere. After an hour of it I was forced to pitch my tent. Seventeen kilometres.

The slog continued. Navigation becomes painstaking. Ideally, you follow a bearing off your compass, find some sort of feature in the distance (which is not always possible, depending on the light) and ski towards it. Among big sastrugi, though, you can't see far enough away to latch on to a landmark, and even if you could you would soon lose sight of it because you are constantly having to focus on what's in front of you. It adds further to the stop-start nature of your progress, checking your compass, flexing your extremities, climbing over sastrugi, checking your compass, all the while becoming colder. In a whiteout, it becomes almost impossible.

Now my date with the plane on 25 January was in jeopardy.

I was in contact with Steve Jones, ALE's operations manager, who advised me that there was the possibility of a pick-up on the 28th, as long as I was there by midnight on the 27th. He also told me that he'd flown over the area, and the sastrugi continued towards the end of the 88th degree. In other words, I had more than another 100km of this shit.

Day thirty-two, I twisted my knee; day thirty-three, it was head down into a full-on blizzard (a ground blizzard, to be precise, where the snow in the air is blown from the floor rather than the sky) that conformed to every Hollywood stereotype of a movie in Antarctica. Fifteen kilometres, but at least I just scraped into the 88th degree. And the weather proved a distraction to the pain in my knee.

That night (19 January), I took a difficult decision. Food was becoming the next issue. I was pushing to make this plane, and I didn't have enough to last me until the 27th, which would be forty-one days after I'd set off. It was with misgivings that I arranged for a drop from ALE. This would mean I lost my unsupported status, but it was more important that I continued safely. I had to keep reminding myself that this was, first and foremost, a research trip. It was a trial, not a Test match.

With the pressure eased and the light completely flat, I decided to start the next day in my tent, taking in a couple of extra meals. That made me feel much better, but any optimism quickly turned to despair. The light would not improve. I managed to steal about four hours from 11 p.m. on the 20th, during which I was blessed with a stunning quad helix – that rainbow feature around the sun that I'd encountered in the Arctic – but the 14km I skied then were all I managed in two days. That did not represent the kind of progress I needed.

Worse still, the conditions were making it impossible to land a plane. Even my precious food drop, planned for the 21st, had to be aborted. Those two days were the bleakest I have ever known on expedition. My body fat was virtually non-existent, which meant I was colder than I'd ever been. I've no idea what the ambient temperature actually was – this was Antarctica, so it wouldn't have been much – but my wasted frame at that altitude felt the chill as never before. Now that the food drop had been aborted, my decision to eat two days' worth of meals the day before seemed naive beyond belief. I hated myself for it. It was almost in the name of self-flagellation that I allowed myself only half-portions the next day. Truth be told, I was running out.

The psychological pressure of my situation was becoming intolerable, holed up in the most remote tent in the world (I was the last expedition on the ice) with my lifelines, if not broken, then seriously compromised, and with not a thing to be done about it. I was weak, cold and not myself anyway, but two days of that sort of confinement turned up the emotional fever dangerously.

It was at 10 p.m. on day thirty-five (21 January) that I made my next mistake. The light had become marginal, by which I mean I could just about make out shapes and shadows. Or maybe I just told myself I could. I had to move.

Precious energy was wasted packing up my tent. Within minutes I was among the sastrugi again; within a few more any marginal visibility that might have developed had evaporated. I was stranded in a sastrugi field, unable to see a thing. All of the usual problems recurred, the reasons I had stayed put in the first place – the inability to navigate or move quickly, the temperature, the threat of injury from an ill-judged step. Within an hour I was becoming dangerously cold. My GPS told me I'd moved a kilometre. But I was in trouble now, because I couldn't find anywhere to pitch my tent. In light like that, you can't even see the ground beneath your feet. It is effectively pitch-black. Except it's white. I started searching urgently around me, trying to find some level ground. I could feel that I was on sastrugi, each about the height of a kitchen table, densely packed. To pitch a tent on these would be impossible. Normally, you'd carry on until you found suitable terrain, but I was too cold and weak and the dexterity in my fingers was deteriorating fast.

It began to dawn on me that I'd made a mistake I might not be able to get out of. There's a special kind of terror when that happens. My situation seemed so innocuous. These were sastrugi, not clifftops or crevasses, yet this peculiar combination of circumstances rendered them potentially lethal. My decision to waste energy on striking camp had seemed a mere strategic error. Now it was presenting itself as a good deal more serious than that. These were repercussions from a simple mistake you could never anticipate without first making that mistake yourself. I'm grateful for the lesson now. Wasn't at the time.

I don't know how long it took me to find a patch of level ground. I obviously did, or I wouldn't be writing this now, but my fingers were grinding to a halt, not to mention my body. Erecting the tent was a painful experience. Climbing inside it, though, was one of pure relief.

The weather cleared enough the following day to organise the food drop a couple of kilometres away. I had to remain stationary to receive it, which meant a third day of stagnation, but at least I had extra supplies. I even got to speak face to face with a couple of humans! And, no, such fleeting contact does not affect your solo status. When I opened the sack, there were Post-it notes all over the food from my friends at Union Glacier. 'No stopping till the Pole!' they read. 'Crispos make sastrugi disappear!' Little touches like that can feel like life-savers. I stuffed my face with the Crispos (the Chilean answer to Pringles).

I still had the best part of two degrees to travel, roughly 220km, and six days in which to do it. Conditions overhead were almost perfect the next day. The sastrugi were still densely packed, though, and by all accounts there were another 70km of them. That day I broke 30km for the first time in ten days.

But I had to push too hard to achieve it. In my condition, this pace was not sustainable. It was ten out of ten, rather than the six or seven required earlier in the expedition. And I made another error that day. Trying to make up the time, I was working beyond my aerobic threshold and into anaerobic ter-ritory. My breathing was so heavy that my face mask clogged up, so I took it off. Within a few hours my nose had developed frostnip, which is a milder form of frostbite. It was another miscalculation, and a sign that it was time to stop. There are no margins for error in Antarctica.

I was dangerously underweight. There were bones sticking out of me I didn't know I had. I'd lost weight off my feet. Even my boots felt baggy! My mouth was full of ulcers. I managed 4.27km in three hours the next day and lay awake tossing and turning afterwards, trying to reconcile an impossible equation in my head. I had 190km still to travel and three days left. Even at my strongest, if I did away with sleep for two nights and blitzed it, I couldn't cover that. There was no way I could reach the South Pole now. I had to accept that after thirty-eight days and 974.68km, at 2700m altitude in the 88th degree, I had run out of time.

In the moment, it felt like a defeat. To have travelled so far and been through so much, not making it to the South Pole was tough to take. But by the time I was back in Punta, having been picked up on the ice by a Twin Otter on 25 January, I was already assimilating the lessons. Bar reaching the South Pole, every objective of the expedition had been met. Even the act of calling the attempt off had demonstrated to my family, my sponsors and those at ALE that I was capable of making smart decisions in a hostile environment under intense pressure, that for as long as it remained within my power I would be coming back from this and any future endeavours. My systems, strategies and equipment had been rigorously tested. The tent, cooking equipment and clothing had proved a resounding success; other areas, such as my food system and physical conditioning, would need more work. I had data that I could not have gathered any other way. And, most of all, I had experience.

Next time, I would be ready.

10

Towards the end of the expedition in Antarctica, I was told that Channel 5 had commissioned a series of four one-hour programmes to cover my year ahead, culminating in Project X. Talks had been well advanced before I'd left. Jonny and I had approached them about a possible one-hour documentary. I'd detailed the type of training I would be putting myself through over the course of that year. There would be a cycling component for fitness, a deprivation component for mental and physical resilience and somewhere towards the end a big, brutal endurance test to send me off. In other words, the aim was for me to be chewing barbed wire by the time I left.

The executives nodded their heads, taking it all in. They seemed to be listening.

And, bloody hell, were they listening!

Not only did they expand the original idea for a one-off

documentary into a series of four, they came up with three events that catered for each of the components I had high-lighted, around which the first three episodes would be based.

You want a cycling event? Try the Yak Attack, the highest mountain-bike race in the world, a 400km ride through the Himalaya, reaching an altitude of 5416m. Deprivation, you say? We give you the Jungle Ultra, a 230km run through the Peruvian jungle, with more than seventy river crossings, in temperatures of up to 40°C and humidity up to 100 per cent. And, as for your last big, brutal endurance event, we've found this thing in Wales called the, well, Brutal. It's a double iron-man triathlon wending its way through Snowdonia, the double marathon of which involves running to the top of Mount Snowdon itself. And, don't worry, we'll be with you all the way, filming the whole thing in high definition.

Shit.

First things first, though. I was so excited and proud to be given a television series. There are lots of people out there doing amazing things, but not many of them have the oppor-tunity to share it on network television. This was a real privilege. And, joking aside, those three events sounded just the kind of thing I needed. No doubt when they were chosen it was with one eye on the viewing figures, but there was method in the madness, too. I could see how they corre-sponded quite precisely with the vision I had outlined for my year ahead. I wouldn't necessarily have chosen those events myself, but they each represented the kind of challenge I could learn from.

The first sounded brilliant. I love cycling; I love the Himalaya. Why would I not love the Yak Attack? Well, at almost any other time in my life I would. But when they told me about it in late January 2013 it was not just any other time.

Picture the scene. I've arrived back in Punta Arenas, flown off Antarctica after thirty-nine days of expedition that have completely battered me. I am a skeletal wreck of a human being. When I stand on the scales for the first time, the final quantity I am left to ponder is my weight, back down to its post-Everest low, 79kg, or 12½st. It means I've left 16kg (2½st) of myself out there on the ice. My body is racked with pain and injury, my frost-nipped nose an absurd sight under the dressing they applied to it at Union Glacier. I am an absurd sight. The mirror reveals a man I barely recognise. And then Tracy tells me about my first race for the Channel 5 series. What's more, this Yak Attack thing starts on 1 March, little more than a month away. I will be flying to Nepal to acclimatise in three weeks. And I'm still in Chile.

Excited, proud, privileged – yes, I feel all those things. Nervous, vulnerable and really quite seriously concerned? All those, too. My mind is reeling almost as much as my body.

When they'd picked me up from the 88th degree in the Twin Otter it was a relatively warm day, but I was shocked when the pilot told me the ambient temperature was –27°C. That meant for the previous week at least it must have been well below –30°C. I've experienced colder on Denali, but never in such a wasted condition.

I knew I had travelled a long way in my thirty-nine-day epic across the wasteland, but flying back over it was mind-blowing. It took us four and a half hours to return to Union Glacier, which is next to where I'd started at Hercules Inlet. On ground level I had focused each day on any landmarks, or even just details, I could make out ahead of me – and sometimes they were just a few metres away. Bit by bit, day by day, moment by moment. This flight put all those little pieces into perspective. I had skied 975km, which sounds a lot, but I hadn't really thought about what it meant. Seeing it laid out in front of me made me feel better. If I'd set out from Cardiff, pulling a pulk across the frozen wastes of Ice Age Europe, 975km would have taken me around 40km past Toulouse – which, I see, is at 150m altitude, not 2700m.

My good friend David Hamilton, the Jagged Globe leader on Everest, was at Union Glacier. He literally took my hand when I stepped off the plane, led me to the food tent and fed me. A few days of adjustment at Union Glacier might have helped me rehabilitate myself, but it just so happened that the Ilyushin was leaving for Punta Arenas pretty much straightaway. Within ten hours of being picked up in the 88th degree, I found myself back in Chile.

I was like the savage thrown into civilisation. Nothing seemed to make sense. It took me two hours just to buy a pair of pants. I had longed for so many days to be back in the land of the living, eating a full meal, but here I was, missing the simplicity of life on the ice. That bloody steak I'd been dreaming of didn't quite taste as good as I'd imagined, and my stomach didn't know what to do with it. My pulk was delivered to my hotel room, straight from the ice. Being reunited with it was weird, like seeing an old friend from another time and place. My poo was still inside, now fully thawed. Antarctica's final joke on me was the revelation, back at Union Glacier, that I hadn't needed to carry my own waste after all. I'd misread the contract. That's only in the last degree, where the traffic on the continent is at its greatest. Everywhere else, you can bury it. I just couldn't believe it. I'd been carrying all this shit with me – and I use the word advisedly – for no reason. I had become only the second expedition in history to do so. And the other lot carried theirs for scientific research. Fucking typical.

The glare of society came at me from all sides – the darkness after forty days of light; the company of others after forty days of solitude. I felt like a primary school kid again. Everything was overwhelming. David and the others from ALE would lead me out of my hotel room and take me for something to eat. Then they put me on the plane back to the UK, where my parents, along with Amy and Tracy, would take up the responsibility of helping me reintegrate.

A new person stepped into my life at this point, someone who was to play a vital role in the year to come. Well, not really new – I'd known Dr Nicola Phillips for years. She'd been a physio at Pontypridd back in the nineties. Then we'd been reunited at a Sport Relief event I'd been involved with a year earlier, when she acted as physio for Team Wales. So she knew already that I had changed shape quite dramatically from when she used to work with me as a rugby player. Now the broken shell of that man turned up at her door.

Tracy, being Tracy, had foreseen something of a car crash developing when the Channel 5 series had been signed off while I was away. She'd phoned Nic and asked about her availability. Would she be able to perform some emergency work on me when I returned from Antarctica? Oh, and would she mind going with me to Nepal for the Yak Attack in three weeks' time? Surely she had some leave she could take from her job as reader at Cardiff University and consultant for Sport Wales High Performance Unit ...

Thank God, it turned out she had. Even more incredibly, she said yes! Here was the latest person to give freely of their time to help me out. In the end, we squared it as part of her work for Sport Wales, with whom I was working increasingly, but my reserves of gratitude were being plundered again by more incredible people. And for Nic to give up holiday to accompany me to Nepal (she'll say it would have been negligence to have let a man in my state go there without support) was taking things to another level. Doing what I love is motivation enough for these challenges I take up, but it is redoubled by the desire to create a business model by which I might one day pay my team a reliable income.

Nic set to work immediately. The trouble was, there was not much that could be done for now. Rehab was what I needed, and not just injury rehab but rehabilitation into everyday life. I needed to feed myself up and reintroduce myself to the concept of sleeping at night. There were injuries, too, mainly just wear and tear. I'd been in good shape when I left for Antarctica, but not good enough for what I was about to take on. I had serious soft-tissue damage to the psoas muscle (which is at the front of the pelvis) and hip flexors on my left-hand side and in the erector spinae muscles on the right. In short, my back was shot through. Nic couldn't understand why only one side was so affected.

It was my frost-nipped nose that accidentally revealed the answer to that mystery. Like everyone, she was intrigued by the mildly comic nature of the cold injury, which was most pronounced on the left of my nose. Why was that? Because the prevailing wind had been from the south-east, I told her. That was when she twigged. Not only had I been hauling an 80kg pulk uphill on skis for thirty-nine days, I must have been doing it while leaning into a south-easterly wind. I confirmed that this had been the case.

These were all weaknesses to be worked on later in the year. Of more immediate concern was this insane mountain-bike race I'd been entered for. Nic's assessment was that these injuries would normally require six-to-eight weeks of rest before training could resume. This was early February. I was leaving for Nepal in two and a half weeks. The race was starting in four. In my favour were my fitness and powers of recovery. Aerobically, few people on the planet could have put themselves through as much work as I had over the previous couple of months. And my nose gave me a boost on the recovery front. When Ian Williams, my vascular surgeon, removed the dressing, the tip of it came away with the bandages to reveal a nose beneath almost as good as new. I do seem to heal well. It's pretty much established now as clinical fact.

Bearing all this in mind, Nic was prepared to entertain the idea of this race in Nepal.

'I think I can get you there,' she said, 'but I have no idea how you're going to perform.'

She knew me from my rugby days, so she knew how competitive I could be about such things. I had to let go of any aspiration to do well in this race. This was just a part of the curve that led from the end of Antarctica last time to the start of Antarctica next.

'You have to see this race as part of your rehab,' Nic said. 'See it as a four-hundred-kilometre recovery session.'

We left for Nepal on 20 February 2013. My nerves were in a hell of a state. Throughout my life as a sportsman I have drawn almost all of my confidence from preparation. I was coming into this race on the back of none. Apart from the fact that this was the first bike race I'd ever entered, my training had amounted to a few sessions treading water in a hydrotherapy pool and a catastrophic outing in the Peaks on my spanking new Specialized road bike. Specialized provided me with a mountain bike for Nepal, too – it was so beautiful, I was happy just looking at it! I took the road bike out from Amy's house in Sheffield for a first and final test of my condition. After about an hour I stood up on the bike on Winnats Pass, and my back went into spasms. If the film crew hadn't been there, I'm not sure how I would have made it back home.

Back home? How was I going to make it through 400km in the Himalaya?

Meanwhile, some of the other riders I was meeting in Nepal had been clocking 800km a week. There is a strong community spirit among these racers, bound by the amount of work they put into their sport – then up I rock, a complete novice with no preparation. And, worse than that, I have a seven-man film crew in tow. It was embarrassing, to put it mildly.

But nothing compared to my performance. I remember the warm-up ride on 1 March, the first morning of the race – a 13km ride in 30°C heat from the hotel in Kathmandu, climbing 500m to the race's start in the Shivapuri National Park. If I have nothing else I do have the ability to dig deep, and I'm not weak, even if I was in a severely compromised condition off the back of Antarctica, but every single fibre of my body was screaming at me, 'What the fuck are you doing?' And that was just to get to the start line. I carried on smiling, but any show of confidence was a veneer across a vortex of doubt and pain.

The first day's ride was 42.5km, climbing 890m to Nawakot, along terrain of road, gravel and dirt. It was searingly hot, the temperature rising to 35°C. There were lots of fast and lethal sections in the first few stages. It's a game of 'chicken'. Hurtle round a bend in the middle of the road and it might be for the last time. These roads were narrow, sometimes with sheer drops to one side, but you shared them with oncoming vans, lorries and colourful buses overflowing with people. There's barely enough room to pass, even at snail's pace. Every one of us had close shaves throughout the ten-day race, every one of us had falls.

But, for all the fast sections, it was the climbs that dominated. Day one's biggest kicks in at around 30km. Bang! Five kilometres into it, I imploded. My back was in agony, my legs seizing up. I was already towards the back of the field, but I was forced to push my bike now. In the final kilometres, five other 'riders' passed me pushing theirs. I knew this was not meant to be about performance, but the sense of humiliation that racked me was instinctive and unavoidable. I limped past little rustic settlements, the beautiful locals, young and old, sitting serenely outside their homes. I couldn't help noticing, either, that, but for these bewildered spectators, a few competitors pushing their bikes faster than me and the odd yak, I was completely alone again. I was sick of it. No sooner had I returned from soloing across Antarctica than I was cycling and walking on my own at the back of this insane race. The occasional flyby of the film crew to capture my indignity did at least provide some relief on that front, but I can't say I enjoyed the idea of this being recorded for posterity. I had an HD camera and battery pack sitting on my head and another camera strapped to my handlebars. No matter what agony and distress I suffered, there was this dispassionate lens staring at me throughout. There was nowhere to hide. I felt so vulnerable.

I finished day one in thirtieth place, in a field of thirty-three. It was as if I'd been smashed over the head. As soon as we got inside the tea house I collapsed on the floor. I just wanted to get on the first plane home. Over to Nic. My pocket rocket, as I call her (she's not the biggest), set straight to work, kneading her elbow into parts of me she had no business reaching. The pain was indescribable. She could see I was in agony, physically and psychologically, tortured by my inability to do this race or myself justice. She kept telling me that just finishing a day was a victory for someone in my state. And then she would make way for the camera crew, who wanted to know how I felt.

Now, I'm a nice boy. My parents did a pretty good job with me. I don't like to be rude or negative. I knew that to reveal on camera the full extent of how I felt would have been to violate those principles, but for some reason it feels OK to do it in a book. Honestly, I felt like a cunt. I know I should have a vocabulary wide enough to avoid using a word like that, but I genuinely can't think of another that quite does the job. I'd returned from Antarctica at the end of my tether, and three weeks later I'd left my girlfriend, family and friends again to come out here to a part of the world I love as much as any, only to turn it into the most hideous, embarrassing, ill-advised experience from hell. And this wasn't even supposed to be my deprivation event.

I didn't use the C-bomb on camera, but I did try to explain the extent of my misery and despair that evening – and the evenings to come when the same routine would be acted out: rubbish (though gradually improving) performance in the day; pain, exhaustion and physio in the evening; interview to camera afterwards about how it's all making me feel.

Nic watched the latter with some concern. Her experience in high-performance sport is extensive. She is used to being able to call the shots when it comes to the recovery and handling of her athletes. She normally allows them to unload after an event, but the focus quickly shifts from that to buoying the psyche up after disappointment or pulling the ego back after triumph. Although sports psychology is not her specialism, it plays a key role in her line of work. She knew that endlessly poring over the trauma of the day just gone was not conducive to tackling the next in a positive frame of mind. I knew it from my own background in elite sport. Normally, an athlete wouldn't be so honest – or at least not at such length and so often. If you are constantly articulating how bad you feel, you are constantly reaffirming it as well. It's a basic tenet of sports psychology that in bad times you talk yourself up with positive affirmations, even if they belie the way you really feel, but that is not as good for television as a man racked with doubt and pain.

Channel 5 and Zigzag, the company producing the series,

wanted as much of the raw emotion as they could coax out of me. It was important that I cooperated. I wanted to. They had given me this opportunity to share my experiences. They had injected much-needed funds into the operation. Honesty was non-negotiable. Having a film crew follow me round for the next year was an inconvenience, of course it was, which shifted the dynamic significantly – and the need to carry equipment and film myself on my solo expedition to Antarctica for the fourth episode was even more than that – but it was a reality I had to deal with.

In my anguish, I might not have picked up on the subtler aspects of what was going on here, but Nic saw it immediately, which was invaluable. Not only was she on hand after each interview to try to talk me round into a more positive frame of mind, but she was ideally placed to identify the issue and help me develop a technique for dealing with it. Although there would be no film crew in Antarctica, I would be filming a video diary at the end of each day. On the Yak Attack, Nic saw first-hand how I ended up telling the camera how bad everything was; on my own, I could so easily slip from there into a downward spiral. It was essential that I learned to open up to camera, then close the door behind it and prepare for the next day.

As tough as the Yak Attack was to handle at the time, though, we derived so much from it. The agony was punctuated by some wonderful times. I don't need to go over again what the views in the Himalaya can do for the soul, and the camaraderie that developed between the racers was uplifting. The race itself is the most fantastic institution. It was set up in 2007 by a property developer called Phil Evans, who is passionate about mountain-biking in Nepal. Every western competitor subsidises one of the Nepalese entrants. The best of the Nepalese (and some really were among the most naturally gifted athletes I've ever had the privilege to compete with or against in any sport) go on to race professionally. The way they dance on the pedals while the rest of us labour and groan is astonishing. No westerner has ever won the Yak Attack. The race is nourishing a growing sport in Nepal. I'm so proud to have taken part in it.

It was a success for me, too, on many levels. I can see that now. If nothing else, it highlighted weaknesses in my physiology. My back and core muscles were exposed as needing serious attention once I was back on an even keel. They were already severely compromised by Antarctica, but my adductors really suffered, too, as I tried to control my bike on the uneven terrain. This was another vulnerability that could be shown up on a pair of cross-country skis in a sastrugi field. Having adopted a rehab strategy up to and throughout the Yak Attack, Nic and I started the transition into prehab after it – in other words, taking steps to ensure that next time Antarctica wouldn't do to me what it had the last.

There was no better environment than the Yak Attack for experimenting with recovery strategies. Sport Wales had bought some Firefly recovery devices for their athletes and asked me to test some. These are small electronic devices you attach to your lower legs. They emit electronic stimuli that cause muscular contraction, accelerating the flushing out of lactic acid from your muscles, thus aiding recovery and reducing delayed-onset muscle soreness (or DOMS, as it is known). I wore them at night under compression socks, which I was also asked to test. The current makes your toes twitch, so they're not often worn in bed, but I'll sleep through anything. The recovery protocols we tested that week were a resounding success and were incorporated into my strategy for Antarctica.

I grew stronger as the Yak Attack progressed. The agony never lifted, but that's the nature of the race. We were all suffering, hence the camaraderie that developed. It's just that some were doing it at higher speeds than others. I moved gradually through the field, partly as people dropped out, partly as the altitude increased and I grew stronger. Day nine was the most brutal day, the one everyone had been dreading. We had to carry our bikes up and over the Thorong La Pass – at 5416m one of the highest in the world. Normally, you can saddle up and ride on the other side once you climb down to 5000m. This year, the heavy snow meant we had to keep carrying on the way down for another three hours before we cleared the snowline and could actually start riding. In the end, we cycled a mere 16km to the end of the stage, having hauled our bikes up and over a pass in the deep snow for six hours-plus. After the dust and searing heat of the first three days and the gradual climb of the ones that followed, this was a shock to the system. One of the Australians, Steve Hammer, developed frostbite in his toe. We called him Aussie George Clooney on account of his looks. For some reason, Nic was especially quick to treat him. Sadly (and nothing to do with Nic's treatment, I might add), I believe they amputated the top of his toe back in Australia.

The Aussies took a bit of a pounding on those last stages. Another one, Aussie Pete, copped a serious blow on day ten, the last of the race. It was an accident waiting to happen. We had all suffered close shaves. Pete was lucky to escape this one alive. He'd careered round a corner, avoiding an oncoming lorry, but this one was carrying those rods they use to reinforce concrete. He got clotheslined by one of them, ripping his throat open and breaking his nose. Everybody who was behind him stopped and helped him off to hospital. Out of respect, we decided to ride to the finishing line together.

I finished the race twenty-third out of thirty-three. It was a stage race, so your finishing position was determined by the aggregate of your times. I'd done well to recover from the misery of the first three days. I was racing with others by the end, lifting the loneliness of the early stages. Those dancing Nepalese were still way ahead, but if the general trend was of riders tiring I was bucking it by becoming stronger. Had we not ridden in together on the last day, I think I could have made further inroads. I was the only rider to put on weight over the race, although I started from a low base. Half of the 16kg I'd lost in Antarctica had been restored by the time I reached the start line, and I added a further 5kg before the finish.

Most of all, though, I'd reinforced the confidence in my body's capacity to endure. The effort required to climb the big mountains is intense, but there are rest days interspersed throughout. The dynamic in a big Antarctic expedition is one of relentlessness. It had proved a little too much for me earlier in the year, but this kind of exercise in the Himalaya was further enhancing and underscoring my confidence. Anyone can run a marathon, or ski in Antarctica for eleven hours, or ride a bike through the Himalaya for six; it's getting up to do it day after day after day that is the real challenge. There are no short cuts to prepare for that. It can't be incorporated into a conventional training programme. You just have to keep exposing yourself to extreme situations. That's what the year's three races were for. I'd turned up to this first one in all sorts of trouble. Ideally, there would have been a couple more months between it and Antarctica. Then again, if I'd been stronger I might not have had to endure so much agony. As an exercise in forging mental resilience, it had been invaluable, despite the misery I'd been through. In fact, it had been invaluable precisely because of that.

11

It's fair to say my memory of the Yak Attack may be more negative than it should be. I do remember returning from it in quite a positive frame of mind – positive that I'd survived and grown stronger throughout. I certainly haven't overstated the depths I plumbed during it, but if I remember it less positively I suppose it's because I didn't fare as well as I feel I could have. I'm quite a good cyclist, and I hardly need to elaborate on my love for the mountains. It would be wonderful to give the Yak Attack another go some day.

I'm a better cyclist, at any rate, than I am a runner. And, if I love the mountains, I simply hate the jungle. This didn't bode well, then, for the next event in my year – the Jungle Ultra in Peru.

I returned from Nepal in much better shape than I'd returned from Antarctica. I had picked up injuries to my shoulder and neck from carrying a mini-cam and battery pack round on my head for ten days, but otherwise there was nothing significant to report beyond fatigue and the usual aches and pains. So, after a week's holiday in the Canary Islands with Amy at the end of March, I was ready to hit the ground running.

But not literally. Now we entered a calmer, more methodical period of planning and prioritisation. After Antarctica, Nic had been thrown a bag of bones at the last minute, with the instruction to help me through the highest mountain-bike race in the world. It was an exercise in damage limitation. Now, though, we could start to plot a strategy together. There was a delicate balance to tread. The ultimate goal was Project X in Antarctica at the end of the year, but along the way we had two more extreme events to negotiate. If we were smart, we could use them to enhance my preparation. What was absolutely vital was that they did not jeopardise Antarctica, or even detract from it. From Nic's point of view, both were events I could do without, particularly the Brutal, which was little more than a month before I left for the ice.

Like the Yak Attack, the timing of the Brutal was not ideal, it is true, but I was adamant that all three events had a role to play. As the deprivation event, hand-picked to make me as uncomfortable as possible, I wanted to run in the Jungle Ultra even less than Nic wanted me to, but for that reason alone it was a crucial part of my psychological training. And, although the terrain and conditions of the Amazon could not be further removed from Antarctica's, there are many crossovers when it comes to performance in a hostile environment.

The main problem with the Jungle Ultra was the need for

me to run. I carry many legacies from my days as a rugby player. None of them would be a problem if I led a normal life, but pushing my body as much as I do tends to stir them up. My knees, back and shoulders are constantly having to be managed on expedition. The concern for this event was how my Achilles tendons would hold up. I have mild tendinitis in both. They had not been a problem on the 737 Challenge, but after Antarctica and the Yak Attack they were starting to grumble. Running would surely trouble them even more. Not that I could be sure of that, because I'd never run further than a half-marathon. In Peru, I was going to have to run the distance of five and a half full marathons over five days through the twisting, turning, rising and falling Amazon jungle.

We just didn't know whether my Achilles tendons would hold up, so we took the decision to go gentle for now on the actual running and focus instead on my technique. It had been established that I was fit, which needed to be maintained rather than improved, with a view to peaking for Antarctica. What required attention was the efficiency of my form and posture.

This dovetailed with our broader strategy for the year. I was now entering the prehab phase of my training before Project X. We had seen how my body had been placed under strain the first time round; the aim for the rest of the year was, effectively, to improve its specification. I had to be more efficient in how I moved, and, linked to that, I had to be stronger. It was also important that I became heavier to help me haul my pulk in Antarctica and to act as a buffer against weight loss from the calorific deficit. But this was where the balance in our strategy became delicate. Extra weight would be of no help at all on the Jungle Ultra or the Brutal. Worse still, it might place my body under too much stress. The scenario that kept me awake at night was for injury in either of the next two events to put an end to Antarctica. More than that, though, I needed to return from both in a fit enough state to build on the momentum. I couldn't afford to lose any of that through having to rehab.

In this next segment before Peru, biomechanics was to be the focus. What we'd found in Nepal was that I didn't have the strength endurance to be able to shift down a gear on the climbs, which was a weakness relevant to (and exposed by) Antarctica. Nic devised some basic but specific exercises designed to work on my core stability, stimulating and managing the relevant neuromuscular pathways.

And so I spent much of the ensuing weeks, for example, with one foot on a wobble board and another attached to a TRX band suspended from the ceiling, practising single-leg lunges. The reps were minimal. As soon as my muscles were unable to maintain their stability, I stopped. With these exercises, if you train on bad form it's counterproductive. The key is to teach your muscles the right habits and build up their ability to repeat them, establishing and consolidating the neuromuscular memory. I progressed quickly, performing exercises like these two or three times a day. Nic put me through a few light running drills at this point, but overwhelmingly my training was static. Then, in the second half of my pre-Peru programme, we introduced some interval work.

Still we were keen to protect my Achilles tendons. Through my good friend Peter Thomas, the chairman of the Cardiff Blues Rugby, we were offered use of the Blues' anti-gravity treadmill. This is a treadmill with a waist-high sealed-air unit around it, which you zip yourself into. When compressed air is pumped into the chamber, it supports your bodyweight. The amount of support can be adjusted. It's an invaluable training tool for those recovering from injury, and it suited our needs perfectly. Through it I was able to build upon the biomechanical exercises without placing undue stress on my Achilles. I got through some really hard interval work on that machine. Meanwhile, my prehab exercises had advanced to the point where I was performing them with weights. The net effect was an increase in the precision and endurance of my core muscles. This had huge benefits for my running technique, which would apply equally to skiing in Antarctica. In short, I was starting to move less like an ex-rugby player and more like Mo Farah. Well, a bit more.

But I still hadn't run further than 20km. We were taking a gamble on how my body would cope with the stress of an ultra-marathon. It was a calculated gamble, though. Fitness wasn't an issue, and I had a good track record for digging deep when the situation demanded. One way or another, I was confident I would finish the race. The challenge was to minimise the damage. Nic's precision programme had given me the best chance of doing that, simply by increasing the efficiency of my biomechanics and my functional strength.

I was not in Peru to win this race, any more than I had been in Nepal to win the Yak Attack. I am no one's idea of a world-class runner, but my prospects of a decent finish were actually improved by the terrain, much though I hate the jungle. This was not going to be a fast race along neatly kept roads. We would be battling over inclines and drops, through mud, roots and rivers. Other skills, beyond those of the runner, would come into play, including the sort of expedition techniques that I was well practised in – managing systems, carrying loads, sleeping as and when you can.

It was a self-supported race, which meant no external assistance beyond the facilities provided by the organisers. Nic was not going to be able to accompany me on this one, as she had for the Yak Attack. This was a key step in my training, forcing me to put into practice my own recovery protocols each day. And anyway she was running out of annual leave. She did come with me to Peru mid-May, a week before the race began, so that we could do some filming and continue my preparation. The ancient cities of Cusco and Machu Picchu reverberated to the sound of my drills. Fair play: the Incas loved their steps. Nic had me running up and down them, honing my technique.

One day, in Cusco, the film crew announced that we'd been invited to eat guinea pig at a local farm. Guinea pig is a delicacy in South America. I'd tried it in Ecuador three years earlier, but that was at a market, where they sold it in strips, so I thought nothing of it. This time, however, they handed me Roland Rat on a stick – teeth, eyes, bones, everything. The camera was rolling, so there was no way out of it. Nic and I looked at each other, both thinking the same thing – a dodgy stomach was the last thing I needed. But this lovely Peruvian woman was standing there, smiling sweetly at me with a tray of fried guinea pigs in her hand. Offending her was not an option. Without further thought, I grabbed the nearest one, closed my eyes and bit into its back. I had my mouth round a sizeable chunk of guinea pig, but the skin wouldn't break. It stretched like an elastic band across the animal's back. For a moment I was stuck like this, my stomach turning, the cameras rolling. I wanted to back out, but everybody was watching. Conjuring up some primeval instinct from deep within me, I bit down harder and wrenched the guinea pig away, the skin snapping back against my hands. And that was it for me and food for the day. My appetite had gone.

If only that were to prove my last encounter with the animal life, or otherwise, of Peru. As the race-goers gathered, we were all subjected to the dangerous animal debrief. If you see this snake, make no sudden movements; if you approach to within x number of metres of this tree, you will be overcome by fire ants. That kind of thing.

I was more worried about the race. The nerves were building, now that we were all together. The next day I would have to run 38km (four shy of a marathon), twice as far as I ever had in my life. Once again, I felt awkward. As with the Yak Attack, the field (of twenty-six) was mixed, from the pros at the top, through high-quality amateurs, to those just hoping to finish. Nevertheless, no one enters a race like that without being deadly serious about their running. Here I was, again, without a single marathon to my name – and yet *with* a seven-man film crew. For all the talk of deadly animals, the only things on my mind at that first meeting were my Achilles and the fact I had a camera following me round.

I confess, at that stage I had mixed feelings about the television series. I never regretted that we were doing it – and the guys at Zigzag, the production company, were brilliant throughout that year, not only filming but embracing the spirit of each of the events – but there's no point pretending that it doesn't change the dynamic significantly. Once the race had started, the responsibility for filming became mine. Where this differed from the documentary for the 737 Challenge was in the equipment involved. We had signed a contract to film 80 per cent of the series in high definition, so instead of a hand-held camera a few hundred grams in weight I had to run this race with 3.8kg of equipment about my person, over and above the 11kg of survival gear we were all carrying in our rucksacks. I had a camera on my shoulder throughout, a sound pack and a long-life battery pack, and another camera on my wrist or head, according to the producer's wishes. For some of it, I had to run with this ridiculous camera stretching out to one side of me from a bracket, which kept catching on the trees.

But it was a relief just to get underway. I had been so nervous as we waited, all the more so when Nic said goodbye before the start. She and I had put so much work into my preparation. Now was the moment of reckoning. Would the gamble pay off?

The Jungle Ultra begins 3200m up in the cloud forest of Peru. The first half of the first day takes in 12km of steep climbs and descents, the second a long, torturous jeep trail. Unlike on the Yak Attack, I was in good shape for this and fell in with a group of runners of similar pace. Not that there was a huge amount of running as you and I would know it. Negotiated fresh, that first half of the day was a lot of fun, scrambling up and over, down and through the steamy forest, but it softened up the knees and quads, turning the second half into a long trial of agony. The jeep track was 24km of mud that seemed never-ending. Sometimes it's easier to run on an incline than it is a down slope, and this gradual descent was an example, its gradient just steep enough to throw you off balance. Together with the uneven surface, it was impossible to establish any rhythm. Every bend was the equivalent of the mountaineer's false summit, straightening up to reveal yet more purgatory ahead.

A little more than five and a half hours after we'd started, I made it to the first day's finishing line, full of the usual aches and pains, but, crucially, in one piece. This was the furthest I'd ever run – not quite a marathon, distance-wise, but when you factor in the uneven terrain of the cloud forest at least as much hard work.

The river was the closest thing I had to an ice bath, so I plunged in it. Then it was a case of stretching, feeding, hydrating, filming, Fireflies, compression socks, hammock and sleep. I was in my element at this point. Part of the deprivation for the others was the lack of sleep. A hammock between two trees is not everyone's idea of a four-poster, particularly when those trees and all the others are alive with the sounds of Amazonia – birds, insects, river and the loud, thieving monkeys. But I am well practised in the art of sleeping anywhere, and stringing up a hammock is a lot easier than pitching a tent. I slept like a baby throughout. Indeed, sleeping with my legs raised assisted the recovery process. I was sore the next day, of course, but nowhere near as much as I'd thought I would be.

Day two, though, was when the race dipped into the jungle for the first time, my idea of hell −38°C in the shade, 100 per cent humidity and alive, everything alive. I ran on my own for much of the second day, feeling stronger and stronger, but also feeling constantly as if I was not alone, which I wasn't. Animals are all around. You can hear big things bounding through the vegetation. Stop for a moment, and within seconds your feet are swarming with ants; rest your hand on a tree, and its bugs soon welcome you as part of it. It's an incentive, at least, to keep moving. Not helping on that front, though, is the ground beneath your feet, sometimes thick with mud, sometimes treacherously slippery. I twisted my knee on day two, then suffered an attack of diarrhoea about 10km from the finish line. But after five hours I'd made it through another 34km.

Day three was a mere 33km, but the mud and heat were relentless. As were the river crossings. These were a feature of the race throughout, but the third stage – named Logging, after the trucks whose wheels had churned this path through the jungle – involved countless traverses of the Rio Tono, sometimes by boat, sometimes by zip wire, mostly by wading through rushing water. Locals were detailed to wade across with each of us for support, not that many of them were big enough to stop me if I'd slipped and caught a rapid. Dangerous though some of the crossings were, they were welcome opportunities to cool down and wash the mud away, before the next coating.

What they weren't so good for was the chafing, which was horrific. And, bizarrely in my case (you won't want to know this), not in the usual place, but on my perineum – in other words, just behind my bollocks. That night, I peeled off my compression shorts with extra care. My condition had been building up over the previous three days. In such humidity, it is very difficult to dry your kit out. Because you're carrying everything, you take minimal equipment. I had one dry set of gear, which I wore in the evenings, and one for racing in, which never became drier than damp. And I chose not to carry a towel in order to save weight. By the end of stage three my chafing was really angry, agonisingly so. It's an insane place to be when agony like that actually helps by drawing attention from the pain coursing throughout the rest of you – my twisted left knee wasn't getting a look-in. That night, I talced up, as always (I carried rations of talcum powder in sealed bags), and put on my dry shorts. Next morning, the shorts had become one with my nuts. What should I do? Keep this pair on or put on my race shorts? If I stayed in these, I would then have two wet pairs and nothing dry to sleep in. And wet gear is heavier to carry. But if I removed these shorts ...

I removed the shorts. Away they came, pulling with them the scab that had formed overnight, revealing livid, festering, raw flesh that would take another two weeks to heal once I'd returned to the UK. The threat of infection is everywhere in the jungle, so the medics put me on antibiotics, just in case. Not that it did anything for the pain, which was unspeakable. There is no choice. You must run on. And after a while, about half an hour in my case, it becomes so great that it sort of numbs itself. Or becomes normal. I'm not sure which.

There were only two more stages to go, but we weren't even at the halfway mark, kilometre-wise. The fifth and final day is called the Long One, which it is, at 92km – more than two marathons. It is some testament, however, to the fourth that the Long One is not even considered the hardest. That honour goes to stage four, which is called, evocatively, the Lull. It is only 33km, but it runs through the densest, steepest sections of the jungle. In fact, there's not a lot of running at all. At times, it's more of a scramble on all fours, up and down banks, thick with vegetation and life. The terrain seemed more alive than ever in this section. And when you weren't scrambling on banks, you were wading through mud. In 40°C heat and 100 per cent humidity. It was the toughest stage of the race, all right.

That was the day my left knee reclaimed the limelight as the most agonising part of my body. It had never had a chance to recover from when I twisted it on day two. There would be periods in the Lull when it was fine, but then, as I was scrambling down a steep slope, it would suddenly lock up, as if to bend it would be to snap it. To a passer-by – and there were a couple of Danes who did pass me in that section – it looked as if I had no chance of finishing. I am told they were preparing a rescue party for me. But somehow I ran through it and arrived at the next checkpoint before my rescuers had had a chance to set off. From there, I ran the rest of that stage with a top guy from Yorkshire called Mark Roberts, who I'd finished stage one with. We completed the Lull in eight hours eight minutes.

Now it was my feet that needed attention. Blisters are a common affliction on any endurance event, be it skiing in the Antarctic or climbing a mountain. I'd managed to avoid them so far. All the runners had their feet dressed well by the medics, who were excellent. But now I had blood blisters beneath three of my toenails from all the down-scrambling and the banging of my toes against my shoes. In camp, Brett the doc drilled holes in my nails. It sounds unpleasant, but it doesn't hurt, other than for the split second the drill bit breaks through. Then the pain gives way to pure relief as the blood drains off and the pressure eases.

People were starting to drop out now. Three had withdrawn after the third stage, and the Lull claimed three more. A seventh, one of the pros, was forced to pull out at the start of the Long One because of an injury she'd been struggling with all race.

This was where it really started to matter to me. The longer I lasted in the race, the more invaluable the training. There is no other way to replicate the kind of mental and physical challenges you will face on an extreme endurance test than to go through them for real. Here I was, having covered 138km in four days, with the prospect of another ninety-two to come. No lab or chamber can recreate the suffering and deprivation you must endure to reach that point, no matter how hard you flog yourself. It's very rare that you have the opportunity to be in this sort of situation. I see it as opening doors to new rooms inside yourself. Normally, when you have to enter those rooms there is peril involved, whether it be pushing for a summit or pushing for the South Pole. To be able to go there in a training environment is a very rare and special opportunity. It's the reason I was there. This last 92km was what had stood out about the Jungle Ultra. After four marathons in four days, another marathon wouldn't have provided enough of an edge to the challenge. It had to be this. I wanted my body – and, just as importantly, my mind – to face the prospect of another stage of more than two marathons in length, while already racked, hungry and exhausted. It's the only way to discover how your body and mind respond and to develop the resilience required to perform in those situations.

I was ready and amped for that last stage.

Every night it poured with rain, and the night before the Long One was no exception. Luckily, I find the sound of rain hammering on tarpaulin comforting, so I got away with a good few hours' sleep every night. On this last night, the rain was so heavy that some of the others had to take refuge in a sort of shed near the camp.

Because of the rains, our 6 a.m. start was delayed twenty minutes. I ran with Mark for the first few hours along reasonably comfortable terrain (relative to the day before), interspersed with many river crossings, including one in a basket along a 200m stretch of zip wire. Another section of the route had us wading for a few kilometres in river that was waist-deep in places. Mark twisted his knee in the water and was having real problems with his feet. He was forced to retire at the next checkpoint, which meant that after four hours I was on my own again.

To be pushing myself alone like this was perfect training for Antarctica. I tend to enter a sort of dual-speed consciousness in such situations. On one level I am aware of the pain coursing throughout my body with hotspots on this particular day centring round my left knee and both feet. I think of home and I want to get back there. But on the other level I am in lockdown, focused and relentless. I love it, not that you would find me saying so in the moment. But, as I always say, it doesn't have to be fun to be fun.

At about 5.30, after eleven hours, night started to fall, and

I was on the edge of the next stretch through the jungle. Checkpoint 4 was a couple of kilometres behind me, the next about fifteen ahead. The course was marked with red flags, which were never more than a couple of hundred metres apart. Navigation had been straightforward throughout the race, but a red flag a hundred metres away in the dark is not easy to find. And the darkness in the Amazon rainforest is as total as you may imagine.

I stopped on the edge of the jungle to eat and drink and put on my head torch. A head torch, mind you, is a mixed blessing in the jungle at night. It attracts a bombardment of animals, most of them small and on the wing. So, despite the sweltering heat, I donned my waterproofs, tucking in my trousers and zipping up my hood tight around my face. That helps to keep the bugs out of clothing and ears, but the face is still being bombarded with them. It pays to run with your mouth closed as much as possible. Even so, animals will end up bouncing around in there from time to time. It's important to spit, not swallow.

I might not have been able to see much but I could still hear everything with clarity. That feeling I was not alone was heightened in the dark. I could hear creatures crashing through the undergrowth alongside me – they might have been ox, they might have been pigs. They might have been jaguars. My field of vision was restricted to the single beam of light from my torch. In it, I could see other lights from the jungle wildlife, some flying round, some stationary and watching. Occasionally, something substantial would run or fly across that narrow tunnel of vision. In daylight you thought nothing of an animal crossing your path; at night, each appearance suddenly became a split-second shock to the system. It played havoc with my senses. The simple terror of darkness. This was like the pitch-black I saw to my left in the crevasse on Denali, only now it was all around. For all the big things you'd think you might fear in extreme environments, like death and frost-bite, nothing quite touches the primeval nerve as surely as darkness. It renders the mind irrational. I kept expecting to see a person materialise in the beam of my head torch, as in a horror film. Maybe it's the movies that are to blame.

Navigating was the main problem now. Not only were the red flags difficult to see, but some of them had been removed by the locals in search of souvenirs. If I couldn't find a flag, I would return to the previous one and fan out again until I found the next. It slowed my pace to a painstaking crawl.

The final blow struck at about 7 p.m., when the mother of all thunderstorms broke out. The noise was incredible. My insides rattled with every crack and boom. It was right on top of me. I had reached a section of the race, where the course zigzagged back and forth across a river. If the dark had been unnerving, now I had the opposite problem, with Mother Nature switching on and off the lights. The entire river would suddenly appear in a flash of lightning, then hide again in the dark. They weren't blink-of-the-eye flashes either, but charges of electricity that sparked up and grew among the clouds for what seemed like seconds on end. And the rain ... the word torrential doesn't do it justice. Big, fat balls of water ham-mered out of the skies. My head torch became useless. Its light just bounced back into my face off this curtain of water.

The river crossings had become treacherous. It was pretty much impossible to follow the route now. A lot of the crossings were not perpendicular, so the flag on the other side could be straight ahead or it could be a hundred metres downriver. We had no maps or GPS systems for this race, but I'd studied the route before each stage. I knew this zigzagging section led to the next checkpoint, which sat on the riverbank. My only realistic option of finding that checkpoint was to wade directly down the river. The waters were rising noticeably. Within an hour, they had grown from ankle-deep to knee-deep. The slippery rocks on the riverbed had been a feature throughout the race, injury posing a threat at the best of times. Now I was tired after 60km and thirteen hours or so on the fifth day. And it was dark. Slip and bang your head here – you'd be gone. It was a genuinely dangerous environment. Exactly what I needed, in fact. It was one of the most exhilarating experiences of my life, to be alone in survival mode deep in the Amazon.

Unbeknown to me, I was the last runner still out there. The four behind me had been found in the jungle by a search party and the one still running ahead had been stopped at Checkpoint 5. The locals were worried because the river was rising so fast. The race director, Wes Crutcher, had suspended the race because of the dangerous conditions. Checkpoint 5, which was an overnight camp, had been relocated to higher ground.

At 9 p.m., after a couple of hours wading 5km down the river, and nearly fifteen hours after we'd set off, I saw some lights to my right. They could have been fireflies, they could have been my mind playing tricks, but I headed towards them. It turned out they were head torches. I had reached Checkpoint 5. The race officials were pleased to see me because it meant we were all accounted for. One of the other runners, Kerry Reed, was also there. The waters were too high now even for the massive logging truck that had been sent out to the checkpoint, so we sheltered in a tent for the night, four of us sleeping on top of each other in our soaking wet gear.

The rain had stopped when we woke the next morning, but the devastation had to be seen to be believed. The geography of the riverbank had completely changed. New channels had been cut; trees and bamboo lay broken all around.

For those of us still to finish the race, a new start time was put forward for 9 a.m., while Wes and his team performed safety checks along the river. There were 27km left from Checkpoint 5. Kerry and I were ready to go. She is a very strong runner, who has run the Marathon des Sables (not as tough apparently). We were both set on finishing. Then, just before we were about to head off, the rains came again. With the forecast for more, Wes decided to abandon the race.

It was the right decision, of course, but I was gutted not to be able to finish. I had felt stronger each day and never more so than on the last. The six of us whose race had been ended by the weather were classified as finishers. I came thirteenth out of the twenty-six runners who'd started, which I was pretty pleased with, considering I'd never run a marathon before. The irony is that this, my deprivation event, the one hand-picked to make life as miserable for me as possible, ended up being the one I enjoyed the most. In retrospect, the Yak Attack was the real deprivation event, if we measure deprivation by the levels of misery that had to be endured. I was in much better shape for the Jungle Ultra, and although my running is weaker than my cycling I took so much from the way I grew stronger as the race wore on. What's more, for all the pain and discomfort I suffered, my Achilles had not caused any problems.

The expectations I have of my body are constantly evolving, and this was the consolidation of a new level. I know now that I can run four marathons in four days in hostile conditions and then on the fifth go for, well, it was 60km in the end, but I have no doubt I would have finished the ninety-two. It all represented new territory, new rooms inside myself. Once you have been to them, you get to keep the key, which means you can go back. And from there, who knows, maybe venture a little further again.

12

This was an important time in my preparation. I was back in the UK in early June, which gave me nearly five months before I left for Antarctica and nearly four until the next planned event, the Brutal at the end of September. Nic and I had identified this as the longest period that I had between events and the only one suitable for an adaptation phase before Antarctica. It was time to get stronger and heavier.

Our three-phase programme was entering its final stage. The first two had gone as well as could be hoped. Rehab had been painful, but my recovery from Antarctica last time was more or less complete by the end of the Yak Attack. From there we had addressed the core imbalances of my body, recalibrating my biomechanics, so that everything moved as efficiently as possible. The Jungle Ultra might not have felt very efficient at times, but for a 93kg former rugby player to have run five marathons in five days on that kind of terrain, remaining injury-free, was a testament to just how well Nic and I had fine-tuned the moving parts of my body. I returned from it on a high, full of confidence, ready to launch into the third phase of my training, which was, essentially, to increase my horsepower.

The trouble – or challenge, depending on how you looked at it – was this double ironman that loomed as a big, fat obstacle a month before departure. Nic knew I had to do it, but it went against every principle by which she's led her incredibly successful career. She's been to five Olympic Games with Team GB, seven Commonwealth Games with Team Wales. She was chief physio for Team GB at the Beijing Olympics. She has honorary fellowships and life memberships all over the place. There aren't many more respected physios in the world, let alone Britain. (She'll be blushing if she ever reads this!) At no turn in her career would she ever have condoned something like a double ironman for one of her athletes a few weeks before the main event.

For those unaware, an ironman triathlon is a tough event, more than four times the length of an Olympic triathlon. You swim for 3.9km (the distance of a forty-five-minute walk), then cycle 180km (a couple of hours in a car on the motorway). And then you run a marathon. For a *double* ironman, it's ... well, what it says on the tin. Except the Brutal, for some reason, has an even longer bike leg (187km for the ironman contestants, 374 for the double).

If I picked up a significant injury during this, there would be no time for recovery before Antarctica, and the risk of that was high. At best, Project X would be compromised; at worst it would have to be abandoned. The entire year's work would have been for nothing. And, regardless of that, a double-ironman triathlon is not an entry-level event. Even if I'd competed in a triathlon of any kind (which I hadn't), it would take months of specific training to bring me up to speed. The programme I was on for Antarctica was not compatible with that. And the extra weight I would be putting on was an out and out disaster for a race of that length. Another consideration was the fact I was going to have to train for a new skill altogether. I'm a good swimmer by everyday standards, but swimming for nearly five miles is not a thing to try without a concerted training programme. Would I even have time to fit it in among the rest of the work I was being put through?

I understood all of Nic's points, and I agreed. Of course, what she said was spot-on. You'd never catch Bradley Wiggins or Mo Farah or any high-performance athlete risking themselves in an alien event as brutal as this so soon before departure. But where my next challenge differed from the disciplines Nic specialised in was in the lawlessness of it. There's an element of simple savagery to what I was going to be attempting in Antarctica that does not apply to the clinical world of high-performance sport. Even with the Tour de France, which to my mind is the most incredible sporting event in the world, the daily calorific output of an athlete on a big mountain stage would be roughly equivalent, I guess, to what mine would be in Antarctica (around 9000 calories), but they are surrounded by support teams and medics and just human beings in general. Where I was going there would be nothing. I would have to be self-sufficient. I was attempting the longest solo, unassisted and unsupported expedition in history. There were no rules, no established practice. I knew that from a clinical point of view competing in a double ironman without any experience in the sport was an insane undertaking so close to Antarctica, but the purpose of the Brutal for me was simple: to find out where my empty was. Not my uncomfortable, not my painful, not my wits' end, but empty, nothing left, pure and simple. The last room inside myself.

In the end, it was the Tour de France that imposed upon me a solution to the swimming conundrum. Nic had lined up a swim coach to start work with me in July. Before that, Amy and I hired a campervan and spent a couple of weeks training, while following the Tour. It was one of the best holidays of my life. If I won the lottery, the first thing I'd do is buy a campervan. In the second week, though, we were cycling the seventeenth stage of that year's Tour – between Embrun and Chorges in the Hautes Alpes – when I came off my bike and fractured my left hand in two places.

It was a timely reminder of what could go wrong on the Brutal. An injury like this in late September would put an end to any expedition in Antarctica. Fortunately, we were now in mid-July, so there was just enough time for it to heal, but it meant cancelling my swim sessions. Nic put her foot down. I wasn't going to be able to do any swimming until about a month before the race. If I'd been an experienced swimmer it might have been OK, but the swim for the Brutal was in the icy waters of Lake Padarn in Snowdonia. For a novice open-water swimmer to launch into a five-mile swim in that on the back of next to no training would be foolish, full stop, let alone with another 455km to bike and run straight after it and an expedition to Antarctica a few weeks after that. And, as Nic reasonably pointed out, at least on a run if you're struggling you can walk. In a lake that option is not available.

The sportsman in me bridled at her insistence that I pull out of the swim section. As a young man I would probably have refused to accept it, but a gung-ho attitude only gets you so far in the wilderness. Unless you're happy never coming back, the ability to make informed, rational decisions is one of the most important assets in your armoury. It's the difference between pushing the boundaries of human performance and striding out to certain death. I have acquired that mindset now. My life was never going to be in serious danger if I swam in the Brutal, but the chances of its compromising what I was hoping to take away from the rest of the race, not to mention what I had planned in the weeks after it, were now sufficiently high for me to accept what Nic was saying. It was time to overrule the defiant chest-beater in me and pull out of the swim. I didn't like it, and neither, understandably, did Channel 5. But episode four of our series was more important than episode three, even to them – overwhelmingly so to me. And I was pretty sure that watching me try to cycle and run 455km would provide plenty in the way of good television.

So my training continued in the gym for strength work and on the roads for fitness. My strength was increasing exponentially. What had started after Nepal as standing on one leg on the floor had now evolved to single-leg squats on a wobble board and TRX band hugging 50kg to my chest. I was dead-lifting more than I had as a 107kg rugby player. And then there was The Sled. At the Sport Wales High Performance Unit in Cardiff, they have this metal sled, which you load up with weights and drag along a carpet. Sprinters use them, for example, to develop strength endurance and a good sprint position. They'll haul it for 25m then stop, 25 then stop, completing maybe ten reps. My task was to pull it non-stop back and forth along this 25m stretch of carpet for an hour. It became my weekly progress marker and it was absolutely brutal. We started off with 100kg on the sled, but by the time I left for Antarctica I was pulling 180kg. I used the same harness as I was going to use out there. The idea was to mimic the activity but with a heavier sled and much higher friction on the carpet than there would be on snow. Nic oversaw the first few sessions and tells me I was completing fifty-plus circuits (there and back) in my hour, but then I started to do them on my own with no encouragement bar that from whatever music they might have playing in the gym. Physically, it was horrific – by the end of some sessions I was on all fours dragging this bloody thing, throwing up – and psychologically it was mind-numbingly tedious.

Perfect training, then, for Antarctica.

If training for Antarctica was going well, logistics had hit up against a serious problem. The place I had planned to start my expedition from in Antarctica fell outside the operating permit of ALE, my logistics provider. If I wanted to set off from there, I would have to apply to the Foreign and Commonwealth Office's Polar Regions Department for a permit of my own. ALE would help to grease the wheels, but the application was unlikely to go through in the timeframe required.

The obvious solution was to wait another year to make sure all the pieces were in place, but we needed a finale to the television series. Besides, the idea of delaying the expedition for another year after all the work I'd put in was unbearable.

So it was put to me that I attempt Christian Eide's record of twenty-four days for the fastest solo, unassisted and unsupported coast-to-pole journey in Antarctica. I knew the route. It did make a lot of sense.

But it wasn't what I'd been referring to publicly as Project X, the details of which I had kept under wraps, other than to say that it would be a world first. So we announced that Project X would be a two-part endeavour, attempting the longest and the fastest solo, unassisted and unsupported expeditions, with the first leg, the fastest, to be attempted that December.

Changing the objectives of my expedition so close to D-Day, after over a year of preparation, was tough, but it also took me a while to come to terms with the idea of attempting Christian's record at all. It's a weird feeling. Normally, a sportsman is champing at the bit to compete against others. I'm no different. But the dynamic changes somehow when the field of play is set in the most remote corner of the planet. I was there when Christian broke the record in 2011, as excited and amazed as anyone at Union Glacier as we charted his progress. Trying to break it seemed a bit vulgar for some reason. Maybe it was to do with the fact that I know the guy – indeed, I was to go out and see him in Norway later in the year. ('Hi, Christian, let me buy you a drink. I'm trying to break your record ...')

I was offered another alternative – to try to break the record from Berkner Island. That has a slightly longer route – around 1300km – but a much more forgiving target of fifty days. But this is where the defiant sportsman reared up. Attempting it from Berkner Island would have been a cop-out. No sprinter earns the respect of his peers by setting out to break the 120m world record. They take on Usain Bolt and the 100m.

It wasn't long before I got my head round the speed-record idea. It was a huge challenge. Self-filming would be much harder on this than it would have been on the length record. But I was in the shape of my life. Christian Eide is a much better skier than I am; I am stronger than he is. I was amped about it! And, anyway, I had unfinished business with the Hercules Inlet–South Pole route. Last January I'd run out of time, but I was battling some of the worst conditions they had ever seen out there and I was on a research and development expedition. I had aborted at thirty-eight days and only 200km short of the finishing line of a 1140km course. This time the game was on. To beat Christian's record I would have to transform my performance. Not a problem: I'd spent six months working towards just that. Already, I was a very different animal from the one a year ago.

Before I could take on Christian's record, though, I had to take on that special breed of person that is the extreme triathlete. Any triathlete at all has my utmost respect. I can't speak highly enough of the Brownlee brothers, whose performance at London 2012 was, I thought, a masterclass in athleticism and tactics. As for the thousands of amateurs who fit in the training requirements for three disciplines around busy lives, I think they're incredible. Those who do so for something like an ironman, I don't know how they manage it. A *double* ironman – words fail me. I didn't even realise there was such a thing! I'm a very fit man. I might not conform to Nature's prototype for the perfect cyclist or runner, but I can cycle and run, and cycle and run well. As we shall now see, I lined up in Snowdonia with sixteen other contestants for a double iron-man on 21 September 2013. I sat out the swim. And the 455km that followed took me to a place I'd never been before. The very edge.

It was exactly what I wanted. Of the three races I entered that year, the Brutal was by far the most valuable. The others helped me practise what it is to stretch myself day after day; this one showed me where breaking point is. Or maybe it didn't, because ultimately I didn't break, and that very fact turned it into the most powerful and influential experience. I learned new lessons about what could be endured.

I remember the other contestants taking to the icy water at 7 a.m. There were three races running concurrently – a half-ironman, a full ironman and ours, a double ironman. That meant 136 contestants taking to the water. Sorry, 135. There was one guy with a film crew following him, this time around a dozen-strong, who brandished a sick note excusing him from the swim.

I'd always known that this was going to be a difficult moment, and it didn't disappoint. I felt such a dick. If only it had been a moment. Actually, I had to stand there like a lemon for four hours before I was allowed on my bike. I know none of the other contestants would have even noticed – they had far bigger things to worry about – but the organisers were obviously unimpressed. And the HD cameras kept rolling. I breathed deeply and repeated to myself, 'this is a training event this is a training event', but really I was like a caged animal during those four hours.

The organisers had told me I could set off on the bike at 11 a.m., the first cut-off time. Triathlons have cut-off times at the end of each discipline. If you don't meet them you have to stop. For the double ironman that day, anyone not out of the water after four hours would have to retire, likewise anyone still on their bike twenty-six hours after the start of the race. By 1 a.m. on Monday morning, forty-two hours after the start, the race would be officially over, no matter who might still be out there running.

Come 11 a.m., I was finally allowed on to my bike. One guy from the double-ironman race had been pulled from the lake with cramp. Otherwise the fifteenth and last contestant had emerged from the water around a quarter of an hour earlier. My pride wounded, my frustration acute, my legs more powerful than they'd ever been and my new bike lighter than any I'd ever known, I set off like a rocket. Couldn't help it. Long-distance triathlons are all about pacing. I thought I was pacing myself, but I was way off. The bike leg was 374km, eight laps of 47km, including the nasty climb to Pen-y-Pass, more than 300 vertical metres. I miscalculated badly and covered the first lap in an hour and forty minutes, reaching speeds of 70km/h, overtaking cars. I have heard ironman triathletes use the analogy of a box of matches. We have a finite number for the whole race and must burn them wisely. I reckon I went through a fistful of matches on that first lap. Nic was waving at me to slow down, but I just felt so good, and I guess I had a point to prove after missing out on the swim.

Every athlete in the double ironman had to bring their own support team. I had wanted to race without one, to try to simulate the dynamic in Antarctica, but that had been another example of my naivety. There's no substitute in these races for experience. Fortunately, the organisers knew better and insisted that a support team for anyone racing the double iron-man was compulsory. It turned out I needed one.

Team Parks – Mum, Dad, Amy and Nic – set up camp out-side the Saracen's Head Hotel in Beddgelert, about halfway round the loop. On lap three, five hours or so into the bike leg, I was starting to struggle. It was still a laughing matter, but when I took my first pit stop by the car it dawned on me that, with 120km completed and another 335 to go, I was in trouble. This was shaping up to be the test I'd wanted all right.

Night started to fall towards the end of lap four, and the wind picked up. Amy offered to cycle lap six with me, an offer I gratefully accepted. But she tells me I was zoning out by that stage. She didn't get a lot out of me. Most of what I can tell you from this period I know from what others have told me and from the camera footage. I see, for example, that I passed out for twenty minutes in the back of the car at around 5 a.m., between laps seven and eight. Can't remember it. I look as if I'm drunk.

I finished the final lap of the bike at 8.15 a.m., forty-five minutes before the cut-off time. It left me with sixteen hours forty-five minutes to complete the double marathon. With the sun up, I felt a degree of composure return. My next task was to run up and down the 7.5km track to the top of Snowdon, 1000m above me. Then it was eight laps of Lake Padarn at 8.2km a pop.

I reached the top of Snowdon at around 11 a.m., twenty-four hours after I'd set out on my bike. Twenty-four-hour climbs are nothing new to me, and I've performed them at higher altitude than Snowdonia, but this was way out of my comfort zone. I'm an extreme-environment athlete, not a cyclist or a runner. And the requirements of the filming ...

It was on that race that I reached my lowest point with the cameras. A few weeks before the Brutal, I'd started working with a psychologist at Sport Wales called Cath Shearer. After Nic's heads up about it in Nepal, Cath and I had been working on how I dealt with the cameras. It was a love-hate relationship I had with them, which was troubling me. Jonny McWilliams and I had worked very hard to secure the series, and I was massively committed to it, but on an operational level it hindered everything I was trying to do.

On the way down from Snowdon, for example, they wanted to film footage from the helicopter they'd hired for the day. I had to repeat the same 200m section on the mountain four or five times until they'd got what they wanted. I was basically performing shuttle runs up and down Snowdon after twenty-four hours of exercise. In the transition zone at the end of every bike lap, we were spending five to ten minutes changing cameras and battery packs. The infrared camera equipment I carried on the bike at night actually weighed more than the bike itself.

But another invaluable benefit of the Brutal was that I finally came to terms with the responsibility of filming. Cath had tried to change the way I looked at what lay ahead in Antarctica. The challenge was not to try to break a record and film it; it was to film myself trying to break a record. It was a subtle shift but absolutely vital if I was to avoid letting the camera get me down. She encouraged me to incorporate the camera into my everyday life. If I was ever running late (a commonplace in my world), I had to make myself stop for five minutes and do some filming. The filming and the record attempt were one and the same thing, each as important as the other. It was a reality I had to deal with. After the Brutal, I finally stopped fighting it.

The film crew themselves were always brilliant. The series producer was Dale Templar, who became a really good friend, as did the cameraman, Rob Taylor. They came out to the Jungle Ultra and both would come to Antarctica. In Peru, another of the camera crew, Mark, had a nightmare waiting for me to pass at various points along the route with creatures crawling all over him! They were all here for the Brutal, too. Dale, Rob and Mark ran a lap of the lake with me, as did Amy. Yes, I really did need that support – and I got it.

Not so much of it from the race organisers, though. No one thought I was going to finish. At 2 p.m., eleven hours away from the final cut-off time, they were mumbling about calling me in. The winner of the race had finished by then. He was pretty unimpressed. The triathlon community – and particularly the ironman community – are very tight-knit. They are superb athletes and hugely dedicated to their training. I am to mine, too, but this was not my event. I do understand why there might have been grumbling about my using it as part of my own programme. If only I could have been so reasonable at the time, but after twenty-seven hours of exercise, punch drunk with fatigue, it's not easy when an administrator with a clipboard, or an elite triathlete who's just finished the race you're barely two-thirds of the way through, starts pronouncing on your performance. It's a sure way to stir up the defiance in a man.

But I needed more than just defiance now. By the end of lap three of the lake, we were worried about my feet. I had sharp pain in the fifth metatarsal area of both. If it was a bone injury, I had to stop. Nic pulled me in to examine them. She set up an impromptu surgery on the stone wall alongside the path and satisfied herself that there was no bone damage. After a bit of strategic taping I was back on my feet again. Nic the physio had done her bit again, but she was proving to be so much more than just a physio.

She had noticed that about three-quarters of the way through the Yak Attack I had started to wobble mentally, by which I mean losing sight of what I was there to do and letting thoughts of home and loved ones affect my performance. Here I was again, three-quarters of the way through, and I was starting to bargain with myself. Just finish the first marathon, I was thinking. That would be respectable; thirty hours of exercise is a lot in anyone's book. You came here to find out where empty was. You've found it. Let's call it a day after lap four.

Nic had seen how I was losing momentum in the transition zone between laps, with Amy and Mum and Dad around, offering encouragement and generally being lovely. Oh, go on then, let's just stop here awhile ...

So Nic had set up shop a kilometre shy of the transition zone. That patch-up on the stone wall was not quite as impromptu as it had seemed to me. It was part of her calculated plan to keep me going. She gave instructions to Rob and Dale to keep me moving through the transition zone.

How blessed was I to have someone with that level of intuition in my corner! As my physio with the big game still to come, she wanted me to stop this thing. She'd never wanted me to start in the first place. But she understood what the purpose of this event was for me, even after I, in my exhausted delirium, had started to lose track of it myself. The foot was fine structurally, so it was safe for me to continue. Though it may have violated every principle she had worked to in her life, she recognised the psychological value that finishing this race would yield – and the damage it could inflict if I didn't make it to the end.

I'll tell you where I was, meanwhile. I'd entered what I assumed to be that final room inside myself. As discussed elsewhere, an endurance athlete's operational existence is largely a dialogue between body and mind, the latter overruling the protestations of the former, insisting that more can be endured, no matter what the pain may say, that there is always another room to reach, deeper within.

Until that Sunday afternoon, my mind had always won out, but now even it was accepting that the farthest point of navigation had been reached. If I hadn't had my support team with me, I would have pulled out. And I would have thought that there, where I found myself that day at around thirty hours and 400km, marked my empty.

I would have been wrong. After my mind had accepted the end was nigh, it was my family and friends who took over. Their emotional support and their mere presence showed me the way to new rooms within myself. They would not be with me in Antarctica, but with their help I was discovering now that these rooms were there. My mind was keeping notes. Next time, it would know. This state I was in did not mark the end. There was more that could be endured.

After Amy, Dale and Rob had taken it in turns to run with me during laps five, six and seven, I insisted on running the last lap alone. This was the final 27km I never got to run in Peru. I simply had to finish this on my own.

When I set off on the last lap of the lake at 11.35 p.m., there was less than an hour and a half before the race was over.

'We're taking the race banners down at one o'clock,' one of the organisers warned me as I left.

'You can take your fucking banners down,' I thought. 'I'm finishing this race.'

Might even have said it. Hard to know.

I couldn't imagine how I was going to get round that last lap. It's difficult to explain how it felt physically. I want to say that my body was screaming at me, but that's not right. The body can start screaming on a normal bike ride or day one on a mountain. It went much deeper than that. The pain was universal, obviously, but it had developed into the kind that is warning of imminent collapse. I could feel every muscle twitch and spasm, as if it were on the threshold of cramp. My feet were in agony, as if every step were into a bed of razor blades. I barely had the energy to lift my legs anyway. The weight of millennia was bearing down on me, my DNA, the inheritance of evolution, fight or flight, pleading with me just to stop; for God's sake, please stop.

By now I was hallucinating. All I could think about was the next 20m. I knew the route so well. Behind this gate were some steps; beyond that bench was a tree. Next 20m, next

Testing at GSK's
Human Performance
Lab. Wonderful pain!

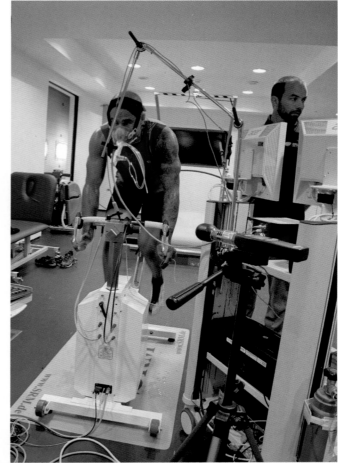

The 'Pocket Rocket'
Nic helping rebuild me
in a Nepalese tea house
before The Yak Attack
mountain bike race.

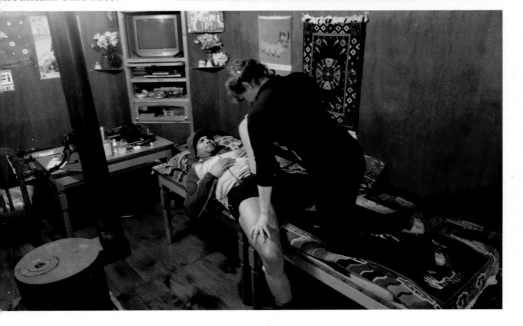

The morning of the 5416m Thorong La Pass stage of the race. Not the most encouraging sight first thing!

Some of the Yak Attack racers at the finish line. It's amazing how quickly you can forget the pain and smile!

The final day of the Yak Attack. All that climbing was worth it to let the brakes go and rip the descent!

Nic and I drinking traditional Peruvian Chicha made from maize the day before the Jungle Ultra Marathon.

Going through my recovery systems at the end of the first day of the Jungle Ultra before my first night in a hammock.

250km self-supported through the Amazon rainforest. All my pain (and some pleasure!) caught in high definition.

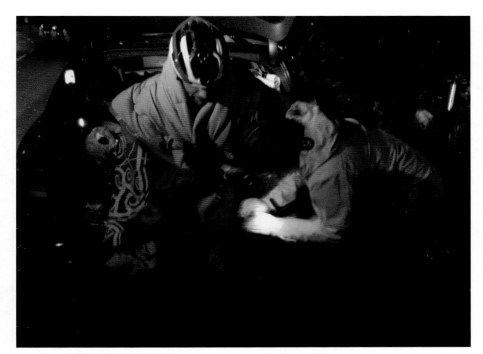

I didn't get many pics from The Brutal double ironman. Everyone went through the mill over those 38 hours. Nic treating my legs on the side of the road at 2am.

-42°C in Pontypridd! Testing my Antarctica camera equipment in the environmental chamber at the University of South Wales.

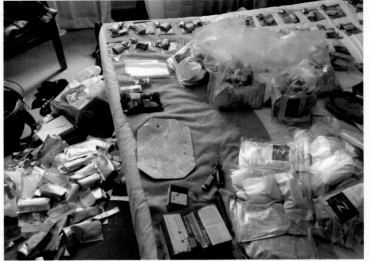

It's in the detail. Packing my daily food bags in the hotel room in Punta Arenas. Just the pile of excess material I cut from them saved me 900g overall. Light is right!

With Rob Taylor, Dale Templar and David Hamilton on the Ilyushin aircraft flying to Union Glacier Camp. After three weeks of weather delays we were full of smiles. If only we knew there would be even more when we got to Antarctica.

Waiting . . . waiting for weather in my ALE tent at Union Glacier.

Antarctic sensory deprivation. Skiing inside a white box/ping pong ball

Antarctica gives you good weather too. At the end of a day's skiing there was no time to stop until I was melting snow inside my tent, out of the elements.

Pride, gratitude . . . and exhaustion at the South Pole.

Physically and emotionally empty back at Union Glacier Camp for my medical checks.

20m. My eyes kept flitting between each route marker and my watch. As I laboured up the steepest section of the climb halfway round the lap, I saw in the light from my head torch Amy, Nic and my parents just ahead, holding a Welsh flag. How on earth had they made it up to this point? By the time I reached them, they weren't there.

No matter. I could feel myself growing. With every step the hardware in my mind was being rewritten. This new level of experience was being catalogued, the good work consolidated. I was going to finish. That idea had seemed impossible so many times over the previous thirty-eight hours. A kind of euphoria was overtaking me.

As I ran through the forest, I thought I saw my dad again. This time, instead of dissolving into thin air as I approached, he kept shouting encouragement at me. It really was him! My dad, a man of seventy-nine, a cancer survivor with a knee replacement, had somehow hauled himself up the hill through the trees to cheer me on in the dead of night. What an incredible man! I wanted to cry with gratitude. If ever I needed motivation for the last couple of kilometres, I had it now.

At 12.55 a.m. on the Monday I crossed the finish line, five minutes before the man with the banners had his moment, 455km, thirty-seven hours and fifty-five minutes after I'd begun. This performance of mine was not going to trouble the historians of extreme triathlon in the years to come, but it was one of my most important achievements. As an act of defiance, as a triumph of will over failing muscles, it marked new territory. I'd found what I thought must be my empty, and I'd gone beyond it, way beyond it. No stopwatch or data sheet could capture what this meant, but it felt every bit as tangible as any read-out from Sport Wales.

As a final test before Antarctica it was exactly what I needed.

13

When you push yourself to take on these extraordinary ventures, like Antarctica, or the 737 Challenge, or even just playing professional rugby, you find that generous people say a lot of nice things about you and to you. The least you can do is to return such praise with gratitude and humility, but it is also true that sometimes it is hard to know where to look. I have always struggled with compliments. Instead of making me feel warm and fuzzy inside, as I know such praise is intended, it can make me feel awkward, as if I'm a fraud. This is entirely my issue, in no way the fault of the praiser – and what a sad world it would be if we stopped complimenting each other – but I tend to let any praise wash over me and not to let it stick.

I know it's sad, but my instinctive reaction is, when are they going to realise I'm just not that special? Any one of these people praising me faces up to major challenges or crises in their lives and overcomes them without acknowledgement. So why should they be acknowledging me now, just because I chose to climb mountains, or chase an oval ball, or cross miles and miles of frozen wilderness?

Don't get me wrong. I know I'm physically fit – and so I should be when I've devoted the best part of twenty years to professions that have required me to be just that. But, like many sportsmen, I am haunted by the feeling that I'm not remarkable, or indeed that I fall short of the acceptable. I suppose it's the very paranoia that drives us on. When we fail, the white room awaits. Life becomes an exercise in running away from that.

Some sportsmen are able to take great confidence from praise, or at least from the perception that the praise is a result of certain unarguable qualities in their make-up. I don't mean arrogance, although there's a fine line; I mean confidence, the belief that there *is* something remarkable about them.

As a rugby player, I gained my confidence from meticulous preparation. If I dropped a restart, for example, I would stay out after training and get Paul John to kick restart after restart at me until I felt confident. The same attitude has applied to my life in the mountains and wildernesses.

But there was an encounter around about this time, just before my departure for Antarctica, when I may just have acquired a measure of confidence from what people said, when I did benefit from the identification of something unusual about me. It may have helped that these people were scientists.

I was undergoing a VO_2 max test in the Human Performance Lab at GlaxoSmithKline. GSK are my science partner, and this was the first stage of my baseline test before Antarctica. In a week I was off to Punta Arenas. I'd been tired and stressed, and I had a bit of a cold. I wasn't feeling great.

The drill was to maintain the same cadence on a static bike, while they gradually increased the wattage. They told me the norm was to last six minutes, but that a few have been known to go for twelve. For some reason, I decided in my head that I would go for nine. They have a chart they put in front of you at various points throughout the test, on which you indicate your level of exertion on a scale from one to twenty, where one is completely comfortable and twenty is about to blow up. I almost always end up lying, and so it was this time, when I settled on the policy of pointing at fourteen and never admitting to any more, no matter how hard I was pushing. I would later tell them that I had lied, and they replied that they suspected as much, because there came a point when I was so zoned out I didn't even notice that they'd put the chart in front of me.

The usual process was endured, the continual overriding of the body's instinct to stop. Needless to say, I worked myself hard and slumped forward on to the handlebars the second I'd reached nine minutes. As they lifted me off the bike and deposited me in a crumpled heap on a bed, my immediate thought was, why did I stop there? I should have gone harder. The answer was because I'd decided beforehand that I'd go for nine. Why hadn't I gone for ten? I would have made it if I had, I was sure.

When I came round, back into the land of the living, there was a real buzz in the room. 'We've never seen anything like it,' said the physiologists.

What? *What?*

'Physiologically speaking, you came back from the dead about three times!'

Apparently, by all the conventional measures of exhaustion I should have collapsed on a few occasions in those nine minutes, yet found ways through it time and again. My carbon-dioxide emissions, heart rate, blood lactate, all of which are monitored, had passed the point of no return. This is a state-of-the-art training lab, so they see high-performance athletes from all sports pass through. When others hit the levels I had, it becomes a slippery slope; the test is over. But I kept on pulling it back.

I wasn't sure that I had indeed squeezed every last drop out of myself, but this was an eye-opener. It was consistent with what we had seen in the Brutal a month earlier, when nobody, myself included, thought I would ever finish. I suppose what they were saying is that I am able to dig deeper than most. I'd probably always known that, but to have it identified, quantified and rubber-stamped like this by men in white coats was a significant shift in my perspective ahead of Antarctica. Could it be that this was a genuine point of difference in me?

There's a safety switch hardwired into the brains of all of us that is triggered before we reach a critical point of no return – in other words, breakdown, or even death. The reason it's there is obvious. The question an endurance athlete asks is just how much of a buffer is there between the switch being triggered and actual breakdown. It is generally accepted that the brain's safety alarms go off some time before the body is in any serious trouble. I seem to have a gift for, if not overriding that switch, at least holding it open for longer than others. I still maintain – indeed, I believe it has been established as fact – that everyone has that same facility, which they resort to when they have to. It's just that I seem to be able to do it on a bike that is going nowhere, or in the name of reaching a finish line before some bloke takes down a banner – as opposed to in the name of a great cause, or childbirth, or simple survival.

The Brownlee brothers were the next in the lab. Their VO_2 max far exceeds mine, not to mention their speed and technique. I imagine they could go way beyond nine minutes. But when they hit the wall they hit the wall. The GSK scientists had given me a little something here. I didn't know how extraordinary it really was, but as a consolidation of what I'd experienced in the Brutal it just might come into its own for what lay ahead in Antarctica.

If only it could have helped me in those weeks before departure. Truth be told, the build-up to every expedition is a stressful period, but this proved to be the most stressful yet. I'd never been in better shape as an athlete, or more confident about the challenge that lay ahead, but with the pressures of filming and managing the logistics I was struggling to keep all the plates spinning.

Those stresses reached a new pitch when one of my key sponsors pulled out, just a few weeks before departure. I understand that it was just a business decision, and I was far from the only one of their sponsorship projects to be affected by what was basically a restructuring of the company's strategy. There was no malice in it at all. But that doesn't alter the fact that, in terms of the impact it had on my little universe, the decision was devastating.

And that wasn't all. Next body blow – my food provider was hit with financial problems a week before departure. I had been working with Fuizion and its owner, Tony Simmonds, for over a year, developing dishes and calculating calories. Working alongside GSK, he had customised all of my food for me, down to the last calorie in a vat of Thai green curry. All that was left was for him to freeze-dry it, when the trouble struck. Now it looked as if I might have to start again, right at the last minute.

With his own business on the rocks, Tony managed to meet a few of his key orders, mine included. Here was another person who went beyond the call of duty. Happily, having averted my crisis, Tony managed to avert his own. Fuizion is still going strong – and no company deserves more to be so.

Again, I found myself surrounded by people going the extra mile to help ease the pressure on me. When I finally flew to Chile it was with a measure of relief just to be away from the white noise and stress. As soon as I arrived in Punta Arenas, though, Mike Sharpe, one of the ALE owners, called me in and asked me to take a a seat. There was a problem. I knew Mike well by this point, and he's a lovely guy, but he had to tell me that the logistical costs of my expedition hadn't been paid yet, because of the loss of my sponsor. Jonny McWilliams, my manager, had shielded me from all of this while he'd been working on a solution. Mike had been happy to extend him more time. ALE knew me and trusted me. The trouble was, the television company didn't know me so well and weren't prepared to pay their bill until I had paid mine. I'd already spent

£10,000 of my own money on the project. This was yet another ramping up of the pressure.

I couldn't tell anyone. I was adamant that Mum and Dad should be shielded this time. They would have helped if they could, but I'd seen the stress the 737 Challenge had placed them under. That could not be allowed to happen again. Besides, when I returned from this, I was moving out of their house into a flat in Cardiff. They were already busy enough helping with the paperwork for that. Amy and I were moving in together, so she had plenty on her plate applying for jobs in Cardiff. Nic had put so much time and passion into my preparation. Tracy was still being Tracy – tireless and hard-working. So many people had invested so much into the expedition, not least me. And now I was suffering a financial crisis like the 737 Challenge's all over again, only this time I couldn't share it with anyone other than Jonny. Everyone knew that the margins for this record attempt were minuscule, even if everything were to run smoothly. I couldn't admit to any of them that, psychologically, I was cracking under the pressure of these logistical crises.

Over the course of the ensuing few weeks, Jonny worked with my partners, the University of South Wales, GlaxoSmithKline and his own company, Wasserman Media Group, who came through with the vital funding, but those weeks waiting in Punta Arenas and then at Union Glacier were agonising.

The reason we had them to wait out at all was the next area for concern. I arrived in Punta Arenas at the end of October. Nobody was going to be flying on to the ice just yet. The temperature at the South Pole was −56°C; at Union Glacier, which is near the coast, it was −38. The winter had yet to blow through. But it was blowing, all right. At Union Glacier the winds were past 60mph.

Although I refused to let myself engage with them, these updates were bad news. One of the most critical margins my record attempt would be relying on was the weather. No expedition to any extreme environment is above meteorological considerations, but when a speed record as fast as Christian's is being attempted the weather becomes more decisive a factor than ever. I would not have the luxury of missing a day here or there, sitting out a storm. Christian's record is considered unbreakable not just because it was set by an elite polar athlete at the peak of his powers. It also coincided with some of the best conditions anyone could remember in the Antarctic.

On the verge of implosion I might have been when it came to the logistical problems, but when it came to the expedition itself I was defiant. I spent a total of four weeks waiting for a chance to set off – ten days in Punta, two and a half weeks at Union Glacier. That's a lot of time chewing the fat with people who were experts in Antarctic travel. Advice came at me constantly, all of it well meant from people who had become friends by this time, my third Antarctic summer in four years. To begin with, though, it did nothing to alleviate the stress. I could see the look in their eyes when the latest weather reports came in from the ice, or when they saw the amount of camera equipment I was supposed to be taking. None of them thought I had a hope in frozen hell of breaking the record.

By the time I was at Union Glacier, I was at peace with the advice, because my systems were constantly being subjected to scrutiny. If I accepted someone's advice and modified something, it meant there had been room for improvement; if I didn't, it simply reinforced my confidence that I was dialled and ready to go. Some invaluable adaptations were introduced over that period at Union Glacier. Hannah McKeand, whose British record of thirty-nine days from Hercules Inlet to the South Pole I was also trying to break, was a great help. There's a wonderful sense of community down there, on the underside of the globe. In any other walk of life, there might be jealousy and hostility over the idea of someone breaking your record, but in Antarctica it is seen as furthering the achievements of the human race, of which we are all a part. Christian had been open and friendly when I'd visited him in Norway the month before; now Hannah was offering insight gleaned from her six (a world record) successful expeditions to the South Pole.

My food strategy was changing this year. Instead of loading up on calories at the start and end of each day, as I had last time, now I would be taking on a drip feed throughout the day. My plan was to ski in tabs of one hour and fifteen minutes, followed by a five-minute break, during which I would take on 350 calories of flapjack. That equated to segments of one hour and twenty minutes, which corresponded to how long I was taking to run each lap of the Brutal. I had learned that this is an optimal time for me – any longer and I would start to drop, any shorter and I wasn't squeezing enough out of myself. Hannah, though, had tended to fit a twenty-five-minute break into the middle of the day, during which she would take on something substantial and hot, as much for psychological reasons as for performance. I liked this idea. I also knew that I was going to have to ski longer hours than planned, because of the weather. So I worked a twenty-minute break into my strategy, at the end of my fourth tab, when I would take on 989 calories of rice pudding. The GSK dieticians had identified rice pudding as a good meal to be taken during exercise, easily digested and high in calories. Fuizion's rice pudding pouches had worked really well on the Brutal. My plan for Antarctica had been to eat one as a pudding at the end of each day, but I liked Hannah's system, so I decided to move it to that new twenty-minute break in the middle of my day.

Another adaptation I took from Hannah was to lengthen the arms of my compass mount. Your compass is obviously vital in an expedition like this. I chose to wear it constantly on a bespoke harness, strapped around my neck but with two arms propping it up against my waist, so that it was always held out in front of me. In a whiteout or in flat light, you have nothing else to navigate by, and the ache in your neck from looking down at it all day can become a problem. Hannah's system alleviated that by extending the arms of the mount with old tent poles. It was a simple and brilliant modification that could only have been suggested by someone who knew what it was like to navigate in Antarctica off a compass.

I'd trimmed every last gram of extra packaging from my freeze-dried food. Dale Templar, the series producer, and Rob Taylor, the cameraman, were out there with me during those weeks waiting (unaware, I should add, that there was a problem with the paying of their bills). They were rocks of support. Rob and I shared a tent at Union Glacier for two and a half weeks. Together, we stripped back to a bare minimum the camera equipment I would have to carry. Channel 5 had wanted me to take not only the camera equipment but Rob himself. The documentary would obviously benefit from the expertise of a professional cameraman. But it was out of the question. There are too many people out there claiming to have achieved things they patently have not. One of the classics is to claim that you're solo and unsupported when there's a film crew following your every move. If we don't have integrity on these expeditions, we have nothing. As much as I would have loved Rob to have looked after all the filming, it would have invalidated my attempt to break Christian's record before I'd even stopped for my first flapjack. Solo means solo. Channel 5 accepted that, but the trade-off was the 13kg of equipment they issued me with and the training days they sent me on to show me how to use it. At Union Glacier, we whittled that equipment down to 5.4kg. It was another vital modification, as were the straps and grips I had devised in Wales to help me operate the camera with my mitts on. I'd used the environmental chamber at the University of South Wales to test all the electronic equipment to −40°C.

The first ten days at Union Glacier involved countless such tweaks. By the end of it, my pulk was down to 68.2kg (10st 10lb). I had settled on 5815 calories of food per day, the flapjacks cut into 350-calorie pieces, eight of them to be crammed into my jacket pockets each morning, the Jelly Bellies (my treat at the end of a day) rationed out into portions using an espresso cup from the hotel in Punta. It was all separated out into twenty-five bags of 1.2kg, one for each day.

Carrying so little food was the next decision to raise eyebrows. Steve Jones, the operations manager at ALE, was very sceptical of my bullishness. To me, it was logical. I was there to break a record that stood at twenty-four days. I also had to carry as little as possible. Twenty-five days' worth of food seemed to me to cater for that.

Steve, who is another good friend, cocked his head. 'There's been a lot of snow,' he pointed out. 'The going will be hard. It'd be a real shame if you missed out on making the Pole because you ran out of food.'

It was the closest anyone came to saying that the record wasn't on that year.

I couldn't afford to think like that – and I can honestly say that I didn't. In Punta, I was stretched to breaking point, I confess, by all the uncertainty surrounding the finances, but as the expedition approached my attitude hardened. I have always taken confidence from preparation, and my preparation had been meticulous. More than that, it had been brutal. I was in the shape of my life. So what if the snow was heavy? I would just ski longer. I might not be as good a skier as Christian, but I would counter that with my strength and fitness. I had so much confidence in my ability to dig deep. That experience with the Brutal, when nobody, including myself, thought that I would ever finish, together with the findings of the physiologists at GSK, had transformed my outlook.

But I was ready to go now. I'd flown out to Union Glacier on the second Ilyushin of the season, the first having taken a skeleton crew to set up ALE's camp. Digging out the metal containers in which the equipment has spent the winter was a tough job that year. When I got there on 11 November it was easy to see why. The weather was poor for the first week, but by the time we were ready to go it was practically extra-terrestrial.

You could be standing 10m away from your tent and not be able to see it through the wind and snow. At least it meant we were able to film for the documentary some convincing stock footage of me skiing in a snowstorm, but it didn't bode well.

That last stretch of waiting was hard. Like waiting in the tunnel for the biggest game of your life – for ten days. I just wanted to get out there.

On 28 November, a precious window appeared.

My plan for departure had been simple. If I arrived at Hercules Inlet in the morning, I would set off there and then; if in the afternoon, I would camp a 'night' and set off first thing the next day. Sod's law, the Twin Otter touched down just before midday. It was the first flight to Hercules Inlet of the season, so a few of the ALE crew had come to check the safety of the sea ice. Rob had come with us to film my start, so I did a quick piece to camera, then thought, fuck it. Let's go now. I switched on my phone, sent a GPS signal to prove my location, then phoned Welsh Dean at Union Glacier to advise him of my departure time. The others gave me a mock-heroic countdown, and I set off into the great white emptiness, as if it were the most natural thing in the world.

That first day was bluebird overhead but soft underfoot. I knew immediately that it was going to be a tough first few days, after which, hopefully, the snow would harden up and offer more in the way of glide. Nevertheless, I put in a good shift that day, climbing 500m over 25km in six hours. Christian averaged 47km a day, 45 if you discount his 90km push in the last twenty-four hours, so 25km in half a day on a steep incline over soft snow was a solid start. Day two, though, the weather turned again. I skied for nine and a half hours in a whiteout, navigating off my compass, with no features to take a bearing off. It snowed, too, doing nothing for the glide of my skis, which were sinking an inch or two with each step, or that of the pulk, which felt so much heavier in those conditions. Every time I looked up from my compass to give my neck a rest, I suffered vertigo gazing into the featureless white void with no horizon. I skied 27km that day, not much more than I'd skied in half a day on a steeper incline the day before. Not good enough. I knew then that I was in trouble. This was not world-record pace. I didn't have the luxury of letting days like this pass through.

But, equally, you can't let a bad day derail you. I decided to sleep on it, even though I knew a miraculous hardening of the snow was unlikely to occur overnight. When I removed my eye-mask the next morning, my heart sank. I could hear the howling wind already, but by the light in the tent I knew it was overcast again. When I opened the zip to my tent's vestibule and looked out through the vent to the weather outside, I could see there'd been more snow overnight. It looked as if it were still snowing. It wasn't – it was the fresh snow being blown up off the floor.

I didn't want to get up, I didn't want to go out. I couldn't even see the point of carrying on. There was no way I could ski any more kilometres in this than I had the day before. I'd do well even to match it. I knew then that Antarctica wasn't going to be offering up any shots at a record that week. And one bad week, one or two bad days, was all it needed to put paid to my attempt.

I reached through to the vestibule and turned on my stove

to heat up the water I'd melted in it the day before. While it rewarmed, I hauled myself out of my sleeping bag and pulled on my trousers and the liners of my boots, then sat with my legs in the pit I'd dig out each evening in the vestibule. It's a foot or two deep. The snow from it acts as the day's water supply. I emptied my bowels into the pit and buried the result in snow. At least I had a proper grasp this time of the continent's poo protocol. Then, over what I call a mountain mocha (one sachet of coffee, one of hot chocolate), I stared out into the driving snow and considered my position.

It was bleak. Only a fool goes to Antarctica expecting unbroken sunshine all the way. Only a fool goes out there expecting not to be involved in some seriously hostile weather. Only a fool, then, I started to tell myself, goes out to try to break a record like Christian's. Because you might not need unbroken sunshine all the way, but you surely need to avoid weather like this. I thought back to my first visit to Antarctica in the 737 Challenge, the very time Christian was flying across the ice. For the couple of weeks I spent in the last degree and at the South Pole that year the sun barely stopped shining. The weather was more mixed at Union Glacier, with plenty of whiteouts while we waited for the fuel strike in Punta to lift, but there was none of this.

The demons were circling again. It's not just the bad day that weighs on you, but the previous twelve months, the previous six weeks in particular. And the solitude. And the camera in the corner that reminds you there is a programme to be made. This wasn't good television. Or maybe it was, but I certainly wasn't enjoying it.

After 1002 calories of porridge, I packed up my tent,

gritted my teeth and headed off into it. My pulk had never felt heavier in the thick snow. The year before, it had started the expedition almost 15kg heavier than this, and with all the poo I'd chosen to carry that year it pretty much stayed at the same weight. Now my pulk felt like the sled I'd hauled on the carpet at Sport Wales. This snow was effectively doubling its weight. As for my skis, they were disappearing in the powder. That may not sound much, but when you have a speed record to break and a pulk to pull that feels twice its 70kg weight it sucks further energy from your muscles and morale. After three hours, my GPS device told me I had travelled 4.5km.

Enough. I pitched my tent, for safety reasons as much as anything else, and jumped inside. But mainly it was anger. The decision I made then to stop was a perfectly rational one, which, in retrospect, I stand by. At the time, though, I was an angry schoolboy in a strop. Fuck this. I'm not playing any more. I phoned Union Glacier and told them I was coming back in.

With the storm raging outside, another struck up in my head. Part of me wanted to crack on regardless, fight through the wind and snow, even though the game was lost. Part of me just wanted to go home. And I mean real home, Wales. My sister was over for Christmas. I'd been away for three of the last four. I'd not shared one with Amy yet. An extra incentive for breaking the world record had always been that I would be home in time for Christmas. I wanted to go home.

My mind was still swirling. I hadn't really thought through what returning to Union Glacier would mean for the expedition. Now I can see that it would probably have meant the end. I didn't have the funds to pay for another flight from Union Glacier to Hercules Inlet.

Then I got a call from Tim Hewette, ALE's field manager, offering me another option. There was a flight scheduled the next day to drop some more expeditions at Hercules Inlet. They could bury a cache of extra food for me while they were there. In effect, I could return to Hercules Inlet and start again.

Returning there hadn't occurred to me, because I would have used five of my twenty-five days' rations by the time I'd arrived, but now this option had been presented it was a no-brainer. I had extra food supplies at Union Glacier. Tim would send ten more days' worth. By the time I'd returned and spent a day or so resting before the restart, I would be left with twenty-eight – in other words, the amount Steve had always suggested I should take.

The storm didn't blow through till the next day, 1 December, when I set off back the way I'd come. In absolutely glorious weather. The snow under foot was still very sticky, although it's less of a problem when you're skiing downhill, but the irony of returning in bluebird conditions was not lost on me. I wasn't really bothered by that. The whole episode had served as the release of a valve. I felt at peace now. I would go back and give this another go.

What was harder was passing other expeditions coming in the opposite direction. On day three of my return to Hercules Inlet, I saw a lone skier on the horizon. A little later, I came across an American pushing his bike uphill. Three people were aiming that year to become the first to cycle from the coast to the South Pole. Someone had failed the year before, so this season others were attempting it. A Welsh woman and friend, Maria Leijerstam, became the first, although you can't compare, because she was accompanied by a truck and didn't set off from Hercules Inlet like the other two, who ended up having a shocker getting there. It was a bad year for skiing the route; bad, as well, it turns out, for cycling.

Next I met two skiers, one of them a sixteen-year-old from Bristol called Lewis Clarke, who was aiming to become the youngest person to ski to the South Pole. He was with an ANI guide, Carl Alvey, who had buried my cache for me. I wished Lewis well – and I'm pleased to say he succeeded.

Later that day, I reached Hercules Inlet, uncovered my cache and pitched my tent. The weather was so beautiful – sunny, no wind, around –10°C – that I actually took an Antarctic shower, which involves stripping down to your pants and boots and rubbing snow all over yourself. That time at Hercules Inlet was the one period I completely chilled out. I wasn't operating on a spartan 3000 calorie deficit. I could eat a flapjack just for the hell of it and not because it was at a particular point of the day.

That afternoon, I was lying in my tent when I heard a plane outside. I poked my head out, and there, pulling up to within a few metres of my face, was ALE's Twin Otter. Out popped Troy and Andy from ALE, full of the joys. It was great to see them, a genuine morale boost. They were dropping off a Spaniard, who was the third of the cycling trio. I didn't like to say that the other bloke had a head start on him. Troy and Andy jumped in the plane and flew off, leaving this Spanish guy and me to speak in sign language to each other. It pained someone as anal as I am to watch how chaotic he looked. He had bits hanging off his pulk; he was carrying snow boots, skis, a bike. But he was a lovely guy. He offered me this sort of pasty, which was a traditional speciality from his hometown. I told him to keep it – he would need all of his food – but he insisted I had it. I later heard he ran out of supplies (he was the only cyclist travelling unsupported) and survived the last week of his forty-six-day expedition eating leftover nuts, cocoa powder and sunflower oil. I wish he'd kept his pasty.

I rested for another day, before I set off at 7 a.m. on 5 December for attempt number two. I don't think I had consciously abandoned hope of the world record, but the fact that I was taking more food with me this time suggests my mindset had shifted towards the barely less demanding challenge of making it there at all within my rations.

The first three days were satisfactory. The weather overhead was perfect, but the snow was still heavy and the headwind fierce. You climb more than 1000m in those first three days, so progress is slower than it will be later on in the expedition. By the end of day three I had covered 98km. That was behind the pace I needed, but not so much. I was still in the fight. Day four, though, the wind picked up even more, and I scraped 30km in eleven hours. My veneer of optimism started to chip away.

That wasn't the only thing disintegrating. I was wearing a new fabric called Stretch Neoshell, which is extra windproof and breathable but less waterproof. It is also very comfy, as it has stretch properties. But I had been skiing ten- or eleven-hour days now for more than a week, and in my trousers the two layers the fabric is made of had sheared away from each other around the crotch. The inner, windproof membrane

285

disintegrated, leaving my privates protected by nothing more than a stretchy outer layer the thickness of a T-shirt. Into a headwind as fierce as the one that morning, this was dangerous. After a few hours it dawned on me that I couldn't feel my penis. I put my hand down there. Nothing. It had turned completely numb.

You might laugh, but frostbite of the privates is more common than you'd think. All of the normal threats to fingers and toes apply in exactly the same way down there. Which is to say, in severe cases, they are amputated. That idea terrified me. For the rest of that day, I stuffed a spare glove and a hat down there, but managing this development was another serious issue to wrestle with, in addition to the kilometres that weren't being covered. It was a problem that could threaten the entire expedition. I wanted this world record – but not that badly.

Then came day five. Oh, day five.

There was a new weather type that year I'd never experienced before – bluebird skies above but a wind so low and fierce and in your face that the fresh snow it kicked up rendered visibility close to zero. Day five was just such a day, with 50mph winds. I didn't know that at the time. All I knew was that skiing against them was savage. They battered my body and spun my mind like a weathervane. I battled into the storm for three hours and covered 9.6km.

Not good enough. Not good enough. The record was gone. For the second time the record was gone.

I felt an implosion coming on. The weight of the previous year building towards this, the weight of the delays and uncertainty, the weight of those looks from people who thought this record was unbreakable, who thought I was aiming too high. Had I aimed too high? The weight, literal and metaphorical, of that camera that I knew, even now, was sitting on its ridiculous bracket, hanging off the side of my pulk, staring at me, unblinking in this furious shit storm. I hope it enjoyed what it saw next. I stopped, weak, vulnerable and for a moment defeated. And the next gust of wind blew me clean off my feet. I hit the ground like a felled tree.

That was it. Or at least I wished it could have been. There is no 'it' on your own in Antarctica. You can't shout fuck off at the world and slam the door behind you. You have to pitch a tent first. When mine was up I threw in my sleeping system and dived after it. On the cold, icy ground I broke down in tears. Proper, loud man sobs above a howling gale. It felt as if I'd wasted a year of my life.

I have a very special relationship with my tent on any expedition, but particularly when solo in Antarctica. From the moment I pack it away at 7 a.m., I look forward to pitching it again. There is nowhere like the wide open emptiness of Antarctica for making the traveller feel tiny and at the whim of Nature. My tent is the one little pocket of that vastness I can control. Not a huge amount has changed on the vulnerability front – all I've done is put a film of material between me and whatever it is outside – but the relief provided by even just the illusion of security is something to be grasped. Within it I can arrange the items of my life as I see fit, in a way I can't when the tent is down.

Erecting it is a skill I have honed. I can do it with my eyes shut now. I keep my tent and shovel on the outside of the pulk, so I can get at them easily in an emergency, without opening up the inside of the pulk to spindrift.

The first thing to be done is to secure the tent to something. You must never let go of it, so I fix the back end into the snow with one of my skis. I was using a tunnel-design tent, so next I align it with the wind, which is almost always blowing from the south. I secure the four corners, then assemble the two poles, each in two halves, and erect the tent. Starting at the back and working clockwise, I quickly dig in the snow skirts, before digging a hole in the vestibule. The displaced snow becomes my water supply for another 24 hours, and the hole doubles as the next morning's toilet and a place to allow me to sit down properly.

I then pull my pulk to the entrance. First out is the sleeping system – a long bag that contains my inflated Therm-a-Rest mattress and Rab sleeping bag – which is thrown straight into the tent. Next follows a daily food bag, and two insulated bags, one holding my cooking hardware, the other the camera gear, electronic equipment, first-aid kit and other miscellaneous items, such as notes from friends and family, a batch of which I allowed myself to open every seventh day.

From taking off my skis to climbing in, my PB was nineteen minutes, which was set towards the end of the trip. Every day my goal was to beat the day before, and that applied not just to pitching my tent but to everything – from time taken getting dressed, cooking food, eating food, taking a piss, packing up, right the way through to hours and kilometres skied. Relentless, detail-driven focus became the best way of handling the peculiar challenges of this lonely attempt at a seemingly impossible record.

The OCD meticulousness of my routine continues within the tent. With the storms raging outside the canvas and within my head, this is a haven of order. Sitting on my sleeping system, looking towards the vestibule, I had my two flasks to the right, always in the same order – the two-litre flask up against the canvas, the one-litre closer in. Behind me, the camera was set up on a tripod for my video diary. I had the next twenty-four hours' food laid out in front – breakfast, flapjacks and drinks for the next day, and for that night a meal (could have been anything from Thai green curry to spaghetti bolognese or chicken jalfrezi) and my treats, which would have been hot chocolate, Horlicks, Jelly Bellies and half a Maxitone Sculptress bar (it's a diet bar, but it has just the right balance of protein, carbohydrates and fat – and I really like it).

Because the tent was generally pointing north, away from the wind, I could tell roughly what time it was by the position of the sun on the canvas. I kept my clothes on the morning's sunny side, so that they had a better chance of being dry and not freezing cold when I put them on the next day. I never took off my base levels. I wore a Rab Vapour-Rise jacket at all times. It's the most simple, light and efficient of fabrics – and I swear by it. On warm days (i.e. −15°C or above) I would ski with just that one layer on, generating enough heat through my exertion to remain comfortable. On colder days, it would form a base layer underneath my outer shell jacket.

At the end of each day, I turned on my satellite phone, which would immediately activate an iridium beacon, transmitting my coordinates to ALE, my mum and dad, Amy and Tracy. It was my protocol that year not to ring anyone at the end of a day, when I might be tired and emotional. Setting up my phone to send that signal meant that just by switching it on I could let everyone know my position and that I was alive. If need be, I could then retreat into the 'cave' and smash my head against an icy floor. I've got a feeling, although I couldn't say for sure, that day five might have triggered a phone call home, but generally speaking phone calls or texts were for the next morning, when I'd had a chance to sleep on things.

This represented a departure from my more haphazard policy of the year before, when I would phone home as and when. Quite apart from the bills we racked up, unloading your problems down the phone to loved ones who are powerless to help can prove counterproductive. Hearing someone you care about rant in the middle of a raging storm in Antarctica does not generate a positive dynamic at their end. And at mine, when I'm tired, lonely and vulnerable to psychological implosion, hearing a familiar voice talk about the sort of everyday matters I long to be a part of again is sometimes catastrophic for morale.

In the year between expeditions, I worked with Cath Shearer, the psychologist at Sport Wales, on the distinction between dissociative and associative coping strategies and knowing when to use them. The year before in Antarctica I had leaned too much on the dissociative, which is basically daydreaming, escaping it all, thinking of home. Actually phoning home. This does have a powerful part to play and can boost morale if used at the right time. Too much of it, though, like rich food, can overwhelm you. When times are tough it is important to pull your horizons in and focus on the details of what you're doing and where you are – your body temperature, the direction you're moving in, the next step. This is the associative coping method. It is what had worked so well for me at times on the 737 Challenge and is based on the adage that if you take one step at a time you will get there eventually.

For the methodical among us and indeed the flighty – especially the flighty – it's not a bad discipline to live life by. Easier said than done, mind.

I didn't let myself eat on day five. If I was to lose a day's skiing I couldn't afford to lose a day's rations as well. It was then that I accepted once and for all that the challenge was no longer to beat Christian's record. The challenge was just to make it to the South Pole before my food ran out. The shift in emphasis from the former to the latter had been gradual over the twelve days since the expedition had begun, but the last hopes for the speed record had finally evaporated. It was now all about getting there. I had taken less food than any unsupported expedition in history. Even Christian took more than I had. I was aiming to cover the distance in less than thirty days, or bust. No one other than Christian had achieved that before. In these conditions, it was a bold statement of intent. I could see that now.

On the plus side, I had a new clarity of purpose. If the turnaround a few days earlier had felt like the release of a pressure valve, this was the blowing off of its top. I had serious words with myself in the tent that day, but only after the warring voices in my head had had their say. One voice insisted I had made the right call. The energy I would have to expend in these conditions was not worth the minimal distance I would cover. The other berated me for not being out there. Every moment tent-bound was a moment wasted. Did I want this record or not?

Fully clothed, I climbed into my sleeping bag and closed my eyes, just to escape it all. If you'd have offered me an out at that point, some kind of portal from Antarctica to somewhere else, I'd have taken it. That's why we should always sleep on things. Because when I woke I could see my new path clearly.

I'd asked myself so many times over the previous few days – sometimes with anger and bitterness – why are you doing this? The people and things you care about are half a world away, and you're here flogging yourself to the point of collapse in a godforsaken wilderness.

Well, I'd always known the answer to the question. Because I love that wilderness, too. As with anything – or anyone – it's sometimes easy to forget that, but if it's genuine love you are reminded the next time it courses through you. Antarctica is a wonderful place, which I mean in the proper, literal sense. It's a place full of wonder. And wilderness and colours. Not just the blue and white, but the rainbows and the shadows and the light. All of that is bound up with the hostility. You can't have one without the other. I love the way Antarctica makes you work. The sheer hell you have to go through to reach the place where you are in love with her. It's like a rite of passage. You have to suffer before she'll let you in. You have to prove yourself worthy. That very day, Tracy sent me a message that was spookily well-timed. There have been so many coincidences like this along the way. It felt as if Antarctica herself might have passed this one on (although Tracy deserves a bit of credit, too!). It was a quote she'd found from Børge Ousland, a Norwegian who was the first man to cross the

Antarctic continent solo and unsupported (he used kites, so he wasn't unassisted). He'd noted that it generally takes ten to fourteen days to find the inner peace required to survive and thrive on a solo expedition. It's so true. There are no short cuts to that state of mind. You have to suffer the internal storm before you can establish a rhythm. I found my form after that day and although the hard times were far from over I felt in the groove.

The reality was that this was now my job. It wasn't like the 737 Challenge, which was part exorcism, part fundraising. From where I'd started emotionally before the 737 Challenge, the only way was up. It was a one-off. In Antarctica, though, there was a sense that this is what I do now. Jonny, my manager, pointed out that the second album is normally harder than the first. It felt a bit like that. The tough times were more difficult to manage because there was a weight of expectation on me. Conversely, when I hit my stride, it was so gratifying. This is what I do. And I do it well. Like some of the best days on a rugby field, when you're running on top of the ground and feel as if you could go on for ever. Those are the games whose details you don't remember. You're in the zone. It's associative, I guess. Likewise on the ice. After I'd weathered that early storm, I focused in on the next tab (gotta make 5km) and in further on the rhythm of my skis. One of my rugby coaches described an openside flanker as a metronome. It was an idea that had resonated back then and revisited me here as I worked my skis across the snow.

When I woke up again on day five, I was back in the game. To reach the South Pole in less than thirty days, which was the new challenge, represented a mammoth undertaking. Only one other man in history had managed it. After my failure to make it a year earlier, I was all the more determined to do so. I thought of what lay ahead. The sastrugi had derailed me then; this time I felt prepared for them. Would they be as big? If so, they would meet a new and improved version of Richard Parks, mentally as well as physically.

Whereas a year ago, under similar circumstances, tent-bound in a storm, I had gobbled my way through a day's rations, this time I was more disciplined, more stoical. That well-established mantra about controlling the controllables. Associative coping. First of all, I had to identify what it was I could control, then I had to control it, then I had to stay in the moment. That moment of that hour of that day. I reorganised my food. No skiing meant no flapjacks. I was allowed a hot drink and half a chocolate bar. No skiing meant making good use of the time, so I attached my Firefly devices and compression socks and stretched. I planned new tweaks to my day. I couldn't ski any faster in these conditions, so I was just going to have ski longer. If I could squeeze an extra minute from each break, that's nine minutes a day. If I could find another five, that's fifteen, which equals a kilometre. Add them all up and we're making a bit more progress.

Then I addressed the problem in my trousers. I was carrying a pair of insulated emergency trousers with me. It was with uneasiness that I took the scissors to them, but this was important. Having cut a patch, I sewed a PrimaLoft codpiece into my base layer, which took care of the windproofing of my privates. It was a weight off my mind.

Inside that tent, so hastily pitched, a new momentum gathered. I was in the 81st degree now. One down, nine to go. I wrote the coordinates of where I was on my mattress. It felt good. Like a new start line. At the end of tomorrow I would write the next day's coordinates and the kilometres covered. And then the next. I would watch those degrees fall away, bit by bit. This mat, the buffer between my resting body and the ice, would document my progress. According to Union Glacier I had by now gone past the other expeditions that had left from Hercules Inlet. No one lay between me and the South Pole – just nine degrees of latitude that had to be reeled in.

To work.

Day 6 Needed a big day! Am windy; pm good conditions

11hrs 34.8km 81°26'S alt: 704m total: 172.5km

Day 7 Great conditions. Legs tired

11hrs 39.5km 81°47'S 806m 212km

Day 8 Great conditions. Poor contrast, but good

11hrs 40.6km 82°9'S 839m 252.6km

Day 9 Sore legs, tough temperature control

11.5hrs 42km 82°31'S 981m 294.6km

Day 10 Whiteout, soft snow. Tough but great day. Spiritual signs, orange sky, songs

12.5hrs 40km 82°53'S 1069m 334.6km

I hate it when it snows in Antarctica. Especially if I'm in a rush to get somewhere. Progress had picked up. Day six was a loosener, and day seven felt big. I was gutted when I climbed into the tent and turned on the GPS – 39.5km! Just another 500m and I would have broken 40km. After that, I made sure I turned the GPS on before I pitched the tent.

Never mind. I cleared 40km the next day, and on day nine, despite a tough climb and a day of intermittent sunshine that made it very difficult to regulate body temperature, my mileage increased again to 42km.

I was moving through the gears, but to wake up to a fresh layer of snow on day ten was deflating, as if someone had tied my shoelaces together overnight. Just as you think the going underfoot might be hardening up, along comes another dump. This was supposed to be a desert.

The weather that had brought the snow had almost cleared, but the forecast was not good – and ALE's forecasts tended to be spot-on. When I set off that morning it was under an incredible orange sky. Incredible because the sun never sets at that time of year, or gets close to it. This was like seeing a rosy dawn in the middle of the morning. Something about the angle of the sun on the clouds, or through the atmosphere, or through the ice crystals – I don't know what it was creating this effect, but science becomes superfluous when you experience these things in Antarctica in a state of extreme fatigue. In those situations we are transported back to the mindsets of our ancestors, for whom the world was a thing of wonder, to be worshipped and inspired by. I took this orange sky as a sign, which lifted me just as my new-found momentum was being challenged by the latest influx of snow.

But the predicted whiteout descended within an hour or two. What we mean by a whiteout is moisture in the air, basically a misty day, rendered all the whiter by the nature of the terrain. It is at one end of the visibility spectrum with a clear, still day at the other. In between is a range of different weather types.

The day before had been challenging because the sun was trying to break through the clouds. When it did, shadows appeared, defining the landscape ahead. Navigation was suddenly so much easier. You could pick a feature in the distance and take a bearing off it, but actually that feature is no more than interplay between the terrain and the sun, reflecting off some surfaces and casting shadows across others. Then the clouds would block out the sun, and the whole vista would change again. It's not like a cloudy day in the normal world, where distinctive shapes and colours remain visible even after the sun's gone in. The landscape in most of Antarctica is made up of shades of white. Take away the sunshine and everything changes.

The temperature plummets, too. It's not practical to keep changing clothes – and doing so has to be at the expense of precious time skiing, eating or drinking – so I was constantly having to vent and close my jacket, and to intensify and moderate my work rate. You do sweat on an expedition like that, of course, but it has to be regulated. Moisture control is a vital skill in any cold environment. When clothes are damp against your skin, you are more vulnerable to the cold, which means your body burns calories to keep warm. Those are calories that are being directed away from the main task in hand. And, in a worst-case scenario, if you are caught in severe weather dripping with sweat there is the threat of hypothermia. I use a light clothing system and keep warm through exertion. At high altitude you can't always do that, because you have to move so slowly in the thin air, but in Antarctica there are more options available on the work-rate front, so you need fewer on the clothing.

In some ways, it's easier in a whiteout, when you can just whack on the insulation, zip up and plough through. But in many ways it's not. Day ten a whiteout and was the first big test since I'd found my new resolution on day five. Once the whiteout had settled round, it was back to my compass, skiing into nothingness. The difference was that I was enjoying myself now. I'd broken 40km, which was a real psychological barrier. My aim was never to go backwards. My evening ritual with the sleeping mat had sharpened the idea of these degrees of latitude as something to pull in, as if I were chasing somebody. On a normal expedition this might have been the sort of day you would pitch your tent and sit out, but I didn't have that luxury.

My route to the South Pole was more or less straight. There was a slight detour to the south-west at the start to avoid a crevasse field, but once I'd straightened up I was on a straight bearing to the Pole. Although it's not due south. A compass seeks out the magnetic poles, not the geographic. The South Magnetic Pole these days is just off the coast of Antarctica in the eastern hemisphere, about 1900km away from where I was heading. My bearing after the initial detour was around 140 degrees, or 40 degrees east of due south.

In a positive frame of mind, it became a pure exercise in associative coping. My world focused round that little needle in its plate, held out in front of me like a trophy. The crazy thing was that so much of that day passed quickly, despite the lack of visibility, despite the soft snow underfoot. The iPod helped. It was one of those days when every song that came on was uplifting and/or somehow relevant. Until the battery froze later on in the expedition, I skied with an iPod Classic on shuffle mode. I'd flown out with two iPod Shuffles full of songs important to me – Amy had made me a playlist – but their batteries don't last long. If I was skiing ten to twelve hours a day, they would become deadweight pretty quickly. So I took just the iPod Classic. There were plenty of sick reminders on that expedition of some of the rubbish that had found its way into my library over the years. In Antarctica a whole day of love songs is tough to take. The iPod sits next to my skin to help maintain battery life, so you can't flick on to the next one. Whatever comes on must be endured. But on day ten everything seemed tailored for me. It felt as if Antarctica was sending them to help, even as she tested me.

If you can radiate positivity, it will be returned to you – I genuinely believe that.

'I think I'm gonna get there

... almost there

Feel like we've been getting nowhere'

At the end of that day, I stopped at my usual time and turned on my GPS: 35km. Fuck it, I'm doing 40. I ended up skiing twelve and a half hours, ten of them off my compass into a whiteout. All of them on a fresh layer of snow.

I pitched my tent and turned on the stove. Frazzled. That was a brutal day. But I was so enthused, so buoyant. If I can do 40km in a whiteout, there's never an excuse, never a reason to drop below that.

Day 26 Toughest day physically and mentally. So close yet so far. Conditions deteriorated throughout day. Whiteout plus light snow. Very cold and sticky snow. Feeling emotional. Lots of positive self-talk. Very draining. Thank you for an awesome year

13hrs 38.2km 88°49'S 2753m 998.6km

Day 27 Amazing quad helix first thing, but conditions deteriorated seriously. Cold, snowing, whiteout. Ski broke further. Stopped to repair. Faith. Super-tired. Legs sore. Getting worse. Started anti-inflammatories and painkillers. Worried about food but found another bag? Blessing, Footprints, thank you

10hrs 28.4km 89°4'1S 2770m 1027km

Day 28 Mega quad helix. Shat myself twice. Ski broke again

10hrs 31.4km 89°19'S 2760m 1058.4km

Day 29 Great conditions. Ski a pain but held up this time. Shat myself twice again! Out on my feet am. Fell asleep. But strong pm. Just want to get there

13hrs 31.4km 89°36'S 2706m 1089.8km

Day 30

I thought day twenty-six was New Year's Eve. Turns out it wasn't.

There were sores on my face and shoulder, minor cold injuries, but nothing compared to the cold injuries on the backs of my thighs. The one on my left was an open wound the size of the palm of my hand. I remember developing an itch in the area at Union Glacier, before I'd even started. Polar thigh, as they call it, is a non-freezing cold injury, which means it develops over time, unlike frostbite, which can strike in the space of a few hours. Once under way, the itch had become a few blotches, then the blotches merged and hardened. The wind had changed direction for a day or two round day twenty-three. A northerly brings the benefit of any tailwind, but this one was able to sink its teeth into the backs of my thighs. Once the southerlies resumed, the skin on the blotches fell away to reveal festering sores. On day twenty-seven I started taking pills for the infection and the pain, which was excruciating. When the dressing was removed weeks later, the nurse retched at the sight and smell of it. For another few weeks, the people of Cardiff knew me by the slick of damp that ran down the back of my left trouser leg.

So much for the surface wounds. Internally I was a mess, too. Physically, I was digging as deep as I ever had. Sleep is usually easy to come by when you're in a permanent state of exhaustion, but there were times when my leg muscles were so painful they kept me awake.

Psychologically, I was at a critical stage. The world record had passed a couple of days earlier. I'd known that would be so for nearly three weeks – and suspected it for longer than that – but I had worked so hard towards the aim of reaching the South Pole within twenty-four days that the passing of day twenty-three left its mark on me emotionally. And it was brutal physically, the climax of the sastrugi, another whiteout, a 200m climb and, you guessed it, more snowing.

But a day after that I was through the sastrugi. Last year, they had been the biggest anyone could remember. This year they were the same size again, with a few the size of a double-decker bus (you ski round those), but I would say they were less dense. It's the ones about a metre high, which you have to ski over, that take their toll. For months, I had been preparing myself for the day the sastrugi came. They had broken me last year, completely derailed my expedition. I'd sworn that this year the expedition would begin only when the sastrugi did. For the seven days leading up to them I had averaged 44km a day, peaking at 46.7 on day fifteen. But if there is one statistic I'm really proud of, it's that I never once dropped below 40km a day in the heavy sastrugi. I was through in less than six days – more than 200km of them and a climb of 1000m.

It left me vulnerable on day twenty-six. This was where I'd pulled the plug last time, midway through the 88th degree, a wasted wreck of a man after thirty-eight days in the wilderness. To have travelled the same distance twelve days faster was a tribute to the work I had put in over the previous eleven months. What's more, I was fit to finish this one off, even if you might easily have categorised me as a wasted wreck again. But it would be so easy to lose it now. The sastrugi had been overcome. The climbing was all but finished. And yet the game was not over. The best part of another 200km remained.

Day twenty-six was sent to try me. Antarctica kept coming. The environment is constantly trying to derail you. That's the challenge, and that's what I love about it. It's what makes it so different from professional sport, where everything is so managed. Another whiteout, more snow, albeit light. And this on the polar plateau, which is supposed to receive less precipitation than the Sahara. The snow underfoot on the plateau is tough going anyway, and not because it's fresh. The opposite problem arises here. Because snow hardly ever falls and never ever melts, the snow on the ground is old and dry, like sand. My pulk was now little more than half its original weight – twenty-five days of food had been shed, i.e. 30kg, and most of the fuel. Yet still it wouldn't glide. I ended up losing my temper with it on several occasions.

Perhaps I was extra-irritable because of the cold. A whiteout on the plateau means bitter temperatures. That has repercussions on a number of levels. You cannot use your poles as forcefully as normal, because you're constantly having to flex your fingers, or give each a turn tucked under the others to keep warm. Or sometimes you just let the poles hang from your wrists altogether as you clasp your hands together. With each stride you are scrunching your toes. Rhythm and momentum are compromised. It affects you cognitively and psychologically. You can feel your mind slow down. And on a straightforward, everyday level it's just demoralising. When the sun is shining, you want to go out. When it's cold and miserable, you don't. Simple as that.

The New Year, real or imagined, has always been a poignant time for me. Because of rugby and now expeditions, I've hardly ever seen one in drunk. For me, it's always been a time for reflection and gratitude, of stock-taking and projection. On the night of day twenty-six, I was emotional, reviewing what I had been through, what I might still achieve. Would I ever go through another year like that? Could I? The pressure had been relentless – on the body and mind, on relationships and bank balances. And yet what incredible places I'd been to – the extremities of the world, the rooms deep, deep within myself. How privileged to be able to go there! Farewell, 2013! I have loved you, but you have not been easy. Like you, Antarctica. Like life.

Day twenty-seven – the New Year. I opened my tent to be greeted by the most incredible quad helix. I was weary and emotional at this point, stripped back to a more primitive mode of existence. This multi-coloured halo around the sun made a deep impression on me. To see it at the dawn of the New Year was a euphoric, awesome experience. You can't fail to be uplifted by such a beautiful phenomenon. In my condition, I interpreted it as a blessing at the dawn of the year from Antarctica herself.

And then, almost immediately she turned nasty again. Was I worthy? How much did I want this? Within an hour, I was plunged into another bitterly cold whiteout. It started snowing again, more heavily this time. Unbelievable. Some desert.

But conditions underfoot were improving. Typical, then, that my right ski should break. Another of my gambles had been not carrying a spare. In the sastrugi, skis are subjected to a lot of abuse. Sometimes the tail of the ski is resting on the peak of one sastrugi and the tip on another, with the middle flexing. That's probably what weakened this one. It didn't break suddenly, but gradually deteriorated, so that at some point on day twenty-seven the front of it was flapping weirdly with each step. I didn't want to stop till the next break, which was when I saw that the underside of the ski, just beneath the heel, had snapped. The top was still intact and I was using a half-skin over the ski's base for traction. The skin covered the break, so I could carry on skiing, but every time I put my weight on my right foot it sank deeper than my left. I was skiing with a limp.

The conditions were foul so I pulled the plug after ten hours. If I'd been an observer watching this, 100km from the Pole without a spare, I might have considered it the end of the expedition. But I was so dialled now, I don't think even a sniper would have stopped me. There was no way I wasn't getting there. I would walk if need be. Faith. I believed I would do it. That poem about footprints in the sand was going round my head. It was read at my nan's funeral. About a guy who looks back over his life with his maker, who has walked alongside him throughout, the pair leaving two sets of footprints in the sand, apart from the periods, it seems, when the guy was in real trouble. For those, there is only one set. Why did you leave me during the hardest times, he asks? I didn't leave you, comes the reply. I was carrying you.

I found an extra bag of food in my pulk that day. The food situation was worrying me. I'd been working on the assumption I had twenty-eight days of food, which meant I should have one bag left. That was going to have to last me the two to three days I had left. But I'd forgotten that I'd not eaten during the wobble of day five. I had an extra bag. What a boost!

I'd forgotten a lot. My mind was suffering as much as my body. That evening I discovered, as well, that it wasn't New Year's Day at all. I felt a bit let down. The quad helix in the morning had not been a sign after all, the brutality of the day that followed not a test of my worthiness to enter the New Year.

Dad had broken the news to me. I'd phoned him to discuss the repair of the ski. The next morning I lay in my sleeping bag, psyching myself up to tackle it. I unzipped my tent and was astonished by what I saw. There, in a clear blue sky, burned another quad helix, even more vivid and sparkling than the one the day before! And this time it *was* New Year's Day! My dad had told me, so it must be true.

With renewed vigour at this second cosmic blessing, I set about fixing the ski. There was a bracket on the side of my pulk on which one of the cameras had been mounted. With a muttered apology to Dale, I dismantled it. The fixing was made of three long, thin plates screwed together with holes along each. It was almost custom-made. Using the self-tapping screws the mechanics at Union Glacier had given me, I fixed a plate along each side of the ski, having cleaned out the fracture and fitted it back together. On went the skin. I was pretty pleased with my handiwork. Until it broke again later that same day. I cleaned it out once more that night and rescrewed the plates. Then I wrapped the fracture in duct tape and reattached the skin. Problem solved. Duct tape's bombproof.

New Year's Day, the real New Year's Day, stayed kind. The weather was perfect. And Antarctica would keep it that way. I imagine her as a grumpy old cynic that year who wasn't going to give anyone anything. But even the harshest taskmasters relent if you prove your commitment. I think Antarctica warmed to me. She let me finish in peace.

It's a shame I was out on my feet by then. My body was

starting to break down. My legs and shoulders were scream-ing. The back of my thigh was burning with pain. I was falling asleep on the skis. For more than a month, including the restart, my legs had performed nothing but the same metro-nomic motion, day after day of it. They were on autopilot now. I could nod off; they would keep going. The iPod had long since given up on me, but I was loving the silence. I spent the last third of the expedition lulled and galvanised in equal measure by the steady swish-swish of the skis and my heavy breath.

Then I shat myself. Four times across days twenty-eight and twenty-nine. The first time I had to empty my trousers as quickly as possible (no skiing on till the next break for this). I wiped my arse with snow. As soon as I was able, I put the waste in a wag bag, covered any stains in the snow and moved on. The second time I was more prepared and able to go into a bag, but I had to be quick. To expose yourself to the per-ishing air of the polar plateau is not good practice. My privates had already taken a pounding from the cold earlier in the expedition. Because of the restart, I'd run out of toilet paper. That night, I took one of my compression socks and cut it up into quarters. This served me well the next day when I had two more emergency pit stops.

I just wanted to get there now.

When I camped on the night of day twenty-nine, I had 45km separating me from the South Pole. With my broken ski and body, progress had slowed to around 30km over each of the past three days.

One big push. It had to be. I couldn't make my food last

any longer than another day. Just another marathon. One last lap of the Brutal. One more push through the jungle. This was what the previous year's training had been building towards. Exploring deep within yourself, as you push to the very edge. I wasn't quite on the brink of endurance, as I had been on the Brutal, because I couldn't afford to be. For the Brutal, I had a support team and twenty-first-century infrastructure to hand; here I was alone in Antarctica. Safety was still paramount. For me that is non-negotiable. You hear stories of people arriving at the Pole so delirious they have left their pulk 20km away and are rushed to the infirmary. That's not doing it, as far as I'm concerned. It has always been important to me to remain self-sufficient, never to risk my safety any more than I have already by putting myself in these environments in the first place. There's a line I won't cross. I spent most of the previous year investigating where it lay.

I was near it now. When I struck camp for the last time, I was no more or less excited than on any other day. The only difference was that, all being well, at the end of this day's skiing it would be over. I was absolutely bollocksed. The mornings had been a real struggle the last few days, more so than the afternoons. I nodded off on the skis again that morning, but the pistons kept pumping. Into the evening the same applied, right the way through to 10 p.m. when I stopped 11.1km away from the Pole, according to my GPS.

The trouble was, I couldn't see it. In that condition, in that environment, it doesn't take much to set off crazy thoughts in your head. It had been a long, long day – twelve and a half hours and counting. Why couldn't I see it? We'd seen it from

17km away on the 737 Challenge. Was my GPS working properly? Was I even on the right track? I did a quick piece to camera. Fatigue was overwhelming me. The sun was shining; there was no wind; it was the polar plateau at its most temperate. But it was still the polar plateau. I was wearing minimal layers. I had to keep moving.

The polar plateau is basically flat, but there are undulations throughout, some of them imperceptible. I must have been skiing in a dip for a few kilometres, because suddenly, barely a hundred metres further on from where I'd stopped, the Amundsen–Scott Station appeared from nowhere, not just as a dot on the horizon, but as the big space age monstrosity that it is. To be able to see an object at all, let alone the one that marked the end of my 1140km journey, was, I think, the most euphoric, jubilant experience I've ever known. Certainly, the equal of reaching the top of Everest or Denali. But, no, it surpassed that, because the journey had been even more demanding. And lonely.

I didn't stop skiing, but I started crying into my goggles. Within a few strides, uncontrollably so. The gratitude and relief that rushed upon me then was the climax of the entire journey. All the emotions you might have expected me to feel at the finish, I felt there. Spiritually that was the moment I reached the South Pole.

But I still had to reach it physically. The Amundsen–Scott Station is a big silver square block. The emotional boost I received at the sight of it kept the metronome swinging.

Off to the right of the station is what looks like a school microscope from a distance but is actually a telescope.

I kept to my systems.

Every kilometre I inched closer, something else appeared – a new colour, a flag, a building.

I had half a flapjack left.

Those last 10km were the longest of my life. I stopped for that last flapjack 3km from the Pole. I can't explain it. It took every ounce of willpower I had to get up and finish the job. I suffered this eerie and compelling urge to pitch my tent. Physically, I was fucked, to put it bluntly. But that wasn't it. I'd been that way for a long time. And when I finally arrived at the station I perked up.

There was something deeper going on. With virtually every step for the next hour between that break and the end, I had to talk myself out of stopping to pitch the tent. I've thought about it since, and discussed it. People wonder if it was fear of the end. For over a year I had focused so relentlessly on this. And not just working-hours focused – twenty-four-hours-a-day focused. Even before we'd decided on the speed record, Project X had always involved a finishing line at the South Pole. Then that focus, that longing for this moment, had intensified again over the previous twenty-nine days and nineteen hours. Was I running away from the end of all that?

But I swear that wasn't it, either. I was not afraid to finish. I wanted nothing more than to be at the South Pole. I had done what I'd come here to do. I wanted to go home. There was, sincerely, no fear of the end.

I shall never know what it was, but I fought it just as much as I fought the pain of my every functioning muscle. As I approached the Pole, now within a few hundred metres of it, I saw someone waving. It was Hannah, the very person whose

310

British record I was about to break. She seemed very animated about something. How nice of her to be so excited! How selfless! Then I realised she was waving me in another direction. I was skiing on the air strip. Of course: the protocol of the Pole. After so many days surrounded by nothingness, the Amundsen-Scott Station, with its vast buildings and colourful flags, is the most vulgar hit on the senses. It's not the South Pole a lot of people imagine and certainly not the one that Scott and Amundsen reached. But it represented the civilisation I was about to return to. I was too tired to argue, but clearly not too tired to observe the rules and regulations, which required me to veer off from my course for that precious metal marker a few hundred metres away and make instead for the correct channel by which to approach it.

When I came to it, I skied past the chrome sphere that sits on the famous ceremonial marker of the South Pole with all its flags and splendour. I was only interested in the more modest marker, the real one. Three days earlier, at the dawn of the New Year, it would have been repositioned in the correct place, to account for the drift of the glacier, so I knew when I skied up and placed my hands upon it that I had genuinely reached the point where the lines of longitude converge. I had reached the South Pole.

Twenty-nine days, nineteen hours and twenty-four minutes. I had become only the second person to complete the journey in less than thirty days. Hannah was a great source of support and positivity beside me, and I know Christian would have been the same had he been there. I hadn't been able to break his record, but I was at peace with that.

I was at peace. The tears I shed then were gentle and

reflective. It was too soon to process what I'd been through, too soon for it to sink in, as it has done now. But, as I stood there gazing at this humble metal marker that represented so very much, I knew most surely that sink in it would.

14

It has sunk in. I think. It has. Mind you, how can you tell when the implications of an achievement have 'sunk in'?

What I can say is that the satisfaction deepens every day. That applies to the 737 Challenge just as much as to Antarctica, even now, years after its completion. Sometimes it blindsides me when I'm doing something else entirely. More people have been in space than have stood at the top of the Seven Summits and the North and South Poles.

Fewer still have skied solo from the coast of Antarctica to the South Pole, unassisted and unsupported. I became the seventeenth. The fastest Brit. The only Welshman. That means a lot. We are a small nation, but we are proud. Wherever I have gone, my Welsh flag and Union Jack have come with me. When I'm not on expedition, they live at the Millennium Stadium.

When they weighed me back at Union Glacier, I was 89.2kg, exactly 12kg less than when I'd set off. I had worked harder than I had the year before, when I'd lost 16kg and returned a broken man, yet this time Antarctica had taken less out of me, literally and metaphorically. I can't give you an accurate calorie count for my output. I spent a long time researching watches before I left, but the heart-rate monitor on the one I chose, which would have combined with the watch to give an accurate reading for calories burned, malfunctioned at the start and never recovered. But I can estimate it, according to weight loss, previous expeditions and how it felt at the time. In Antarctica the year before, I burned an average of 8000 calories a day, the equivalent for someone my size of two marathons. This time, the average was 9–10,000, on some days reaching 11,000, I would say. I was constantly managing my oxygen deficit, pushing on the threshold between aerobic and anaerobic exertion. I couldn't sleep some nights for the pain in my leg muscles, which was a new experience. So I was working harder than I ever had, skiing longer hours, while burning 50 per cent more calories than I was taking in.

Many factors contribute to these figures and to the ultimate statistic of distance travelled per day. My pulk and gear were lighter this year, but the snow much heavier. I was in better shape, stronger and more efficient in my action. Absolutely vital to the reduced weight loss was the efficiency of my absorption of food. The year before my daily intake had been between 5300 and 5500 calories; this time, it was 5815 calories but spread more evenly throughout the day. The body can absorb only so much in one hit, which means a lot of what I was eating the year before was not being taken up. The difference between all of 5815 and, say, 70 per cent of 5500 is massive.

I was a different animal for the Antarctica speed-record attempt. Although conditions rendered hopes of success unrealistic in the end, the difference between the state I was in post-Antarctica 2013 and that of 2014 was a testament to my preparation, as was the simple fact that the second time round I finished the job. GSK performed tests on me when I returned, the findings of which are still being processed. Although I lost 12kg of weight, for example, scans reveal that I gained 3kg of lean muscle mass round my abdomen, which is extraordinary, given the caloric deficit I was operating under.

Weird things were happening to my mind and body. Offering it all to science is an important part of what I do now and what I want to continue doing. It is a privilege to be able to use my experiences to help coaches, athletes and scientists learn more about how the human body performs in extreme situations. Leaving a legacy of some kind from each of my expeditions is just as important to me as the expeditions themselves. For the 737 Challenge, the legacy was to support Marie Curie; for Antarctica it has been educational and scientific. Through my relationships with GSK, Sport Wales, the University of South Wales and many schools, that work continues. I have at least one more expedition to Antarctica in me, which I hope will further develop our understanding of human physiology and the continent's geography. I am passionate about pushing the boundaries of human performance.

But 2014 was to become a year for reflection and recharging my batteries. The previous five years had demanded so much. Training for the 737 Challenge, the Challenge itself, the year of fundraising that followed, then the seventeen months preparing for Antarctica – I hadn't stopped since I'd emerged from that white room where it all started. I cleared my diary. After almost twenty years in high-performance sport, I know that the body just needs a rest from time to time. So does the soul. I wanted to regenerate physically and mentally, to spend normal time with people I care about.

I take a lot from pushing myself in extreme environments. I'm not an adrenaline junky, far from it, but I do enjoy the purity of that existence. Life is stripped back to its primitive, constituent needs. These days those needs, even out there, are met by some state-of-the-art equipment, but they remain elemental – shelter, warmth, food, the ability to travel from A to B. Having wrestled with issues of self-confidence and fear for a lot of my life, I benefit hugely from being able to perform in environments like that. But it makes sense only if I am able to balance it with all the people who are special to me. I'm not a nomad or a loner. I love watching TV or grabbing a coffee as much as anyone. That balance, though, is vital. I wouldn't want to live a life that is driven materially, but neither would I want to live one in isolation and loneliness. I love spending quality time on the sofa with Amy. I love going round to Mum and Dad's for barbecues with Ben the Dog. I love hanging out with family and friends in general.

These are the little things that we can take for granted as we rush about in everyday life. I wish I was as good here as I am on expedition at stopping to celebrate what is around me. I have discussed elsewhere the balance a mountaineer needs to find between looking up the mountain and down it and focusing in on the details of the moment, the things that can be controlled. There's no universal equation for that, because everybody's different, but on an expedition I'm really good at striking a balance that makes me feel perfectly at one with the environment and what I'm doing in it. Then, when the moment takes me, I can stop from time to time, fill my lungs and rejoice at where I am. I know precisely at any point where I'm going, how far I've been, how best to organise myself into taking the next step. Without that balance, we are just floundering aimlessly in the wilderness.

This, the story of five years of my life, began with me lost in a white room. I just couldn't see a way out of it. It felt as if my life, so managed and institutionalised until then, had finished with the end of my rugby career. But if there's one thing I've learned since, it's how our supposed weaknesses so often turn out to be strengths. I am inherently insecure. At times I have been crippled by it, unable to think of that as anything other than a terrible flaw in my personality. In the white room I was terrified when the one channel I had learned to focus my energy through was suddenly closed off.

But insecurity is just that, an energy. Realising it since has been as important a development in my life as learning from scratch a skill like mountaineering. I am very proud to have honed that skill so quickly and effectively, to have achieved a world first in it within two years and to be paid to continue to practise it, but could I have achieved any of that without the meticulousness of my preparation, the relentlessness and brutality of the training?

It is insecurity that drives me to those lengths, the fear of being found out – by my peers or just by the mountain herself. I have learned not to fight it but to harness it. The pressures and torments that threatened to overwhelm me in the white room are still there, bubbling away, but I think I have developed the emotional maturity now to know how to make use of them. It's a bit like the relationship I have with the very mountains and wildernesses that have taught me that in the first place. I don't see them as something to fight against, something to conquer. Mother Nature cannot be overcome. But you can learn to work with her; you can learn to become one with her. And when that happens, not only do you transcend those four walls, you reach places from which you can see farther than you ever thought possible.

ACKNOWLEDGEMENTS

'Stick it in the acknowledgements,' they kept saying. 'Don't clutter up the narrative with name checks and thank yous.'

Well, here it is. There are so many people who didn't quite make it into the story, but whose support in the background has been vital in keeping the whole thing moving. Personally, I'd have found a way to get you all in the book, but these editors are ruthless.

First of all, the countless people who are generous enough to think of me on my expeditions and send messages of support – and in the case of the 737 Challenge to send the donations that helped me raise money in aid of Marie Curie Cancer Care. I receive all the messages and you've no idea how much they mean to me.

Special mention, though, for the rugby community that helped shape me and for the teams in whose colours I am so proud to have played – Newport, Cardiff Meds, Pontypridd, Celtic Warriors, Leeds Tykes, Perpignan, Newport Gwent Dragons, Barbarians and Wales. And to the medical people who have kept me together physically and sent me out for more. It's a full-on job, so my thanks to Geoff Graham, Dave Pemberton, Dr Dee Clark, Ian Williams and Dr David Hillebrandt, among the many doctors and physios whose expertise and friendship have meant so much.

I have so many friends and family I'd like to thank – too many even for the acknowledgement section, apparently. You know who you are, and I hope you know how much your love and support mean to me – not to mention your graciousness in not taking the piss out of me too much.

This book would not have been written at all if I hadn't successfully completed the 737 Challenge and for that I am hugely indebted to so many, not least the brilliant 737 Challenge team of volunteer executives, in no particular order, Bev and Andy Rees, Gemma Hutton, Carwyn Williams, Lindsey Bridgeman, Emma Assender, Gareth Thomas, Nick Jones, Rob James, Liz McKeown, Hefin Archer-Willians and Vida Greaux. For introducing me to the mountain life and ensuring that the 737 Challenge ran smoothly, I owe so much to Simon Lowe, Stephanie Hopkinson, Tom Briggs and the rest of the team at Jagged Globe.

I have benefited from the support of so many partners, who have facilitated my expeditions. I am so grateful to all these companies and people who have believed in me: Nikki Skinner, Matt Gower, Dan Thompson and the team at Rab; Karen Jones and Janet Suart at Marie Curie Cancer Care; Gavin Cleverley and family at Mon Motors Audi; Alex Down and all the team at Limegreentangerine; The Mountain Boot Company; Clogau; Russell Isaac, Dai Camera and the team at Sports Media Services; Huw Davies at the Cameo Club; Louisa Scadden and team at Admiral Insurance; Gusto Events; Geldards Solicitors; HSJ Accountants; the WRU; Morten and Ole at Sportsnett Norway; Specialized; Donna Mead MBE and Linda Evans at the University of South Wales; Mark Langley and the team at GlaxoSmithKlein Human Performance Lab; Brian Davies, Cath Shearer and all the team at Sport Wales; Andrew James at Ace Feet In Motion; Firefly; the Wasserman Media Group; Mike Sharpe, David Rootes, Steve Jones and the rest of the team at Antarctic Logistics and Expeditions; Steve Dalton OBE at Sony UK; the Vale Healthcare; Danny Fenton and the Zig Zag Productions team; Group M; Dale Templar, Rob Taylor, Mark Challender and team at One Tribe; D2G; JV Graphics; Ortlieb UK; George Madine from Circle Within; The National Multiple Sclerosis Therapy Centre for use of their hyperbaric chamber; MSR; The Cardiff Arms Park Male Voice Choir; The Revd. Robbie and Diane Dennis; Chi Eta Phi Sorority Inc; Gethin Jones; Nicola Williams; Lyndon Polley; Bisley Office Furniture; Sigvaris; the late John Hughes, Richard and family at The World of Groggs; Harriet Davies and team at the New York Deli in Cardiff; Sir Ranulph Fiennes; Steve Williams OBE; Kev Morgan; Cath and Lou Harris; Matt Parkes; Roger Mear; and David Hamilton. Special mention, too, for Babs and Peter Thomas CBE, Diane and Henry Engelhardt and Dame Rosemary Butler for their belief, support and friendship.

I would like to thank the many schools who have supported me and had the courage to inspire a new generation not to be scared of life outside their comfort zone. And the organisations and institutions that have presented me with awards and honours – your endorsements mean the world.

For the production of this book, my thanks go to Adam Strange and Rhiannon Smith at Little, Brown, Jonny McWilliams of the Wasserman Media Group, Jonathan Conway of Jonathan Conway Literary Agency and my friend Michael Aylwin. I thought skiing to the South Pole was hard – writing this book has been epic! But I've loved it. Thank you.

And finally to those people who are in the acknowledgements *and* in the narrative. I must be doubly indebted to you. Ha! I shan't go into details here. I hope it comes through loud and clear in the book all that you have done for me and how much I value and cherish it. I mean you, Tracy Pinder, Dr Nicola (sorry, Nic) Phillips, Ben the Dog (a man's best training partner), Amy and, of course, to Mum and Dad for, well, everything.